TOTAL QUALITY SERVICE

How Organizations Use It to Create a Competitive Advantage

0 57812 23392 8

Service...everyone is talking about it...few are happy with it ...even fewer are doing anything about it.

Total Quality Service

How Organizations Use It to Create a Competitive Advantage

Stanley A. Brown

Prentice Hall Canada Inc., Scarborough, Ontario

Canadian Cataloguing in Publication Data

Brown, Stanley A., 1946-
  Total quality service : how organizations use it
to create a competitive advantage

ISBN 0-13-923392-X

1. Service industries - Quality control. I. Title.

HF5415.5.B76 1992   658.8'12   C92-094670-4

Prentice Hall, Inc., Englewood Cliffs, New Jersey
Prentice-Hall International, Inc., London
Prentice-Hall of Australia, Pty., Ltd., Sydney
Prentice-Hall of India Pvt., Ltd., New Delhi
Prentice-Hall of Japan, Inc., Tokyo
Prentice-Hall of Southeast Asia (Pte.) Ltd., Singapore
Editora Prentice-Hall do Brasil Ltda., Rio de Janeiro
Prentice-Hall Hispanoamericana, S.A., Mexico

Editor: Glenn Martin
Interior and Cover Design: Carole Giguère
Composition: Suzanne Boehler
Cover Photo: Steve Payne
Cartoons: Bill Suddick
Technical Illustrator: Phillip Allen
Manufacturing Buyer: Lisa Kreuch

ISBN: 0-13-923392-X

  2 3 4 5   RRD   96 95 94 93

Printed and bound in the U.S. by R.R.Donnelley & Sons Co.

C O N T E N T S

(Thinking about the Quality Service journey)

The world today...the new customer...differentiation...the challenge of building a Service Culture...what is quality...competi-
tive advantage...the cost of customer dissatisfaction...the
complaint multiplier...the cost of not putting in a quality service
program...Total Quality Service (T.Q.S.); what makes it different; how it works; how it starts...why use Total Quality Service

(Checking the road conditions)

The PULSE (Program to Understand the Level of Service Excellence)
study...global research on quality and service...what the PULSE research tells us about service needs; are consumers willing to pay
for quality service; the benefits of high customer-perceived quality...practices of quality service organizations...the gap analysis...process redesign...encouraging employee buy-in...creating
momentum...the role of innovation in T.Q.S.

7. Encouraging Excellence 158

(Staying on course and not running out of gas)

How do we stay on top...some thoughts on success...rate response...trust and recognition...the recognition gap...giving rewards that count...award systems pre and post...types of non-monetary awards...awards and suggestions...how to keep the suggestions coming...suggestions as culture...the scope of suggestions that can make a difference...continuous improvement...performance measurement...measuring what's important...going to the customer for suggestions...mystery shopping...the Baldrige Award...a checklist

8. Lessons Learned and Not Forgotten 186

(Some driving tips from the experts)

What we've learned...complaints: a chance to learn...how to measure complaints...service recovery...service guarantees...guarantees and the bottom line...internal service guarantees...a miscellany of lessons learned...do customers care about quality of service...lessons learned in the public sector...warning signs...the ultimate test of empowerment...the pygmalion effect...T.Q.S.: a summary...is the journey over...the nicest customer in the world

Appendices

ACKNOWLEDGMENTS

This book is not the work of one but a collaboration of many. I wish to thank my wife, Rhonda, for giving up the many weekends and evenings required to put this together; thanks also to my children, Cynthia, Brian and Lowell, who each in their own way have had an impact on this book; to Alex Finlayson, who provided much-needed assistance in crafting the words and style; to a long-time friend, Rhonda Sone, for providing guidance on the illustrations and cartoons; to my secretary, Helen Chalmers, who put in after-hours work in retyping and critiquing the book's content; to Price Waterhouse, in particular Tom O'Neill, John Konrad, John Clappison, Len Rutman and John Simke for their encouragement and input; and to the Prentice Hall team, John Schram, Ric Campbell, Tanya Long and Ken Proctor, for helping me to put this publication on the fast track.

Lastly, this book is dedicated to three people who have had a significant impact on my life: Anne and Louis Brown, and Ruth Silverstein.

My thanks to all of you and to those whom, through oversight, I may have neglected to mention.

PREFACE

Has this happened to you? You come to the office, read a magazine, then the newspaper, and you see — again — the words "quality service." Or perhaps someone higher up the organizational ladder calls you into his or her office and says, "Everybody seems to be on the quality service bandwagon — what are we doing about it? We need to be closer to the customer. Our survival depends upon it."

So you immediately call together your senior people and create a task force to look into what your company should be doing.

The task force sets to work. They buy all the books on quality and service. They subscribe to all the newsletters. They attend every seminar that has the word "customer," "service" or "quality" in the title. They meet with a company or two involved in quality service.

They conclude that they must share this knowledge with everyone in the organization to heighten their awareness of the importance of and their commitment to giving the best service possible, both inside the company and out.

So they put in place an off-the-shelf training program based on the principles they've found. The team heads back to their desks eager to see how it goes. Six months later, the task force meets again.

After reading all the books and all the newsletters, after attending all the seminars and all the workshops, after evaluating all possible approaches to service excellence, after assessing all the theories, then educating the organization accordingly, they discover nothing has changed.

The idea hasn't worked.

The organization is just the same as before.

The members of the task force are annoyed, and more than a little baffled. They thought the approach they had chosen was a good one.

So they put their heads together and select a new approach. In goes another training-based service program. Six months later, they meet again.

Still nothing has changed. They are exactly where they started a year ago. They are standing in the blocks while the competition is halfway around the track. Why?

They did all the right things. They thought they'd picked a good plan. What went wrong?

The problem at my hypothetical company is one I see quite often. Too often, in fact. Which gave me an idea.

But I have to backtrack first.

A couple of years ago, in the course of doing a national survey on the successful and less-than-successful service practices of North American companies, I discovered a very simple "first principle," a principle used by businesses and corporations famous for their quality of service. It's the Golden Rule:

Do unto your internal customers as you would have them do unto your external customers.

In other words, exceptional service cannot be delivered to the customer until good service exists within the organization itself. Progressive companies today have developed a service culture within their organizations in order to compete and be successful where it counts — outside, in the marketplace.

I also discovered that in order for companies to sustain their competitive advantage through excellence in service, they must build a foundation on which to support it. I called this foundation REACH — research, empowerment, acknowledgment, communication and help. The philosophy of REACH became the basis of *Creating the Service Culture*, a book I co-authored.

The REACH concept is simple yet far-reaching. It discusses the foundation for building a service culture but does not go into the process: How did leading quality service organizations get that way? How did they start the engine and keep it running?

Back to my hypothetical company. I've met the situation many times. The company's problem was that no one had shown any of its staff *how* to achieve a service culture. They liked the idea of quality service, but they didn't know how to tailor a quality service agenda to their organization and their customers, how to put one in action, and how to keep one going.

Since the publication of *Creating the Service Culture*, "service" thinking has evolved and grown. Business people now speak readily of the need for "quality service" to be delivered to the customer.

And more and more people have begun to ask, "I know the level of service I want to achieve, but how do I go about doing it? How do I get there?"

So, I thought, if my first study (IDEA: Innovation and Delivery of Excellence-in-Service Assessment) established the foundation for quality service, why not do a second study to understand how quality service is achieved? I found support for the project, PULSE — A Program to Understand the Level of Service Excellence, from Price Waterhouse and a number of prominent companies in the service industry.

This landmark study traced the evolution of management thinking on service excellence in organizations right across North America. The goal was to determine today's most successful approaches to service culture.

The findings of the PULSE survey were added to interviews with senior executives from organizations as diverse as Federal Express, Amdahl, Campbell Soup, Manpower Temporary Services, American Express and Canadian Pacific Hotels & Resorts, along with the views of speakers at the Prentice Hall/Price Waterhouse seminars, "Profiting from a Service Focus" and "Total Quality Service." The result was a method for putting quality service into action.

That is what this book is about. How to do it. A manual, almost, on how to turn your organization into one that edges out the competition because only you provide the one thing they don't: Total Quality Service (T.Q.S.).

What you gain from T.Q.S. is the competitive edge.

And EDGE, I think appropriately, is the name of the four-step process that has evolved from the research. I have dedicated one chapter to each of these steps. Each chapter shows you, step by step, how a company may achieve service excellence and thereby acquire and sustain a competitive advantage. There is also a chapter on service lessons companies have all learned, as well as an appendix full of service strategies and customer bills of rights.

It is important to stress that T.Q.S. is not some business cosmetic or an off-the-shelf quick-fix. The hypothetical company in my example is, in fact, very real. There are hundreds like it in the marketplace today. They all believed that training alone was a cure-all for their problems. But, by itself, training is a cosmetic. Combined with other actions aimed at creating a service culture, training becomes a key part of that effort.

Nor is T.Q.S. an approach tied to some vaguely worded and unrealizable standard. It is more philosophical, embodying the full meaning of the words "total" and "quality": T.Q.S. is the belief in, and the practice of, providing the best and most thorough service possible, at all times, by everyone, to everyone.

As in my earlier book, I have heeded the experiences of others and want to share them with you. Innovation is not creativity, but the adaptation and modification of ideas of others and the shaping of them to fit the needs of your organization. I have pulled together the diverse experiences of many organizations, found the common thread, then woven those experiences into a consistent and, more importantly, usable philosophy. The result is *the* how-to book on service excellence.

There are many companies described herein there are many ideas there are many procedures that the reader can pull out of this book and say, "This is something that I can do in my company," or "With some modifications, this is something that I can change."

John F. Welch Jr., Chairman of General Electric, told Fortune magazine that, in the '90s, a corporate Gulliver is doomed without lilliputian virtues. He means speed, simplicity and attention to the customer's smallest needs. His choice of *Gulliver's Travels*, the greatest of all travel books, is an appropriate metaphor.

Because quality service is a journey. Like any journey, it would be fraught with wrong turns, rough roads and dead ends if one were foolhardy enough not to bring a map. *Total Quality Service — How Organizations Use It To Create a Competitive Advantage* is that map.

HOW TO READ THIS BOOK

The book is divided into small sections to illustrate specific points. Each point is a strand in the fabric of the book. Each point follows from the one before it and leads into the one after it.

Therefore, you can open the book at any place and begin, going forward or backward as you see fit. The book moves in a loop, as it were, like Total Quality Service itself.

One of the reasons for writing this book was to provide a guideline for people who want to begin the service process and have on their desks a handy reference to quality service practices.

I also wanted to cut through the jungle of material on the subject and give a clear, simple picture of service excellence and how to attain it. Consequently, I have presented only the best practices I have found in the service field.

I hope readers will find the material inspiring. I hope, too, they will find in it something they can take back to their organization to help it begin, or continue, its quality service journey.

C H A P T E R

1

A LOT OF TALK...LITTLE ACTION
(Thinking about the Quality Service journey)

I am sophisticated — much more so than I was a few years ago. I have grown accustomed to better things. I have money to spend.

I am an egotist. I am sensitive. I am proud. My ego needs the nourishment of a friendly, personal greeting from you. It is important to me that you appreciate my business. After all, when I buy your products and services, my money is feeding you.

I am a perfectionist. I want the best I can get for the money I spend. When I criticize your products or services — and I will tell anyone who will listen when I am dissatisfied — take heed. The source of my discontent lies in something you or the products you sell have failed to do. Find that source and eliminate it or you will lose my business and that of my friends as well.

I am fickle. Other businesses continually beckon me with offers of more for my money. To keep my business, you must offer something better than they.

I am your customer now, but you must prove to me again and again that I have made a wise choice in selecting you, your products, and your services above all others.

That about says it all, doesn't it?

I found this in a publication on front-line service by a Florida company called Innovative Business Education Inc. To me, the person speaking is today's typical customer: more demanding, more discriminating, more fussy. This person is the global customer. I, for one, would not like to lose this person's business.

With customers like this, it is not surprising that "service" is the word on everybody's lips. Extensive literature now exists on the subject; seminars are held regularly; magazines devote cover stories to it; industry leaders gather together for panel discussions — all in the name of service excellence. It's the buzzword of the decade. And it may become the mindset of the next 50 years.

THE WORLD TODAY

We live on a fast-changing globe. There is free trade. There is the European Economic Community. International travel is easier. Information travels faster. Access to information is available at the touch of a button.

Demographic patterns are changing. Populations are older, with the needs and wants of people who are old. There is greater interest in the family. There is concern about the cost of health care. There is worry about the environment.

Changing just as fast are the needs and expectations of the consumer. The same goes for employees, the very foundation of the delivery of products and services.

The shape of business is changing, too.

According to the U.S. Bureau of Statistics, the number of goods-producing workers has declined steadily since the 1940s, while the service-producing sector has grown rapidly. In 1940, service workers represented less than half the workers in the United States; in 1990, nearly nine of 10 workers were in service industries.

Around the globe, expanding multinational corporations compete in narrowing markets: 47 of the world's top 100 economies are now corporations. So few companies, so many customers. Companies are under pressure like never before to offer a consistent product and quality of service worldwide, not just in their own backyard.

SHAPING BUSINESS FOR THE NEW CUSTOMER

The customer base is changing, its needs shifting, its loyalty wavering. Customers are becoming more selective. When you run a business in a market that is the whole planet, quick response to new or changing business conditions is absolutely necessary. A quick response can mean introducing a new product, promptly filling an order, or swiftly dealing with a supplier's complaint.

Companies that follow the teachings of quality gurus like Deming and Juran are using far fewer suppliers than in the past and demanding more from them in terms of quality and service. Companies have found that it is more beneficial to have one supplier with which they work closely than five suppliers with which they don't. For a start, there is no dickering over price. There is less downtime from having to co-ordinate multiple suppliers. And there is no need to repeatedly check the quality provided by the supplier. This last point is the most important. The supplier works closely with the company to supply exactly what the company needs at the time it is needed. Their interests are interrelated and mutual, almost as if the supplier were a division of the company itself, and vice versa.

With business activities spread out around the globe, it is imperative also that a company be structured horizontally. This is old news, but old news worth repeating. Traditional top-down management is unsuited to today's business environment.

A Hay Business Culture survey compared Canadian and American management structures and their ability to formulate and implement business decisions with management structures of five European countries.

The United States and Canada came out fifth and sixth, respectively. Both countries ranked near the bottom in encouraging individual initiative and speedy decision-making. European businesses were generally thought to be more open to change and innovation, and were acknowledged to be more flexibly structured as they face up to the reality of the common market.

Vertically structured decision-making is slow and bureaucratic. There are many "moments of truth" in a business system. Yet decisions about most of these moments rest all in one place, at the top. People at the top are often so far removed from activities on the front-line that their understanding of front-line operations bears no relation to reality.

I see everyday how the predominantly vertical structure of organizations defeats initiative and encourages counter-productive internal rivalry, which is why the pep-talk approach to improving service and quality fails every time.

Decision-making must pass to those nearest to where the decision is being made, because only those closest to a decision can respond quickly and with sufficient knowledge to resolve the matter at hand. Canadian business professor Jeffrey Gandz, in his article "The Empowerment Era," says, "Other things being equal, the speed of response is inversely proportional to the number of levels of approval."

Old-style business hierarchies lose too much in time, efficiency and quality decision-making to be competitive. The unfortunate truth is that if organizations do not change of their own accord, the business environment will do it for them by driving them out of business.

DIFFERENTIATION AND PROCESS TECHNOLOGY

In the period 1950-70, North American businesses and products developed in a world of limited competition. That world isn't around any more. Technology is so sophisticated that a company can duplicate a competitor's product or service in a matter of months. Companies can survive this competition if they operate in a protected environment, but now those barriers have fallen away. You can no longer run business as if it were 1970.

Companies have seen their market grow from being merely national to encompassing the whole world. And their old, safe home market is being besieged by competitors from all over the globe.

There is another fact worth noting, too. North American business succeeded in the seller's market that followed the Second World War. The idea that sheer volume regardless of quality will swamp the competition has long been a trademark of North American business thinking. Another is the policy of planned obsolescence, which makes quality and service concerns secondary. A third is product enhancement, like lots of optional knobs and dials on a stereo receiver, that nevertheless, has the same sound quality as the old model.

In short, the mindset of North American business was to give the appearance of constantly offering newer and better products.

Newer and better products meant greater and greater profits. Until 20 years ago, North America had a terrific technological advantage over just about every other country in the world. The Japanese and the Europeans could not hope to catch up. So they began to improve the processes of making existing products, like cars, rather than banging their heads against the walls trying to come up with better products than North Americans.

The Japanese are now the acknowledged masters of reverse engineering. Their logic was, if you could make a product faster and cheaper than anyone else, you could steal their market.

The fastest company wins.

But there is an upper limit to this. Soon everyone will be using just-in-time delivery, and the advantage of superior process technology will disappear. So a new differentiator, a new competitive advantage, will be needed. It will be service.

THE NEW DIFFERENTIATION

Companies have been slow to realize that value is not in the minds of makers, but in the minds of buyers. In the customer's eyes, value is an attribute of a product; it is not an image derived from advertising or "Quality is Job 1" slogans.

We live in an economy where the relationship between buyer and seller is as important as the actual products being exchanged. No longer does the success of a company rise or fall on product alone. Technological sophistication has toughened the marketplace. You make a product, and in no time at all, imitators are right there cutting into your action. One company's offering looks just like another's. There are too many retail stores and chains that are too much alike. Price wars flare up that cost everybody.

In such a tight space, only companies that excel have the edge. And it is service that separates successful companies from the pack. Service means more than pleasing the customer. It means having an all-encompassing and genuine service culture in your organization.

Many companies that are now service leaders saw the writing on the wall some time ago. Canadian Pacific Hotels & Resorts, which owns or manages some 80 hotels and resorts across North America, is one of them.

"The competition for the accommodation industry dollar is fierce, and is going to continue to be fierce," says Robert DeMone, President. "The sophistication of world travellers is such that you really have to run like hell today to stand still. And the only thing that differentiates one service provider from another is the quality of the service that is provided. People will tolerate a degree of product deficiency if the service is great, but people won't tolerate poor service. And there is always somebody next door willing to provide excellent service and leave you out of the business."

Yet the question everyone asks me is that if service is such a hot idea, why are so few organizations genuinely successful at instituting and sustaining a corporate culture that emphasizes it? The answer is simple, embarrassingly so.

THE CHALLENGE OF BUILDING A SERVICE CULTURE

Large corporations cannot change their practices overnight. Large objects are not shifted easily. At the management level, hiring a new CEO or president, by itself, has never made a true change to the culture of an organization. Putting on a brand spanking new "service culture" hat does not make a new corporate executive. Simply wanting improved service does not make it so.

At the employee level, for example, granting across-the-board salary increases has never translated into long-term changes to corporate culture. Indeed, what happens in many organizations is that company technology advances at a brisk pace while the core business activity — client service — is shoved into a corner somewhere. It's something we'll get around to later, executives say.

Terms like "service excellence," "quality service," and "service culture" are familiar to anyone in business these days, but the subtlety of the concept has eluded many executives.

Over and over again, in the public as well as the private sector, I see that adopting a service focus is thought to mean improving the speed of service or adding new services. But the emphasis on speed — quantity over quality — is wrong. It means that service is solely transaction-based.

To provide transaction-based service is to do only half the service job. While the focus on transactions — the quantitative element — is essential to any firm's success, there must also be quality. It's like in school. When the teacher asks you a question, you provide an answer (transaction). But you also try to give the *correct* and *complete* answer (quality). Companies that have a genuine service culture (and you will find many in the pages of this book) give such answers. Companies that don't are like students who mumble a reply, hoping the teacher will move on to someone else.

SERVICE ABOVE AND BEYOND THE CALL

Here's a way of looking at service. In 1989, an earthquake hit San Francisco. Buildings collapsed, roads split open, the power failed. The city came to a halt.

Yet, out on a street in ruins, a temporary travel office went up. From their makeshift office, employees of American Express worked through the night with flashlights and portable phones, going to hotels, contacting customers who had flight plans for the next day.

The office cashed checks, even for customers from other credit card companies; they provided emergency assistance to cardmembers and non-cardmembers alike; they set up a hotline to the American Express operations centre in Phoenix to provide information to cardmembers about relatives living in the Bay area.

They did this all on their own. No one asked them to do it. No one told them they had to. Nor was it an unusual thing for an American Express employee to do.

The service culture at American Express encourages employees to provide service beyond what the customer might expect. That's quality service.

AMAZEMENT

Let's say you are travelling in a rural area of upstate New York. You begin having trouble with your car. You pull in at the first service station you see. While your car is being gassed up and generally looked over, you watch a mechanic working on a car in the garage.

He amazes you. He changes the oil without spilling a drop. He wipes his hands before touching the upholstery. When he finishes, he backs the car out of the bay very, very slowly. There is not a scratch on it.

Impressed by his diligence and attention to detail, you say to the fellow pumping gas: "Your mechanic does a very careful job, doesn't he."

"Why not," he says. "It's his car."

It was his car.

That, to me, sums it up. The secret of quality customer service lies in one word:

Ownership.

It was the mechanic's car and he took to his job with the pride of ownership.

Does he work on other people's cars this way?

I'd go out of my way to his garage if he did, perhaps even pay a premium price for this service.

Service depends on who is receiving it and how they perceive it.

The goal of an organization should be to amaze customers with their product and service delivery. The organization can do so only by living and breathing a service culture. Organizations are truly differentiated by the quality of their service — delivered consistently and amazingly. They surprise their customers. Customers remember surprises.

In the words of CP Hotels' Robert DeMone: "Our mission commits us to exceeding the expectations of our guests. The expectations of our guests are growing in sophistication day-by-day. If we are not on a continuous automatic program of quality service improvement, we will not exceed the ever-growing demands or expectations of our guests."

Quality service is not defined by the company. Quality service is like truth or beauty — it is in the eye of the beholder. If the customer thinks he or she has received good service, then good service has been given. If they don't, it hasn't. The customer is the sole arbiter of service excellence. Understanding this is the necessary first step toward creating a service culture.

Donald E. Petersen, Chairman of Ford Motor Co., puts it this way: "If we aren't customer-driven, our cars won't be either."

Petersen's statement reflects the much-overlooked fact that service depends on who is receiving it and how they perceive it. There is no point in developing some idea of what service should be like, then offering it to the customer with the attitude that, if the customer doesn't like it, too bad. It is no longer good enough to say, "There are plenty of people out there who like what we do, so lets not worry about a few unsatisfied customers." Many firms make this error. They think that changing the whole organization to fit what the customer wants is too expensive. What they do not understand is the sheer cost of *not* having a quality service culture. But first...

WHAT IS QUALITY?

Quality reflects customer satisfaction. It is the customer's perception of you and what you make as being first-rate.

This might sound simplistic. But look at it this way. Quality is not a variable. There is no such thing as high quality or low quality. Quality is an absolute. The product or service you offer — a brand of track shoes, hot meals, financial management — is either quality or it is not.

What can you do to reach this state?

The traditional method has been what quality guru Philip Crosby calls the philosophy of appraisal. A company conducts a battery of quality control tests, inspections and production audits.

Ideally, these procedures root out production and delivery errors and correct them. If someone does a slack job or offers an indifferent product, it is easy to point the finger at the guilty party. A correction can be made.

With errors eliminated, your organization will function efficiently. Costs will go down, quality will rise, and the customer will be pleased.

Sounds simple enough. But true quality does not work that way.

Quality that is simply error correction is quality that is always one step behind. You are always playing catch-up. The only guarantee of true quality is prevention. In Crosby's view, prevention gets to errors before they occur, not after — and this achieves more, in terms of the bottom line, than simple error correction.

Think of it this way. You are about to head out on a long car trip. Do you fill up the tank before you go? Of course. You wouldn't want to run out of gas halfway to your destination, on some lonely stretch of highway, miles from the next town.

The error correction method would have you leap in your car, take off on the trip, and run out of gas somewhere. Naturally, you'd learn from the experience, and you'd remember next time to fill up before you left. But look at the grief you caused for yourself because you didn't prevent a delay from happening in the first place.

Of course, few of us would make such a blunder more than once. Strangely enough, while we learn this way in our daily life, we don't in the workplace.

Service organizations blow 25 to 40 per cent of their operating costs on correcting foulups and doing things over. Some manufacturing companies waste 20 per cent of revenue on scrap. In North America, shoddy quality and service can cost companies as much as 25 per cent of their revenues. In Japan, where quality methodology has long been advocated, this figure is less than 5 per cent.

True Quality

Money wasted on doing things again indicates that your organization is ignoring true quality. You must reorient your practices by focusing on getting it right the first time: determining customer needs, setting requirements to meet those needs, and fulfilling those requirements every time. On an organization-wide basis, resources won't be wasted cooling off irate customers while you fix something for the third or fourth time.

Quality means doing it right the first time and all the time. "That's good enough" is not good enough. For example, the customer expects to have his shirts properly cleaned and returned undamaged to be able to accept the bill of sale he receives. Think of quality in terms of a medical operation. There is no halfway measure about it.

When employees believe doing things right the first time is not a high priority in the organization, they don't bother to improve the way they do things. So for true quality to occur and to continually improve, a vision of quality must permeate the organization. Yet...

True Quality Is Only Half the Battle

Crosby, a pioneer in quality thinking, says in his well-respected book *Quality is Free* that "if you concentrate on making quality certain, you can increase your profit by an amount equal to 5 to 10 percent of your sales."

This is true, but it is only half the battle. Crosby has focused on the internal workings of the company. Just because you do something well inside your company, it does not follow that your "out front" product will shine. You may produce a product of high quality with zero defects, yet still see it flop in the marketplace.

For there is still the customer, the service you give him or her, the workings outside the company, and how you are perceived.

Firms often begin their quality journey by taking the wrong fork. They dream up an idea of what quality should be without consulting the customer. And the customer may have very different views on quality than the company.

In 1989, a *Wall Street Journal* survey revealed that only one customer in 20 felt that American businesses were listening to what they had to say. That's shocking.

DIFFERENTIATION AND THE CUSTOMER

The importance of the customer's opinion relates to product differentiation. As football coaches or baseball managers say in post-game interviews after a tough loss: "We didn't execute the basics."

Service and quality are not new concepts; nonetheless, many organizations have forgotten them, like the wide receiver who misran the pattern he had learned way back in training camp. He botched the play, he cost the whole team. Make a lot of these miscues and slowly, over time, the team's bottom line — its win-loss record — suffers.

Naturally your team won't thrive if you perform the basics and no more. Your fast-food outlet can provide clean premises, a meal that isn't cold, friendly staff. But that is not enough. Your competition does the same. What you don't have is competitive advantage or, in marketing terminology, a unique selling proposition.

Many businesspeople dismiss discussions of quality service on the grounds that their industry is purely price-driven. They say that once they have met the industry standard, the customer's decision on whom to buy from simply rests on the lowest price.

The trouble with this attitude is that the company inevitably gets stuck on a roller-coaster of cost-cutting and price wars. The company becomes dependent on what the competition is doing. It assumes that the customer cares only about getting the cheapest deal.

But customers aren't like that anymore. They see that many products in the marketplace are much the same, so when they consider their purchase options, they look for a product with something extra, a value-added benefit. If your product comes with something that no one else offers, you have a unique selling proposition.

Mitchell Fromstein, President of Manpower Temporary Services, adds a note of caution: "I'm not sure that you can go for the quality edge with the supposition that people will pay you more for it. I think what you need to do is to price competitively as well as provide quality service. Then price being equal, you get your edge."

EROSION

Product differentiation always declines over time. The competition starts doing what you are doing. A firm makes some change in products or services and sits back waiting for the dollars to roll in, thinking it has done all it needs to do to get an edge.

But quality service is ongoing. To me, a decline in service in a company means it has lost interest in customer preferences. The company drifts back into old habits. If times get tough, it takes the path of least resistance and starts aggressively cutting costs. This is dangerous short-term thinking. It can crush a company faster than if it had left well enough alone.

The famous example is a brewery in the United States that reduced its brewing cycle by half and switched to cheaper ingredients. Profits soared. Then, over a few years, profits plummeted. The customer hadn't liked the way the new beer tasted. Because the company had cut costs and ignored the customer, it almost got knocked out of the market.

PREDICTABILITY AND VALUE

Armand Feigenbaum, another of the great quality theorists, strongly believes in the effect that predictability of performance has on buyers. The marketplace rewards quality. In one of Feigenbaum's studies, he found that eight out of 10 buyers say quality is equal to, if not more important than, price in their purchase decisions. Ten years ago, only four of 10 said so.

Mitchell Fromstein of Manpower put it this way: "A customer's perception of quality is very directly related to ongoing satisfaction — not just initial." But quality does not happen all by itself. That is why Manpower has considered applying for the Baldrige Award (see Chapter 7), not for the sake of winning, but as a guidepost. Fromstein says, "I believe that it's more important to use the application process of Baldrige to measure the quality level of what we're doing than to win it, to get visibility of the quality issue within the organization and bring all forces within the organization to bear on that effort."

COMPETITIVE ADVANTAGE

The competitive advantage stems from gaining high customer-perceived quality for your product or service. Customer-perceived quality relates to how the customer sees your product. There are the minimum requirements that the competitors' products meet, and there are the "extras" that you provide in the way of quality and service that increase the value of your product. This quality edge pays.

The time has long passed when a company, like Henry Ford's, can offer a car in any colour as long as it's black. In other words, a company driven by production quotas, not customer needs, is doomed for the dustbin.

The company must take the customer's opinions and incorporate them into the product. Esteem for the product rises in the customer's eyes when this happens. The customer comes back to you again and again. He or she likes what she sees.

When the customer keeps coming back because you offer quality, you reduce costs and raise profits.

KEEPING CUSTOMERS FOR LIFE

"Why did you stop doing business with a company," ran a question in a study by *Mortgage Banking Magazine* in 1987. Sixty-eight per cent of respondents said something like the following:

"An employee of the company showed an attitude of indifference to me."

According to Robert DeMone of CP Hotels, "If you have excellence of product and lousy service, you aren't going to be able to attract returning guests. If you have some deficiencies in product, but excellence of service, you'll probably attract returning guests."

A repeat customer is one whom you can count on for revenue over the long-term. It's worth the trouble.

It costs five to six times more to go out and get a new customer than to keep an old one. For every customer who complains, another 26 feel the same way — and 18 of those you will never see again.

The Technical Assistance Research Program (TARP) Corporation, an American customer satisfaction consultancy, drew the same conclusions in one of its studies.

It found that unsatisfied customers who do not complain come back 9 per cent of the time.

Customers who complain, but do not have their complaints properly resolved, bring repeat business only 15 per cent of the time.

Resolve those complaints satisfactorily, and the customer comes back 54 per cent of the time.

Resolve them quickly, and repeat business soars to 82 per cent.

Other studies have echoed the TARP findings. Robert L. Desatick, in his 1987 study "Managing To Keep the Customer," noted that 90 per cent of customers who received a poor level of service would not do business with that company again.

Another study showed that of customers who had received bad service in a banking institution, only 51 per cent would continue to bank there.

An Atlanta complaint monitoring company, Sertec, discovered that if a company responds to a complaint within 24 hours, 96 per cent of customers will stay with the company. For every day the complaint is not dealt with thereafter, the company loses about 10 per cent of customers.

The numbers in these studies may differ, but the message is the same.

Listen to customers or lose them.

Losing customers has a nasty domino effect. When the customer is dissatisfied, he or she no longer does business with the company. High customer turnover develops. Profit margins fall. Employees become dissatisfied and quit. A poor working environment results. The customer senses an attitude of indifference from the staff and takes his or her business elsewhere. High customer turnover continues, and down and down the company spirals.

Now turn my scenario around. When the customer is satisfied, he or she continues to do business with the company. Customer turnover falls. Profit margins rise because you have steady customers. Employees enjoy their work. A good working environment is fostered. The customer senses that the staff cares about what it does, and the customer keeps coming back. Customer turnover falls, and so on, up and up.

As you can see, there is a relationship between customer satisfaction and the kind of people you have in your organization. People, in a sense, are the product. Carolyn J. Clark, Robert DeMone's Vice-President of Human Resources at CP Hotels, sees the truth in this assertion: "All along, we've said that we had to upgrade our product, but at the end of the day, the physical plant is basically an empty shell without the people who provide the service."

THE SANDY CORPORATION STUDY

In 1988, the Sandy Corporation published a study that stands as the final word on customer satisfaction. The study defined customer satisfaction as "the intent of a customer to purchase from you again at their next opportunity." And it made a key observation about the role of service and customer satisfaction: service and customer satisfaction is an economic issue, not an aesthetic one.

Service and customer satisfaction, in other words, is not window dressing. Satisfaction of the customer affects the whole organization, not just the out-front look of the product or the company.

This survey proves it.

The cost of customer dissatisfaction, in terms of revenue lost and the costs of replacing customers, is over 10 per cent of annual revenue!

Here's how Sandy Corporation worked it out. It asked service company executives for the reasons why a customer buys from a particular company. Four reasons were given: past satisfaction; availability and convenience; service quality; and, last of all, price.

Most frequently, respondents (banks, hotels and restaurants, and transportation sectors were surveyed) cited past satisfaction. This answer was given 59 per cent of the time. What does this mean?

It means that past satisfaction — demonstrated by the number of repeat customers and the number of referrals or endorsements by customers — is *the* indicator of customer satisfaction.

A Hard Truth

In this same study, the majority of service sector executives said customer satisfaction was their No. 1 priority. They believed their customers were either satisfied or very satisfied with the product they received. By their own estimation, most believed that less than 10 per cent of their customers are dissatisfied but don't complain, and that only 5 per cent will switch to another company.

A widely recognized study by the U.S. Office of Consumer Affairs disagrees.

According to this study, 37 to 45 per cent of all service customers are dissatisfied but don't complain, and 28 to 30 per cent of dissatisfied customers don't bother to complain — they just switch.

If we do some quick math, we see that 10 to 14 per cent of *all* customers don't complain but switch, which means that companies in every service sector grossly underestimate the number of dissatisfied customers they have and the number of customers they are losing.

The Cost of Customer Dissatisfaction

So far I've just been talking percentages. But these percentages, when put in dollar terms, produce some frightening figures.

One can calculate the cost of customer dissatisfaction, whether by company, industry or sector, from four annual figures: number of customers, total sales revenue, promotion or marketing expense per customer, and estimated customer loss rate.

The Sandy Corporation's report did so and found this: Using the service sector's annual customer loss rate of 5 per cent (remember, this is the executives' estimation, not the true percentage), companies lost on average $89 per customer in unrealized revenue and $100 per customer in replacement promotion and marketing costs. That's $189 per customer thrown away!

And this is a conservative estimate, because (as mentioned above) executives tend to underestimate, by a fair margin, their customer loss rate.

To get a sense of the kind of loss I am talking about, consider the study's determination that service sector firms lost, on average, 454,000 customers a year. That translates into $86 million in unrealized revenue and replacement costs!

And There's More

The figures I've cited still don't show the full impact of customer dissatisfaction.

There are many indirect effects. Product warranty costs rise. Legal fees, market research costs and advertising costs go up. The company must spend extra money and resources to combat competitors trying to break into its market. There is the expense of high employee turnover. Customers cease to be a source of new ideas for product or service improvements.

Most dangerous of all, however, is the multiplier effect.

The Complaint Multiplier

The TARP research shows that when a customer has a complaint but either doesn't bother to complain, or receives insufficient redress after he or she does, that customer will tell eight to 10 other people that the company is no good.

A Canadian hotel chain did a similar study. It found that if a customer received bad service at one of its hotels, the customer would tell 12 people within 24 hours. Within 72 hours 23 people would have heard about the experience. And at the end of the week, 72 people would have heard about the lousy service of the hotel chain.

The ripple effect of such negative referrals is long-term. The company's good reputation becomes that much harder to keep.

The reverse is also true, if not so dramatic. If a customer likes the treatment he or she receives, or gets prompt, efficient resolution of a complaint, the customer will not only become a repeat customer, but will tell the good news to four or five others.

The conclusion to be drawn from this report is unmistakable. Customer dissatisfaction costs a bank vault's worth of annual revenue — and most executives don't seem too worried about it!

One doesn't have to think too hard or too long to see that giving the customer quality service translates into more profits. Jeff Rushton, Vice-President, Finance of Mediacom, is big on taking care of existing customers: "It is a lot more profitable to keep and retain existing customers than to try to rebuild a new customer base every year."

A study by Bain and Company found that a 2 per cent increase in customer retention affects the bottom line the same as cutting costs by 10 per cent. The logic is that loyal customers spend more and buy more expensive goods and services over time (a weekend holiday package, then a seven-day vacation, then a luxury cruise).

In the automotive service industry, for example, the profit increase after a 5 per cent rise in the retention rate was over 30 per cent; in advertising, a notoriously tough business for keeping clients, the profit increase was nearly 80 per cent. The lesson is simple: perceived quality of product and service affects the success of a business more than any other single factor. Customers, in the words of Tom Peters, author of *In Search of Excellence*, are "appreciating assets."

CUSTOMERS TELL THEIR FRIENDS BUT THEY DON'T TELL YOU

Why don't customers complain?

Often they don't know who to speak to. The clerk? The supervisor? A senior manager?

Or they feel that complaining won't do them any good. They perceive that dealing with complaints is a low priority for the company.

Or they think their complaint will end up at the bottom of someone's in-basket and never be seen again.

Or they hear the line, "It's company policy."

So the customer thinks, "The company, deep down, doesn't really care. They've got my money and that's the end of the transaction." Rather than do anything about the complaint, the customer decides that it's just as easy to walk out and take his or her business elsewhere.

ASK WHAT IT COSTS NOT TO PUT IN A QUALITY SERVICE PROGRAM

A quality service program has done its job if the level of customer-perceived quality rises, because that means higher profits through reduced costs, which cuts revenue loss, which increases market share.

Look in your books. How much is spent on customer services? How much is spent resolving customer problems and complaints? How much does it cost your firm to settle warranty claims, refund returned merchandise, or handle requests for repeat service? Why is there always time and money to correct a problem or error but never time or money to do it right the first time?

Add this all up and see if these costs are too high *not* to have a Total Quality Service (T.Q.S.) program.

Put another way, if you think quality is expensive, try shoddiness.

It is clear then that both quality and service are necessary for business to move ahead in the '90s. So how do we bring them together?

People seem to think that quality service programs are just for service companies. And they think that quality standards programs are just for manufacturing companies.

The truth is, they are both for both.

WHAT MAKES T.Q.S. DIFFERENT

What distinguishes T.Q.S. from other service-excellence processes is the way it is applied.

Like Crosby has done with the idea of quality, the conventional approach to better service implements "service standards" in the organization. Service standards form an integral part of any service-excellence program to be sure but, like a quality program, they accomplish nothing when used alone.

Preset service standards as a management tool usually involve, first, some sort of quantifiable means to assess performance and, second, the use of a detailed blueprint by management to make sure employees meet those requirements. This method works well in industries where performance standards are easily measured, like the electronic parts or automobile industries.

The methods of Deming, Juran, Crosby and others have proven to be more than useful in the past. The great advantage of their methods is that they are simple to understand and easy to teach. But these methodologies came from another age, a time when manufacturing was the cornerstone of the economy.

That time has passed. We are now in the service era. The forerunners of T.Q.S., because they were geared to a manufactured product and not a service product, made no allowances for the psychological and cultural aspects necessary to instil service quality in an organization.

T.Q.S. breaks new ground because it factors into the service equation the social structure of the workplace. Its goal is to establish an ethos of service commitment that will induce autonomous effort on the part of workers to improve and maintain quality of service.

Remember the mechanic? The goal of T.Q.S. is to build into service excellence a sense of ownership; an employee should wish to give the best service possible without the repeated prompting of superiors or the feeling that they must live up to a code of standards.

MEANS, NOT ENDS

Often the introduction of service standards (indeed, standards of any kind) comes from on high. The boss walks in, drops a list of standards on your desk, expects you to meet them, and walks out. This kind of attitude does not suit the modern workplace. It is counter-productive. Such behavior annoys employees because they will come to think that all their previous work for the company has not been good enough. A service program that fails to encourage employees is about as useful as not having one at all.

According to Karl Albrecht, a quality service specialist, organizations that operate under the principles of T.Q.S. operate by atmosphere rather than coercion, inspiration rather than mandate, shared values rather than standards. Without question, standards have a place in the modern service organization, but they must be thought of as tools, not as ends in themselves.

HOW T.Q.S. WORKS

The chief attraction of a purely standards-based approach to service is the promise that it will provide a blueprint that would work in any organization. The trouble is, using a one-size-fits-all blueprint is like using a highway map of the United States to find your way through the suburbs of Chicago.

What an organization needs instead is a set of practices and processes that can be tailored to its unique needs. It needs a county roadmap.

So let's make some assumptions, based on what I've discussed above.

Excellence in service gives an organization the competitive edge it needs to stand out in today's marketplace.

The implementation of a service culture differs from one organization to the next. What works for a financial services institution won't work for one that retails car parts.

Size makes a difference, too. Larger organizations are harder to change than smaller ones, simply because they are bigger.

Organizations with old, conservative structures, or ones that sell a product that has long been in the marketplace, might find it more difficult to change than an organization used to living on the cutting edge of technological change, like a computer company. Companies that offer price-driven products will have to take a different approach from ones that sell highly differentiated products.

And it's going to take time.

Here's Robert DeMone again: "[T.Q.S.] is a long journey. The older the company, the longer the journey. If it takes 100 years, and it did to get to where we are, it's going to take a few years to get somewhere else. It's not going to happen overnight. There's a significant degree of turnover of people in the hotel industry. We think our turnover rate is better than some other people's, but it's still a significantly high turnover rate. With that turnover rate, if we religiously recruit service-oriented individuals, over time we will have people that have been appropriately selected and trained as the majority of the employees in our company."

And it's a continuous process. "We spend a great deal of time trying to analyse the customer's real need rather than just responding to a customer's request for people," says Mitchell Fromstein of Manpower Temporary Services.

"We'll send people who meet the basic requirements, but then we'll spend quite a bit of time analysing what they're doing, where they're doing it, why our people are being used and what the objectives are in the use of our services. In our business, in particular, it's important to get the right person or group of people into an organization on a timely basis. But the better the match that we're able to make between person and function, the higher the customer's perception of our quality."

T.Q.S. BEGINS AT THE TOP

No matter what the organization, service excellence begins at the top. Management must be devoted to its fulfilment. And here's why it must begin at the top.

For T.Q.S. to succeed, management must translate its wishes to all members of the organization. And that means everyone, from top to bottom, must think in terms of the customer first, whether the customer is the person across the sales counter or next person down the assembly line.

Management must lead by example. This raises customer service beyond the clichéd and frequently misunderstood notion that "the customer is always right" to a level where the organization exceeds customer expectations — "superfaction," not plain old customer satisfaction.

Exceeding customer expectations means everyone must work together as a team so that when the Moment of Truth comes, when the product or service "changes hands," the recipient will know that your organization provides the best all-round product on the market.

Only through a full commitment of resources and energy will a service quality program succeed the way you envision it.

A half-measure investment of energy and resources will only waste energy and resources. You will be back where you started, wondering why these service programs just don't seem to work.

Full commitment means getting everyone involved. There are many who wonder these days about the role middle managers will take in the future of companies. Many uncharitable executives see them as people who impede the work flow.

This needn't be so. Middle managers perform an essential function if they become, in service terms, individuals who coach and guide the service culture process, rather than being people who obstruct work flow and act as mere desk-tidiers.

T.Q.S. IS FOR EVERYBODY

It might be thought that T.Q.S. suits only the business community and that public service institutions need an altogether different approach. Not so.

Times are changing for public service organizations. Governments at all levels have been forced to privatize, and even institutions that have not done so have been forced to behave more like privately held organizations. They have had to become entrepreneurs seeking out innovation. Above all, they have had to consider the customer.

Government agencies differ from private business in the nature of their customers. A business has a narrow market, a certain kind of customer (whose only interest, for example, is buying tires). Public service agencies have everybody, the public as a whole, because everyone is a taxpayer or uses a public service institution in one way or another. And as every taxpayer knows, they don't like to be kept waiting in line at some government office or to be told to come back tomorrow. They want their tax dollars spent well. And that means better service — quality service.

The public sector has two primary impediments to service excellence that the private sector doesn't have. It operates in a monopolistic environment, or at least in one of limited competition, so it feels it needn't worry whether it provides good service; after all, the customer has no choice but to come back.

The public sector is also very hierarchical. Many decisions are made by people far removed from the customer. Many policies and procedures are developed to support the organization internally rather than to support delivery of service externally.

The public sector must balance and respond to the needs of four groups: business, the public, public service employees, and interest groups. An individual can be a member of more than one of these groups, which makes service matters even trickier.

Business relies heavily on its government for assistance to compete effectively both nationally and internationally — it turns to its government for information and research, financial aid, and trade protection.

The general public relies on the public service because that is where its tax dollars go.

Public service employees rely on the public service for career advancement and job fulfilment.

Interest groups rely on the public sector to listen and respond to their demands to introduce or amend public policy.

The public sector must reorient the way it does business, so that the many groups with which it works will continue to receive the service they expect and deserve from their government.

Public service organizations are already changing their attitudes toward service. The Ontario Ministry of Government Services, for example, has developed a one-window concept whereby customers can do all their business at a single booth, rather than be obliged to run around to various offices.

The city of Montreal has installed an information nerve centre that a person may telephone or visit; it provides information about services offered by various municipal government departments. Staff spend one-quarter of their time being updated so that the information they make public is current.

Innovations can be as simple as the Ontario government's Blue Pages in the telephone book. It is a separate listing of government departments and contact numbers at the back of the book, which prevents you having to thumb back and forth through the whole book to find the department you want.

"ALL HAT, NO COWS"

Isn't T.Q.S. just another business cosmetic? Another boardroom fad? A cute-sounding approach designed to make everyone feel good, but one that adds nothing to the bottom line or to job satisfaction?

Many executives think this way, and it is an understandable worry. The reason is as simple as it is well-known. Here's why:

Motivational cheer-leading sessions, promo buttons, witty coffee cups, smile training and poster campaigns may improve the atmosphere in the workplace for a while, but they do nothing to change the culture or shape of the organization.

These short-term cure-alls are asked to do more than they are capable of doing. They work for a while, but then everyone goes back to doing things the way they did before. There has been no change to the way of thinking in the workplace.

It should come as no surprise that employees are cynical about such schemes. Employees want to do their bit, they want to get the most out of their work, but too often they suspect management is merely conning them with fancy talk. They see little touches of cosmetic motivation that strike them as hollow.

"Cosmetic" means touching up the appearance, improving it temporarily, without changing the body. For people, so too for organizations. Putting up posters that say "We care" has as little effect on the customer's perception of service quality as it does on the employee's view of management aims. It is like certain advertising campaigns, where the company hopes the buyer will believe the claim rather the quality of the good being sold.

All of the things I have mentioned above are, of course, essential to the success of a larger service excellence program. I am not saying companies should do away with advertising or motivational programs. I am saying that these aspects of business — in terms of creating a service culture — do little on their own. These ideas need to be backed up with a vision, a vision that lights up every nook and cranny of the organization. Only then do you get long-term results.

WHY USE T.Q.S.?

Listen to Dave Clark, President of Campbell Soup Company Ltd:

"The reason that we have made total quality in service in products, in management, in approach, in discipline, the reason we have made it one of the most important areas of focus within the company derives from the essential nature of our business.

"We are a consumer packaged food firm. A consumer packaged food firm lives and dies on its ability to satisfy, first of all, its consumers, and secondly, its customers. That is to say, the distributors and retailers, through which it must meet the needs of its consumers. Any firm in our industry that doesn't practise quality customer service is dead. There is no other way.

"This is a business that is slow- to no-growth in terms of tonnage; it grows only at the rate of the population overall. There are a number of organizations that are as big or bigger than we are, with as many resources as we have, all of us fighting for a slice of a fixed-size pie. They're battling us and each other. They're large, well-resourced, battling in a stagnant environment.

"If you are not absolutely, totally, 100 per cent aligned to the needs of your consumer and those customers in that environment, you will not last. And I don't care how strong a position you start from.

"So, to us, a focus on the consumer and the customer is the best quality approach I've ever read about, heard about, or experienced. It's fundamental. You can't compete, you can't survive, you just can't do anything unless you start from there."

Dave Clark is saying something very simple. An organization must align its operations and culture to customer wishes. We may be putting out products or products with features that the customer doesn't need. So we must change our products and services in accordance with customer needs. The customer is, after all, the company.

How do we get started? Where should we begin? Do we need more market research? Whom should we train? Should we have a quality standard? Times are tough: will a service initiative take away precious resources that we need elsewhere? What if the employees don't really go for it? How long before we will see any results? And, always, the first question, How much will it cost?

Read on.

CHAPTER 2

WHAT'S HAPPENING OUT THERE?
(Checking the road conditions)

A difference that makes no difference is no difference.
— William James

Service. Everyone talks about it; not everyone is happy with it. Possessing a service culture will be essential to the survival of all organizations in the future, whether they realize it now or not. Worldwide economic upheaval has forced management to find new ways to out-think the competition. And management will have to continue to do so in the future — exceptional "service" may be the last strategic differentiation, the last competitive edge.

To help management take the first step toward gaining that competitive edge, I undertook, with the help of American Express, Canadian Pacific Hotels & Resorts, Federal Express, Manpower Temporary Services, and Rogers Cantel, a study of service excellence. The first study of its kind conducted in North America, it's called PULSE — A Program to Understand the Level of Service Excellence. (A copy of the questionnaire can be found in Appendix I.)

The purpose of PULSE was twofold — to understand consumer needs with respect to service, and to identify the current service practices of organizations from a broad range of industries.

In addition to the basic statistical research, I conducted in-depth interviews and discussions with organizations known for their dedication to quality service — organizations in manufacturing, government, financial services, retail, and health care. I complemented my findings with an extensive review of the literature available on quality service.

The research results gave inescapable proof.

Consumers as well as companies are anxious to do business with organizations that deliver quality service — and they are more than willing to pay a premium price for it.

The organizations to which customers gravitate possess these characteristics:

➤ they continuously research their competitive position and the needs of their customers and their employees;

➤ they demonstrate ongoing, single-minded dedication and commitment to continuous improvement of their service delivery system;

➤ they possess a strong communications program that effectively carries the quality service message to both the customer and employee;

➤ they maintain effective training and reward programs to ensure the long-term interest and involvement of the employee in the quality service journey;

➤ they recognize the role that the internal customer (the employee) plays in the delivery of quality service; in a phrase, they adhere to the Golden Rule of Service: "Do unto your internal customers as you would have them do unto your external customers";

➤ they adopt a culture-based approach rather than a standards-based approach to the development of a quality service initiative; and

➤ they possess a "journey" philosophy — a quality service initiative is a journey, a never-ending journey, not a weekend trip.

My intent is not to make this book a research report. This section should give you an overview of the research, which is a foundation for the material in the chapters to follow.

Before we examine the survey, however, let's first look at an international survey to see how North America fits into the larger global picture.

WHO HAS THE GLOBAL EDGE?

The role of service in business is a global issue. When thinking about service, it is no longer sufficient to worry about your competition at home, because your competition is, and will increasingly be, from firms around the globe. So how does North America stack up against the world's other economic leaders?

A survey by the American Society for Quality Control asked U.S. workers if they were committed to quality; 61 per cent said yes.

Japanese and German workers, when asked if they thought American workers were committed to quality, said no: only 21 per cent of Germans thought Americans were committed to service; 3 per cent of Japanese thought they were.

The majority of Americans — 55 per cent — think they make a high-quality product. Only 17 per cent of Japanese think so.

Buying habits in the three countries differ markedly. Japanese consumers buy a product on performance alone; Germans rank price first in buying decisions; Americans ask the advice of friends.

Consumers in each of the three countries were asked to define quality. To Americans, a product possesses quality if it bears a well-known brand name or if it has been praised by others. Germans feel quality is determined by price and a well-known name. The Japanese equate quality with a brand name and performance.

When it came time to buy a product, the attributes that most influenced the Japanese buyer's decision were performance first, then price. For Americans, they were price and quality. So too for Germans.

The most interesting difference between Japanese and American consumers, however, was this: Japanese rank ease of use and availability of service as the top attributes of a product. Americans, on the other hand, value availability of service and ease of repair. So where the two countries differ is on the importance of ease of use and ease of repair. I think there is a lesson about the business philosophy of each nation in this distinction.

Ease of use implies making the product with the customer in mind.

Ease of repair suggests inferior quality and implies that the customer comes second, or at least comes after considerations of planned obsolescence, ease of production and other company-centred rather than customer-centred ways of thinking.

Let's take a close look at the PULSE results.

THE PULSE SURVEY

The PULSE study examined perception of service (what the term "service" means, what kind of service is given) at various levels of management and among industry segments.

The PULSE questionnaire was divided into three segments:
- Service Practices in Your Organization
- Related Service Practices
- Service Issues as a Consumer

Service Practices in Your Organization

In this section, the study instrument was designed to determine the extent to which quality service was woven into the fabric of the respondent's organization.

It was also important to find out how committed the organization was to quality service; the delivery mechanisms it used to reinforce that commitment; and how the organization had structured itself to deliver quality service.

Related Service Practices

This section probed the respondent's knowledge of both the competitive environment and consumer perception of the organization.

More specifically, it explored how organizations monitor their competition, their customers, and their customers' perception of the organization relative to their competitors. It also investigated practices regarding employee compensation, training, recruitment and performance measurement.

Consumer Service Issues

In this section, respondents were asked to take the point of view of the consumer and assess quality service issues within a number of industry sectors other than their own. They were also asked whether they were willing to pay for quality service and how often they had done so in the past.

Respondent Profile

The survey was sent to organizations across North America. The results below represent replies from close to 1,500 respondents. The results give a picture of North American business as a whole, as well as for each of the following sectors:

- government
- transportation and communication
- financial services
- business services
- retail
- foodservice
- lodging and recreation
- manufacturing

PROFILE OF RESPONDENTS BY INDUSTRY SEGMENT

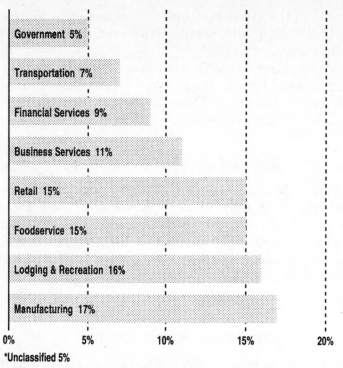

*Unclassified 5%

SOURCE: PRICE WATERHOUSE PULSE STUDY

Just under one-quarter of survey respondents came from the first tier of management — the president, chairperson or CEO; one-third came from the ranks of middle management.

PROFILE OF RESPONDENTS BY ORGANIZATIONAL HIERARCHY

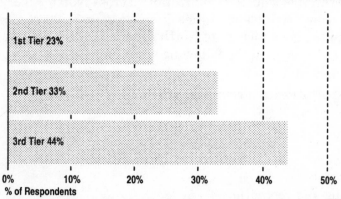

SOURCE: PRICE WATERHOUSE PULSE STUDY

In terms of size, respondent organizations represented a cross-section of North American business. At the low end of the scale, about one-quarter of the organizations surveyed had sales revenues of less than $5 million; two-thirds had revenues in the middle range, between $5 million and $1 billion. The remainder had sales over $1 billion.

PROFILE OF RESPONDENTS BY SALES REVENUE

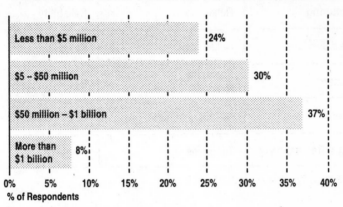

SOURCE: PRICE WATERHOUSE PULSE STUDY

A Consumer Perspective

Past research by Parasuraman, Zeithaml and Berry at Texas A&M shows that, in the eyes of the consumer, quality service bears the following features:

➤ *Reliability*: the ability to produce what was promised, dependably and accurately.

➤ *Assurance*: the knowledge and courtesy of employees and their ability to convey trust and confidence.

➤ *Empathy*: the degree of caring and individual attention provided to customers.

➤ *Responsiveness*: the willingness to help customers and provide prompt service.

➤ *Tangibles*: the physical facilities and equipment, and the appearance of personnel.

In the PULSE study, respondents were asked which of the above factors they, as consumers of services, valued most. They were also asked to identify which of the above features required immediate attention or improvement in their organization.

Sector	Column 'A' Most important Quality Service factors	Column 'B' Area requiring most immediate attention
Retail	Responsiveness	Responsiveness
Financial Services	Reliability	Assurance
Manufacturing	Reliability	Reliability
Business Services	Reliability	Reliability
Government	Reliability Responsiveness	Responsiveness
Foodservice	Responsiveness	Responsiveness
Lodging & Recreation	Tangibles	Empathy

SOURCE: PRICE WATERHOUSE PULSE STUDY

The PULSE research shows that the retail, manufacturing and business services sectors underperform delivery of critical consumer needs (column A above). In these sectors, the service issues considered most important by consumers were the areas that still required immediate attention, or required the most improvement (column B), by the organization.

Retail, for example, believes the most important service factor is responsiveness, the area it feels most requires immediate attention. The manufacturing sector is in the same situation with respect to reliability.

The financial services, government and hospitality (food and lodging) sectors feel they must be more responsive to customer needs. Generally speaking, these sectors responded well to primary service needs, like reliability, but still need to focus their attention on achieving a competitive advantage. This will occur only when they excel in those areas requiring immediate attention or improvement.

ARE THEY WILLING TO PAY FOR IT?

Consumers on both sides of the Canada-U.S. border want quality service from their suppliers.

Despite the claims made by organizations throughout North

PERSPECTIVES ON CHANGES OVER THE PAST SIX MONTHS IN THE QUALITY OF SERVICE BEING DELIVERED

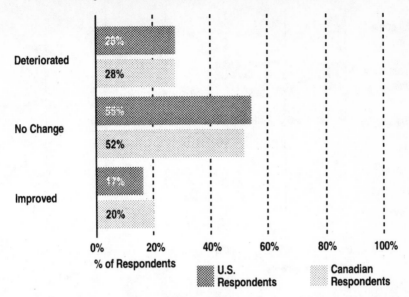

SOURCE: PRICE WATERHOUSE PULSE STUDY

America that they are dedicated to quality service, the majority of consumers believe that, on the whole, quality service has not improved in the past six months.

Rather, quality of service either has not changed at all or has deteriorated. A survey by the *Wall Street Journal* cited in Chapter 1 agrees; it found that only one in 20 customers believed that businesses were listening to their needs. A study by Development Dimensions International in 1989 showed that 97 per cent of customers who received good service — just about everyone who was asked! — said it would have a strong influence on whether they would do business with that firm again.

Consumers prefer organizations that follow through and deliver quality service. Respondents say they are willing to pay a little extra for quality service (as they have done in the past) if they know they will receive it from their suppliers.

Compared to research conducted in September 1990 by the *Wall Street Journal* and *NBC* News, the percentage of consumers who say that they would pay a premium price for quality service has increased in the last few years.

Given the value consumers place on quality service, organizations that outperform their competitors in delivering quality service are likely to achieve a lucrative competitive advantage.

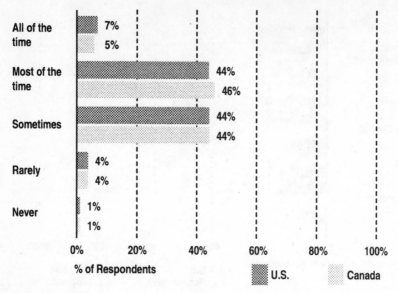

SOURCE: PRICE WATERHOUSE PULSE STUDY

To further emphasize the point, the widely respected PIMS (Profit Impact of Marketing Strategy) is unequivocal about quality and service: "In the long run, the most important single factor affecting a business unit's performance is the quality of its products and services, relative to those of competitors." PIMS research shows that organizations that customers rate highly on quality service

➤ are able to charge premium prices;

➤ increase market share at a rate of 6 per cent per year, compared to a decrease of 2 per cent for businesses that customers rate low in terms of quality of service;

➤ achieve a 12 per cent return on sales versus 1 per cent for those with low ratings; and

➤ achieve a sales growth of 17 per cent per annum versus 8 per cent for low-quality service providers.

Why is this so?

GROSS MARGINS

Many executives say, "Why don't I just stick up the price to increase profits. Then, I won't have to blow any money, time and resources on service programs?"

Executives who try this worn-out approach are assuming that by offering higher quality they will incur higher costs. They assume it costs more to put in a service program than it does not to put one in. The PIMS research shows otherwise.

It is obvious that someone putting out a product with high customer-perceived quality will see a greater return on investment than someone who puts out a low-quality product. The organization that ensures high customer-perceived quality will have a greater market share.

A rise in price, without a loss in market share, will increase gross margins and thereby increase profit. So why not just raise prices and forget this service nonsense?

Because, says the PIMS study, while high relative quality permits a firm to charge a relatively higher price, cost must be factored into the equation. And it is market share, not relative quality, that determines relative cost. An increased market share means higher volumes, so costs go down.

PIMS research ranked firms by perceived quality. Firms in the top 20 percentile saw a return on investment of 30 per cent. The return on investment of the bottom 20 percentile was 15 per cent.

John Groocock, in *Chain of Quality* (1986), tested the PIMS data to see if it held true. It did. He ranked 47 business units by customer-perceived quality. The top two-thirds of the units outearned the bottom third three to one.

BENEFITS OF HIGH QUALITY SERVICE

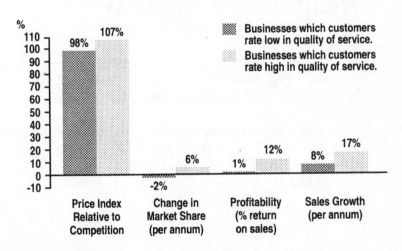

SOURCE: PIMS DATA BASE

DIFFERENTIATION

Here's the bottom line on all this. We live in a commodity environment where, by and large, products all look the same. Any product feature holds a sales advantage for a limited time only. Every day, technology shortens the length of time in which companies can hold an advantage with their product.

As far as pricing products goes, we do not want to offer the lowest price because our competition can easily match us. We would rather be able to charge a premium price. Research like PIMS clearly shows that with a quality service product, one can charge a premium price.

Yet I don't know how many seminars I've attended where somebody has stood up at the end and said, "But my customers buy just on price; they really don't care about anything else — they want the lowest price provider."

The hard reality is that if you believe that old chestnut, you are not going to be able to differentiate yourself from your competition. And the customers will not be able to distinguish either; unable to choose, they will end up choosing the first product they set eyes on.

Competitive advantage means nothing more than being able to distinguish yourself from your competition, and eventually being able to charge a premium price. Failing the latter, you'll at least want the opportunity to get that business, as opposed to not even being included in that market.

THERE ARE HARDER WAYS TO MAKE A DOLLAR

If we can't distinguish ourselves on product or on price, we'll have to spend an awful lot of money in order to get one up on the competition. We'll have to sustain a noise level that people can hear over the din of our competitors.

But the fact remains that advertising is not going to distinguish a product from its competition, and it's not going to bring your customer back to you again, and again, and again.

Only through quality service are you going to be able to keep a customer for life.

So let's put to rest these dated notions of "I'm a customer that only buys a product once," or "I'm a customer who only buys on price." Customers want quality. They will pay for it. And they will come back for it again and again.

Advertising will bring in that customer the first time. But if you lose that customer, you will have to spend more money on advertising to get a new one —five times more.

But if you keep that first-time customer, you will not have to advertise for him or her again. And he or she will buy your product five times a year, 10 times a year, for 20 years, and you won't have to part with another red cent to get his or her business. Good service cuts costs. That is what quality service aims to do.

PRACTICES OF QUALITY SERVICE ORGANIZATIONS

My analysis of the PULSE survey results, combined with a series of interviews with quality service organizations, highlighted a number of practices that leading quality service organizations have used to develop and sustain their quality initiative. They

➤ Prepare a Gap Analysis
➤ Redesign the Business Process
➤ Encourage Employee Buy-in
➤ Create Momentum.

The Gap Analysis

Leading service organizations initiate their quality service journey by first identifying their "service gaps." Such gaps occur when the needs and expectations of those who receive service are at odds with those who provide it. To locate service gaps, it is necessary to study customer needs, employee needs and the service delivery chain as perceived by both employees and customers.

While most organizations conduct some research on service delivery, it appears to be a periodic undertaking (87 per cent of respondents) rather than a regularly scheduled one. The majority of respondent organizations admitted that they had not consulted employees or sought customer input in a formal, structured manner.

Rare is the organization that does not have a few service gaps. PULSE research indicates that in most sectors there exists a substantial gap between senior management's stated commitment to a quality service initiative and the perception of that commitment by the rest of the organization. It appears that, often, senior management is vocal about the need for quality service, but the organization as a whole does not heed the call.

WILLINGNESS TO SEEK INTERNAL & EXTERNAL CUSTOMER INPUT ON SERVICE DELIVERY

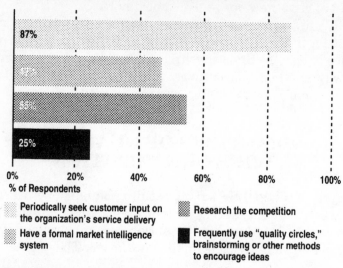

SOURCE: PRICE WATERHOUSE PULSE STUDY

As shown below, the public sector has lagged behind the private sector in service commitment. Responses indicate that public sector management has not fully endorsed the quality message and, consequently, the organization as a whole has not embraced it, as has happened in the private sector.

LEVEL OF COMMITMENT & DEDICATION TO QUALITY SERVICE

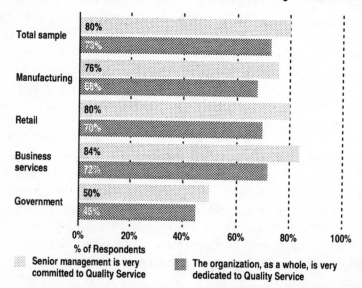

SOURCE: PRICE WATERHOUSE PULSE STUDY

Process Redesign

The objective at this stage of the process is to determine how service gaps are to be closed.

Typically, individuals within the organization work together in teams to design possible solutions to the problems that create service gaps. The result of their efforts shows the organization where the service delivery process must be improved, what standards (qualitative and quantitative) need to be set, and how progress should be measured.

Most organizations have put in place a quality service initiative without, as discussed earlier, having consulted with employees or customers — the first step in creating teams.

It is not surprising, given all the media attention accorded the topic of service, that most organizations have in place strategic mandates or mission statements that emphasize the importance of the employee. However, the employee's role does not appear to be as important as the mission statements would have you believe.

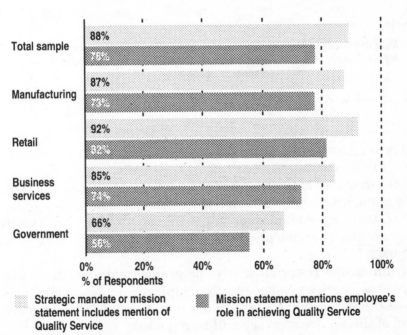

ACKNOWLEDGEMENT OF THE ROLE OF THE EMPLOYEE IN THE DELIVERY OF QUALITY SERVICE

SOURCE: PRICE WATERHOUSE PULSE STUDY

Defining the employee's role in delivering quality service is important for two reasons:

1) It obliges management to hand the responsibility for delivering service quality to those who are closest to the consumer.

2) And it helps management communicate the service message to employees by letting them know that they are part of the plan.

Assignment of responsibility for implementing the quality service program is fundamental to the Design state. PULSE research clearly shows that organizations with more than one department responsible for ensuring that quality service is delivered to its customer base have greater employee involvement in the delivery of quality service.

EMPLOYEE INVOLVEMENT IN THE DELIVERY OF QUALITY SERVICE

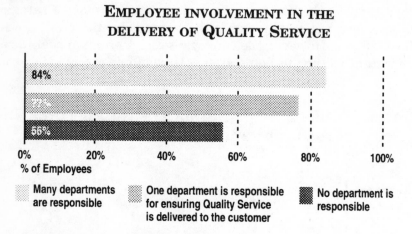

SOURCE: PRICE WATERHOUSE PULSE STUDY

Training and reward/incentive programs also encourage employee involvement.

Less than half of the respondent organizations, especially those in the manufacturing, health care, government and business services sectors, train their employees in the principles of quality service or use reward/incentive programs to reinforce a quality service atmosphere.

Training and reward/incentive programs communicate and reinforce the service message to the employee on a regular basis. Unless these mechanisms are in place and used fairly, communication of the service message will be impeded.

ACCEPTANCE OF THE NEED FOR QUALITY SERVICE
TRAINING & REWARD/INCENTIVE PROGRAMS

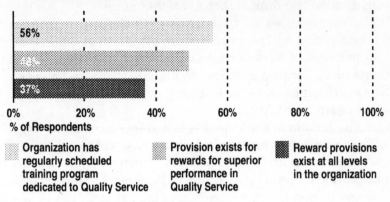

% of Respondents

Organization has
regularly scheduled
training program
dedicated to Quality Service

Provision exists for
rewards for superior
performance in
Quality Service

Reward provisions
exist at all levels
in the organization

SOURCE: PRICE WATERHOUSE PULSE STUDY

Encouraging Employee Buy-In

An implementation strategy or plan must exist for changes to be made to the organization. People, like organizations, resist change at first. The company must use a logical and practical implementation strategy if it is to succeed in making any change to its service delivery practices.

Quality service teams bring an implementation strategy to life. In many companies, teams have designed orientation, suggestion,

ATTENTION TO BE PAID TO QUALITY SERVICE
OVER THE NEXT TWO YEARS

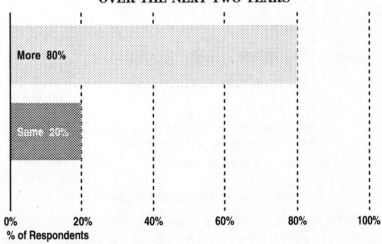

% of Respondents

SOURCE: PRICE WATERHOUSE PULSE STUDY

reward, communications and/or training programs; some have been responsible for performance measurement, or even for training the organization on the importance of quality service.

While everyone seems to be saying that in the next two years their organization will be paying more attention to quality service, only 55 per cent of survey respondents indicated that their organizations had allocated a budget to a quality service process.

Nor do the means exist in many organizations to allow the process to gain momentum.

Communication is the most neglected tool in so many organizations. The organization must inform its members of successes and failures, of what works and what doesn't. Unfortunately, it appears that communication of the service initiative has been handled poorly.

The government sector's score was particularly low — 5.1 on a 10-point scale, well below the sector-wide average of 6.9. Generally, all sectors were poor at communicating the progress of their service initiative — the sector-wide average was 6.1 out of 10.

EFFECTIVENESS IN THE USE OF COMMUNICATION AS A GUIDING ELEMENT

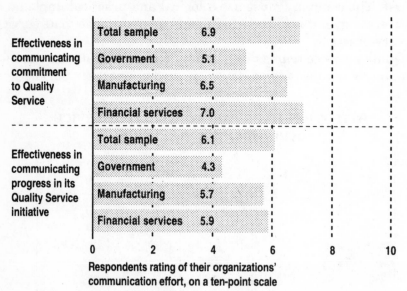

Respondents rating of their organizations' communication effort, on a ten-point scale

SOURCE: PRICE WATERHOUSE PULSE STUDY

Communication and Ownership

One doesn't have to look very far to see that many managers do little to instil in their staff a sense of ownership of the work they do for the organization. Without that sense of ownership, it is unrealistic to think people will act and work like owners, always doing their best.

The same goes for managers. If they lose their sense of ownership in the organization, they too will lose their motivation and desire to do their best. Indeed, they are often their own worst enemies. They spout the service line but are stingy with positive feedback, tight-fisted with rewards, and vague about the long-term plans of the department or organization.

Consequently, they reinforce mediocre behavior, rather than owner-like behavior. It is easy to see that most people won't do their best for management if managers aren't doing their best.

Creating Momentum

A quality service initiative is not something that is performed once and — magic! — your organization is fixed. It's not like getting a transmission job done on your car.

Continuous quality improvement is ongoing; it is an endless journey, not a weekend trip. There will be bends and curves along the way, maybe even a pothole or two.

That being the case, organizations will occasionally be obliged to take alternative and unexpected routes to ensure that they account for every customer need.

EXTENT OF USE OF TECHNIQUES TO ENCOURAGE CONTINUOUS IMPROVEMENT IN QUALITY SERVICE

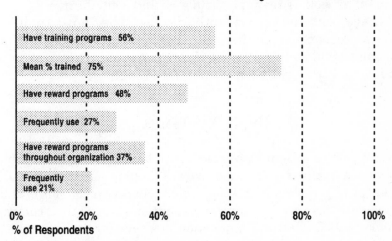

SOURCE: PRICE WATERHOUSE PULSE STUDY

This means ongoing research (the Evaluation stage). Training, too, must not only exist, but be kept up to date. And there must be genuine incentives for management and employees.

As we can see, most organizations not only lag when it comes to establishing programs to encourage excellence, but they also fail to use them when they do have them.

More than half of the respondent organizations possessed quality service training programs, yet only three-quarters of the employees in these organizations received quality service training.

Service delivered to the customer is no stronger than the weakest link in the service delivery chain, so failing to train a quarter of the organization can have serious consequences.

Compounding the problem of insufficient training is that fewer than one-third of the organizations use reward/incentive programs on a regular basis. Without steady employee motivation and reinforcement programs, the likelihood that the organization will achieve total quality service falls dramatically. Mitchell Fromstein of Manpower underscores the importance of training to support a company's vision and culture. In his view, the culture is very dependent on the training provided to the employee base: "Our staff carry the ability in their hand every day to show us as a quality operation or not." Without adequate training, not only in basic skills, but in how to exceed customer expectations, these people are ill-equipped.

By reward, I do not mean a perfunctory Christmas bonus or a jolly handshake. Management must share a portion of the organization's profit with employees — in addition to the employee's base compensation — and they must distribute this share on the basis of individual as well as team performance and contribution.

Management must share authority, too, They must treat employees as responsible adults, just as they treat their peers. They must trust employees to do the right thing and involve them in planning the strategy and operational redesign.

INNOVATION

Innovation plays a significant role in the development and encouragement of a quality service initiative. My 1989 research study, IDEA (the Status of Innovation and Service Excellence in Canada), which complements this book in many ways, suggested to me that, contrary to popular belief, the word "innovation" does not mean "creativity."

Rather to innovate is "to heed the experiences of others." It is to adapt, borrow and modify the ideas of others and shape them to fit *your* needs. It is to pull together the diverse experiences of many organizations, find the common thread, then weave those experiences into a consistent philosophy that will work for your organization. All too often, I come across companies who take the path of least resistance, blindly doing what other organizations have done, without adapting or modifying their discoveries to suit themselves.

The IDEA survey asked respondents to define "innovation."

About one-third of respondents defined it as "new product, service or manufacturing ideas."

Nearly one-quarter said innovation meant "administrative or organizational change."

"Adaptation of outside innovations," which is my understanding of the term as well as that of the majority of quality service organizations, ranked last; 13 per cent defined it this way.

It seems to me that many organizations have little idea of innovation — what it is, what it can do. To many, it is just a word.

TOTAL QUALITY SERVICE — THE INNOVATIVE EDGE

So let's face facts. With few exceptions, a company's products and services are not really that dissimilar to those of its competitors. As far as price is concerned, price changes made by one company are sure to be matched by the competition; a pricing advantage is always short-lived. And as for advertising, it really all sounds the same, doesn't it?

That leaves only one possible differentiator to create a competitive advantage — service. Whether you operate in a manufacturing or service environment, distancing yourself from your competition through the delivery of quality service is the only possible strategic edge.

There are basically three approaches to service: cosmetic, standards-based and culture-based.

Cosmetics approaches take many forms. Some organizations use posters to encourage improved customer service, but they do nothing to correct the underlying mediocrity of the service itself.

Other use video programs, newsletters, lapel buttons, even "smile-training" or "charm schools." These types of motivational courses or training workshops are integral parts of any quality service initiative to be sure, but they are not the process itself. Used by themselves, they never bring long-term, lasting results.

The challenge facing every organization is how to begin the quality service journey and, once started, how to keep the momentum going. Standards-based approaches, like Total Quality Assurance (TQA) and Total Quality Management (TQM), provide a clear, logical methodology for creating quality improvement in organizations where objective standards are possible.

These methods, however, fail to take into account the psychological and cultural aspects crucial to building service momentum — areas where qualitative not quantitative standards are required. This gap is what culture-based approaches fill.

PULSE has pointed the way toward developing such a culture-based approach in an organization.

It is true that every organization has a different culture. "Culture" is more difficult to define than job standards or manufacturing standards, more difficult to measure and more difficult to change. But without addressing it, quality service improvement will be short-lived.

The operative word in T.Q.S. is *total*. Total means getting the entire organization behind the effort. It is less a top-down approach or a bottom-up approach than it is a way to involve the entire organization in the service quality initiative.

Some might think the process they see described throughout this book is a sort of religion.

But to me, religion means dogma. It means telling others what to do. It means imposing set rules. When I use the word "culture," I mean something other than religion. I mean the creation within the organization, of a mood, a spirit, an atmosphere, a place where everyone feels pride, where everyone feels a sense of ownership in what they do.

T.Q.S. is a straightforward concept — perhaps too simple, if not used carefully. It is uniquely concerned with both the internal and the external aspects of an organization; thus, a skilful analysis of the organization's current internal status and external opportunities is essential to its implementation.

The PULSE results, reflecting the responses of close to 1,500 respondents across North America, combined with extensive interviews, discussions and consultations with quality service organizations, has shown us an approach — not a recipe, or "a one size fits all" process — but a logical system of methods that, when working in harmony, will bring about a lasting service differentiation. Let's look at it.

CHAPTER 3

A PLAN OF ACTION

(Planning the journey: what to pack and what to leave behind)

The longest journey begins with but a single step.

— *Chinese proverb*

THE RAMBO APPROACH TO SERVICE EXCELLENCE

Let's say you have a service strategy in your organization. Before you developed your service strategy, did you

➤ consider the competition?

➤ fully understand the environment in which you operate?

➤ assess your organization's internal strengths and weaknesses with respect to service?

➤ assess your current and your potential customer base?

If you answered no to any of the above, you are probably using the Rambo approach to service excellence.

Rambo is a hero. A hero with a fault.

He never takes aim; he never focuses on a single target. He pulls the trigger and sprays bullets everywhere, trying to hit as many targets as possible with one wave of his gun.

He is often successful, but only after wreaking much destruction, expending much effort, and wasting a lot of ammo. It would be more effective — if less spectacular — for him to calmly take aim, fire, hit the target with a single shot, then move on to the next.

Many organizations take the Rambo approach to service excellence, putting on a spectacular display, as if they had money, time and energy to waste.

They take a "broad approach" to their customer base, which is a polite way of saying "So what if we lose a few customers because we didn't understand their extraordinary service needs. You can't please everyone." So rather than target their service effort, they fire all at once, hoping some targets will fall.

What's missing from the Rambo approach is a well-defined strategy. You wouldn't set out on a car trip without a map, an idea of the route you might take, and a plan of what you were going to see and do when you got there.

Yet when it comes to service, many companies don't feel any need to plan it thoroughly in advance. They see service as somehow different from a capital project; they see it as something lesser, a soft option.

Change must be managed. It must be integrated into the organization. Service isn't an optional extra like reclining bucket seats. Service is as important to the success of a business as a capital project.

A survey by J.P. Russell and Associates, the Quality Improvement Process Opinion Survey, asked this question: If you could start the implementation of the quality improvement process all over again, what would you do differently?

The two most frequent answers were "increase management participation" and "develop a better sense of direction."

In other words, have leadership, have commitment and have a plan. Let's first look at the second of these three necessities, commitment.

INSTANT GRATIFICATION

Too often I hear companies say they want a customer service program to make a major impact on their organization within six months. This, to me, speaks of a desire for instant gratification. They are telling me they want to make only cosmetic changes; that they want to give the customer only the *impression* they are providing quality service.

Businesses must be willing to give a service culture sufficient time to take hold. Two years, minimum. And, in a sense, my putting a time frame on it is misleading. "Employee satisfaction, like quality itself," says David R. McCamus, former President and CEO of Xerox Canada Ltd., "is a never-ending process."

Here's another view.

"What worked in our favor," says William J. Sheehan, CEO of Omni Hotels, in an article in the International Customer Service Association (ICSA) newsletter, "was time — allowing enough of it for changes to permeate the entire organization before more changes were added from the top. Feed the plant too much fertilizer before the roots have had a chance to absorb the nutrients and you'll get root rot."

THE MOST COMMON QUESTION

It's much easier to satisfy your customers if you know what they need.

Let's say there is a service excellence plan at a company. After four months, the CEO comes back to the consultant demanding to know why the program isn't working. I've seen this time and again. It seems that executives start wringing their hands almost the minute a service quality program is implemented. They panic because they can't put a dollar figure on service to judge whether it is going well.

Executive worry is understandable. Every organization wants to know how long they must continue to invest in this service idea when they have seen, as yet, no measurable return.

Usually, in this situation, the executive has either underestimated or just plain misunderstood the notion of a service culture.

A culture, an atmosphere, or a mood in an organization is not something that can be picked off the shelf.

Whenever I hear of executives getting cold feet, it tells me that they haven't accepted the service vision in the first place. The executives *say* they have but they haven't; despite all their well-meaning talk about how the organization is committed to service for the long-term, they really saw quality service only as a quick-fix.

Another reason executives get cold feet is that they confuse a process with a program.

A program is a series of steps that, once accomplished, will result in achievement of a goal. The job is done. The program has reached its aims and can now be wound up.

A quality service process is not like that. Whereas a program is something attached to a business system, a part among many, a process is a new way of thinking that touches every aspect of the business. It *is* the business itself. It is ongoing and it goes on forever. It is continuous improvement.

"Quality simply cannot be viewed as a project or even a program because those are typically thought of as being finite in terms of both time and resources," says Cam Bright, Vice-President of Operations at Amdahl. "Both are also subject to cancellation or rescheduling."

Succeeding in a service environment, says Bright, means seeking "continuous improvement, having processes that you continually look at, because what you are engaged in is not a project, but a process. It's something that you continuously look at and work at."

Project approaches tend to encourage short-term thinking, whereas process approaches encourage long-term thinking. David McCamus saw the difficulty, and at the same time the necessity, of implementing a service process at Xerox. "There's no question that investments in total quality have a long-term payback period — sometimes five or six years. It is a factor so basic that without it, no quality program stands a chance.

"Now, I'm the first to admit it's tough to convince CEOs to focus on total quality methodology. I'm a CEO and it was tough to convince me at first! Like many CEOs across Canada, I was accustomed to short-term goals."

QUALITY SERVICE IS NOT A NUMBER

John Young, Senior Vice-President for Human Resources at Four Seasons Hotels, knows that an obsession with the bottom line and superfluous product extras will not translate into differentiated service.

"Fifteen years ago," he says, "Four Seasons could lead the market in room and occupancy rates through physical product alone: a fine building in the right location, elegant interiors, spacious rooms, and the introduction of new amenities like shampoo, robes and hair dryers.

"But anyone with money can hire top architects and interior designers. And innovations are quickly copied by competitors and soon taken for granted by customers.

"We have had to make our edge something that can't be bought or copied: a reputation for outstanding service.

"Service can't be measured objectively like a product. It's a social interaction, highly subjective. More dependent on values, emotions and attitudes. Good service is not what we deliver. It's what our customers believe they're getting, what our customers perceive is worth the price."

BIG HITTERS

In Japan's leading companies, the average number of suggestions per employee each year averages about 50. In the United States, the average number of suggestions per employee per year is 0.14. Even as important, in Japan most of the suggestions are implemented. For example, Toyota, a company that received exceptionally high grades in the PULSE study, implements about 95 per cent of the suggestions it receives.

This suggests to me that the Japanese, in terms of management strategy, do not try to hit a home run every trip to the plate. North Americans, on the other hand, do; they are obsessed with hitting the big game-saving homer, coming up with the big idea.

In North America, top management prefers to send a grand scheme sweeping down from the top, rather than let organizational strategy be directed from suggestions rising up from below.

The Japanese consider quality improvement as continuous, the sum of small changes. In order to achieve continuous quality improvement, they constantly look for ways to improve just a little bit each time. Then a little bit more, and a little bit more.

Says Jeff Rushton, Vice-President of Finance at Mediacom, "True customer service does not mean having new programs and processes every year, but rather it means building on your existing culture and continually updating it through improvements every year, because big successes result from small successes reported daily."

North Americans focus on making the big one-time improvement, the improvement that will solve all their problems at one stroke. Some business thinkers call it the "big breakthrough." Management obsession with the big homer accounts for why, in many cases, North American quality service initiatives never take hold as well as they could.

The Japanese say, "We don't have to hit the grand slam; we want to put together a bunch of singles, a sacrifice bunt or two, a hit-and-run, so that we can edge the process along. It's not the big smash we want, but a lot of little hits to keep the rally going." And that is what employees, like ballplayers, get excited about — keeping the rally going.

THE PARADIGM SHIFT

The flip-side of big-hit thinking is the slash-and-burn approach to change.

To many companies, total organizational change means trimming staff and cutting costs. This leaves the same old organization, of course, albeit a thinner one. This isn't what I mean when I talk about organizational change. It is hardly positive change.

A survey of U.S. corporations revealed that nearly half of today's managers feel they have too much work to do. Nearly 40 per cent of staff feel the same way. Another survey by Gallup said one-quarter of employees suffer stress disorders; burn-out employees lost, on average, 16 work-days a year. Add to that figure impaired on-the-job productivity and errors made when they were there, and we can see the seriousness of the problems of employee overwork and low morale.

A survey of the Canadian public service found employees were apathetic because they could not determine the organization's goals or their part in them. They were cogs in the wheel, in the most negative sense of that metaphor. Public servants want to "do something important," have a hand in creating public policy (it's why they take the job in the first place), but organizational structure has prevented them from doing so. When employees find their work meaningful and when they feel they have direct responsibility for the outcome of what they do, they are motivated and enjoy their work.

To boost employee morale, and hence productivity, organizations need to make a paradigm shift in strategic thinking.

Below are three charts that briefly illustrate the kind of changes that will have to be made if organizations wish to take a more process-based approach to business. A shift from left side of the graphs to the right is the goal of the EDGE process.

EMPLOYEE - SELF DETERMINATION PARADIGM

Old	New
Master/Servant relationship	Employee/Manager partnership
Goals imposed	Control over one's work
Standard hours	Variable hours; alternate work arrangements
Individualism	Team; working with others
Promotion	Job satisfaction
Pay	Personal growth also important
Accept unilateral direction	Leadership/ownership of work
Rigid	Flexible
Hierarchy	Participation/democracy
Differentiation work and personal	Link work and personal
Relocate where required	Two careers — unwilling to relocate
Follow company line	Right to speak out/challenge
Rewarded from above	Rewarded from within/through peers
Loyalty to Company	Loyalty to self/ethics

MANAGEMENT PARADIGM

Old	New
Authoritarian	Coach/Mediator
Rigid	Flexible
Clear lines of authority	Blurred/ambiguity
"Do"	Delegate
Decision maker	Empower others to make decisions
Narrow Focus	Broad Focus
"Own" the program	Employee ownership/manager/ eliminates obstacles
Stifles ideas	Promotes creativity
Keeps information	Shares information
Manages defined tasks	Manages complexity
Train	Develop competencies
Specialist	Generalist
Administrator	Manager
Linear thinking	Intuitive thinking
Manager by control	"Pathfinding"
Top Down	Bottom Up

ORGANIZATIONAL PARADIGM

Mechanistic	Organic
Channels of Communications Highly structured, restricted information flow	**Channels of Communications** Open with free flow of information throughout the organization
Operating Styles Must be uniform and restricted	**Operating Styles** Allowed to vary freely
Authority for Decisions Based on formal line management hierarchical centralized structures	**Authority for Decisions** Based on expertise of the individual, flat position, decentralized
Reluctant Adaptation With insistence on holding fast to tried and true management principles despite changed circumstances in business conditions	**Free Adaptation** By the organization to changing circumstances
Emphasis on Formally Laid Down Procedures Reliance on tried methods, policy manuals	**Emphasis on Getting Things Done** Unconstrained by formally laid out procedures, work under guidelines
Tight Control Through sophisticated control systems	**Loose, Informal Control** With emphasis on norm of cooperation
Constrained On-Job Behavior Required to conform to job descriptions; hierarchies	**Flexible On-Job Behavior** Permitted to be shaped by the requirements of the situation and personality of the individual doing the job
Superiors Make Decisions with Minimum Consultation and Involvement of Subordinates	**Participation and Group Consensus Used Frequently**
Segregate	**Integrate Complexities**
Coordinate Disparities	**Shared Values**
Focus on Means	**Focus on Results**

Adapted from P.N. Khandwalla, *The Design of Organization*, New York, 1977.

LEADERSHIP

In 1990, Gallup surveyed the CEOs of America's largest corporations about their views on quality. Gallup asked, "Did lack of management interest affect quality?"

Amazingly, 62 per cent said no.

Indeed, CEOs admitted that American firms perform poorly on quality, yet were disinclined to blame themselves for poor performance. Over 50 per cent of those asked pointed lower down the hierarchy; the blame for shoddy quality, they said, lies with employee's lack of skills and commitment.

CEOs aren't passing the buck here. They have drawn a logical conclusion. A poor management decision will surface only at a moment of truth between the front-line staffer and the customer. And that management decision was made long ago.

Service problems and solutions begin at the top. The epigraph to a Forum Corporation survey on leadership describes the choice as follows: "You can hand your staff a map and tell them to go to the mountaintop. Or you can give them boots, a compass, the desire to climb — and an invitation to come with you."

The Toughest Leader

John Welch Jr., Chairman and CEO of General Electric, classifies leaders into four personality types. (And, for him, a leader can be a CEO or a plant supervisor.) In the company's 1991 annual report, he says the first type of leader is someone who delivers on their commitments and shares company values. The second type neither delivers on commitments nor shares values. The third type fails to live up to commitments but shares values. The fourth type lives up to commitments but does not share values.

Those in the fourth group, Welch feels, are the ones to watch out for. They are the autocrats of the organization, and executives find them easy to tolerate them because they produce. But in the '90s, they are dinosaurs. For a company to succeed, Welch says, it needs every good idea from every person in the organization; management by intimidation works against that.

Leadership and Rapid Change

The world of business is changing so rapidly that no one knows what will happen next. Business leaders are, understandably, tentative and reluctant to act. They are especially reluctant to put in long-term programs. This rapid change may be one of the chief reasons why management, long accustomed to short-term thinking, shies away from long-term quality initiatives.

Yet management has little choice in today's business environment, but to think in the long-term. Managers must expand their horizons beyond the boardroom table and look out toward the shop floor, out to where the company meets the customer, to free themselves from the tendency to become paralysed in the headlights of oncoming change.

And this means personal initiative. But, by that, I do not mean becoming a Rambo-like business superhero. The business world is too complex for that. What goes for the CEO must also go for everyone below him or her. Decision-making must begin at the top and be passed to all lower levels. Leadership means more than inspiring followers. It means leading by example so that others do the same.

Leaders must lead. They must assess their organization unemotionally and unpolitically. This is an often-overlooked internal barrier to change. There is no room for a CEO or a manager or an employee with a personal power agenda. All must work as a team. They must walk together.

Leadership means getting everyone to row in the same direction (to use a different metaphor). A boat goes forward only if everyone rows in tandem. Giving power to others does not mean you lose your own; rather, you free up the potential of others, which benefits them as much as you.

TWO ROADBLOCKS TO SERVICE EXCELLENCE

When undertaking a service initiative, companies inadvertently put up barriers to its success. These barriers relate to structural change and budgeting.

A study by Bendrick Associates Inc., a New Jersey service management consulting firm, concluded that 40 per cent of customer complaints relate to the structure of a company's service delivery process. The key word here is "structure."

A company can train front-line staff to improve service delivery and still make no dent in their service delivery problems. Why? Because the structure of the company has not been changed. This is management's responsibility. Or, to be precise, the means to solve service shortcomings lies in the hands of management. It is up to them to restructure the company to align it with customer needs.

The second problem is cash outlay. Too often, a company begins the service culture process and immediately defeats it by tacking the initiative on to the training department or shoving a few dollars the way of a newly created customer service department.

A service culture cannot be created this way. Creating a service culture involves retooling the organization. In one of its newsletters, *At Your Service* (April 1991), Bendrick Associates Inc. put it well with a poem:

OUTSTANDING SERVICE IS NOT...
A customer service department,
customer contact employee training,
a single individual,
a title,
a group,
a program,
smile training,
a onetime change,
a marketing blitz
short term planning,
an advertising slogan,
a complaint-handling group,
accomplished by giveaways,
just being nice to customers,
the latest corporate direction,
a quick fix for falling profits,
the people who take incoming calls,
spending as much as possible on service,
a few simple changes or easy to accomplish.

I think this little verse captures neatly all the things executives first think of when they hear the phrase "quality of service" and start talking about cash outlay for a program.

There is a subtler point, however, behind the verse. If a company implemented one or two of the lines of this verse and called it their service program, of course the program would flop. If a company incorporated all the lines in the verse into a service initiative, the initiative would flop too.

What the verse implies is that the goal of a quality service initiative is to establish a service culture.

And what managers often don't see is that the notion of service *culture*, the larger notion of a complete rethinking of how an organization works, is the glue that holds together each one of those actions listed in the verse. The whole is not the sum of the parts.

When it comes to creating a quality service initiative, money must be spent on creating a culture. Budget considerations must begin from this point. That is why, if your organization were to try all the things listed above, it wouldn't acquire a service culture or a competitive edge.

Xerox, a great service leader, understood the distinction I am making. Our "Leadership through Quality" program, says McCamus, "aimed at nothing less than a complete change in our corporate culture and the way we did business."

CONSISTENCY

The PULSE study discussed in Chapter 2 underlined that delivering service excellence is the responsibility of not one individual or department, but the whole organization.

Organizations, whether public or private, that had planned out the service culture process were on the whole more successful than ones with hit-and-miss approaches. They stood out because they offered an exemplary and — this is the key — consistent level of service.

Consistency means offering quality service every time at each service encounter. Consistency is not offering good service once then hoping to live off your reputation for doing that one good deed. Sporadic quality service is, of course, cheaper in the short-term, but in the long-term your business will suffer more than it would have if you had never bothered.

A good customer opinion of your company does not depend on product alone. Coupling your product with consistently high quality service gives you an edge. Consistent delivery and continuous improvement on that delivery keeps the competitive edge ever-sharp. Companies that are unwavering in their commitment to service excellence get ahead and stay ahead.

FIRST STEPS TO A PLAN

Below are a few questions to give you a preliminary idea of what you will need to know to create a service culture that suits your organization. Subsequent chapters will discuss these issues in detail.

To develop an effective service strategy — one that is sustainable and acknowledges each customer's peculiar preferences — you must know your

➤ competition;
➤ business environment;
➤ strengths and weaknesses as an organization; and
➤ internal and external customers.

With this knowledge, you can fight your way out of the Rambo syndrome.

Know Your Competition

➤ How carefully have you considered your competition? Who are they?
➤ Where are they now in terms of products and service. Where do they appear to be going and why?
➤ What is their service philosophy and methodology?
➤ What are their strengths and weaknesses?
➤ How are their management and staff seen by buyers?
➤ Who are their customers? And how loyal are they?

After answering these questions and comparing your practices with those of the competition, consider whether you need to modify your service strategy, or create a new one altogether.

Understand the Environment

By environment, I mean the constraints or "givens" an organization must monitor and to which it must adapt to survive. They can be inside the organization or outside in the marketplace. To understand your environment, you must know

➤ demographics of your current and your potential customer base;
➤ customer preferences;
➤ market segmentation;
➤ customer buying patterns;
➤ the legal and regulatory factors that affect your industry; and
➤ business ethics practised in your industry.

Knowledge of your business environment will help you draw a roadmap on which to trace your service strategy.

Strengths and Weaknesses of Your Organization

Look at yourself as you looked at the competition:

➤ Where are you now in terms of products and service, and where do you appear to be going and why?

➤ What is your service philosophy and methodology? Is it clearly understood inside and outside your organization?

➤ Where do you excel in service? Where can you?

➤ How are your management and staff seen by buyers?

➤ Have you been able to retain customers who have had thoughts of taking their business elsewhere?

Pay particular heed to where your competition has a service advantage over you. Many potential customers may be slipping through the tiniest gaps.

After you have looked at yourself, look at other companies. Throughout this book, I will stress continuous improvement. One key element of continuous improvement is ongoing benchmarking. Benchmarking allows you to compare your business processes with those of the best companies in the world. It is not simply a matter of looking at the best companies in your industry; that is no more than competitive intelligence. Rather it is looking at the best companies in the world. Xerox, a copier company and a service leader, used as its model Komatsu, a tractor company.

There are three questions here: For every one of your business procedures, what company in the world does it best? How do they do it? What hurdles have they overcome?

Know Your Customers

There are three types of customers in a business, three precise sales targets:

➤ your existing customers;

➤ customers who no longer buy your product or service; and

➤ potential customers.

Create a profile for each group. What are they like?

These are the prerequisites for developing a well-targeted service strategy. Remember, these are the '90s. In the '80s, Rambo had a lot of ammunition. He could afford to waste bullets, knowing he'd hit the target eventually. Can you?

THE MOMENT OF TRUTH

The T.Q.S. approach to the customer requires you to manage a customer's entire experience with your company.

Whenever a customer comes into contact with your company, there is a Moment of Truth, the outcome of which shapes the customer's entire opinion of your company. It all happens right there.

The customer's response, often to the smallest transactions — a two-dollar purchase, a brief telephone call — reflects everything about your organization, your people, your facilities, your products (even ones they haven't bought), your advertising, your policies, the way your staff dresses, the look of your bills and invoices. The customer subconsciously absorbs it all, in one brief moment. The image stays with that person long after.

If this is daunting, don't worry. A Moment of Truth is directly within your control.

Before you can improve in this area, you must survey all the contact points you have with customers. I call this "service mapping."

SERVICE MAPPING

Mapping the service-delivery chain is simple. You draw a map or schematic diagram of all the points where the customer comes in contact with your organization.

Identify from the map the points of contact on which you have focused care and attention and the ones that you have neglected. Then determine the points of contact over which the organization has direct control.

Here's an example. A company held a one-day meeting to identify weak points of contact. Its representatives came away from the meeting knowing that 20 points in their service process needed change.

They changed the invoices to make them easier for the customer to read. They made sure that everyone who answers the phone gives their name for the customer's future reference. They resolved to act on all customer inquiries or complaints within 48 hours. And they made customer service responsibilities part of every staff member's performance review.

The company had taken the first step toward customer-first service.

OMNI SERVICE TRADITION (OST)

Here's the service development process one organization, Omni Hotels of Hampton, New Hampshire is undergoing. In the words of its President, William Sheehan from an article in the Fall '91 *ICSA Journal*:

"The Omni Service Tradition [OST] is a simple system: we ask our customers to rate our product, both our physical plant and our personal services, and we involve every employee in our response to both customer comments and their own observations and ideas.

"Each department meets at least monthly, reviews the prior month's customer comment cards, identifies particular problems and compares guests' observations with both the company standards for that area and the internal environment (such as the availability of funds for capital improvements, or overlapping departmental responsibilities which are giving rise to debates over jurisdiction).

"Based on this discussion, the department chooses one problem area and its governing standard as the item which will be improved over the ensuing month.

"All standards must meet minimum performance guidelines. OST forms the benchmark for the continuous improvement. Not only does every department member make a commitment to improving performance, the department's representative (its 'OST Ambassador') carries that commitment to management and to his or her counterparts from other departments. The Ambassador Committee, working with senior management, is responsible for resolving interdepartmental conflicts which might be impeding improvement.

"In the first year Omni Hotels implemented the formal OST program and began a formal database tabulation of customer comments, the 'met expectations' index improved by seven points.

"Our next step was to make examples of employees who showed 'continuous improvement' initiatives — who went 'above and beyond the call of duty' to satisfy the needs of customers or fellow employees.

"We call them 'Omni Service Champions'. For nearly three years Omni Hotels has been providing cash rewards and recognition to employees who exhibit an appreciation for the personal role they play in establishing the quality reputation for Omni Hotels.

"Evenly divided between guest contact people and 'heart of the house' individuals such as banquet housemen, our Omni Service

Champions exhibit the initiative a company must have if it plans to empower its employees, and the team spirit which reinforces our Quality Circle OST program."

TAXPAYER SERVICES BRANCH (TSB)

The Taxpayer Services Branch (TSB) of the Ontario Ministry of Revenue felt it needed to restructure itself to improve customer service. Its basic business function is to get the right tax information to the right people at the right time, quickly. It felt it hadn't been doing that. Good service at TSB is necessary to ensure high levels of voluntary compliance with the tax system. The TSB's goal was to provide one-stop customer tax service — a daunting prospect when one considers how big the Ministry is: its 23 statutory programs (TSB is responsible for six) deal with 1.2 million taxpayers, ranging from convenience stores to multinational corporations; 1 million senior citizens; 1 million farmers; over 1,000 municipalities; and 5.7 million property owners and tenants.

Several structural barriers blocked the way to better service. TSB's telephone service was ancient, with a poor capacity to handle a large volume of calls. Management had little recorded knowledge about the number of people kept on hold, frequency of busy signals or abandoned calls. Staff were ill-trained on referring customers with complicated tax problems to the correct person.

These three problems affected not just incoming calls to the front line. They caused problems deeper in the organization: the antiquated communications system made searches for client information time-consuming, making for frequent customer callbacks, which clogged the system even further.

In 1988, TSB added 12 Ministry programs to its roster of six. The volume of telephone calls doubled, to 450,000. To crawl out from under this crushing weight, the TSB reduced its organizational hierarchy from six management layers to three to speed internal communication; it put in a single 1-800 number on the front line, to be answered by up to 45 well-trained staff. The result?

Service at TSB did not suffer despite the increase in volume. In fact, it improved. One TSB task is to field inquiries about the provincial budget. In 1988, before the program went in, the TSB handled 4,000 calls in six weeks; in 1989, it handled 10,000 in the same time period. Other improvements: over 85 per cent of incoming calls were answered within 20 seconds. First-call resolution to an inquiry jumped to 80 per cent. The branch began to offer services in French and English, and had access to people who could provide service in 25 other languages.

METHODOLOGY

In my first book, *Creating the Service Culture*, I explained the philosophy of REACHing for service excellence. REACH is the acronym I used to describe the five essentials of a service culture.

Exceptional service cannot be delivered to the customer until good service exists within the organization itself.

In other words, progressive companies developed a service culture within their organization in order to compete and be successful where it counts — outside, in the marketplace.

I also discovered that in order for companies to sustain their competitive advantage through excellence in service, the service culture must be founded on five pillars — Research, Empowerment, Acknowledgment, Communication and Help.

The REACH concept is simple yet far-reaching. The organization must first *Research* the needs and beliefs of its customers in the area of service and — this is a big "and" — the needs and beliefs of its employees with regard to service.

Next comes *Empowerment*. Everyone in the organization, from top to bottom, from the chairperson to the floor staff, must be given the power to develop and maintain a service culture in their daily work. Management, particularly, must be given the power to develop the service strategy and have available to them the tools to reinforce it and keep it going.

Acknowledgement. Management must then set the standards of service excellence that its customers demand (remembering that the employee is a customer, too).

And this standard must be *Communicated* to everyone in the organization, so that they all row in the same direction.

Finally, the quickest and most effective way to *Help* employees understand and appreciate the importance of service excellence is to give them thorough training and to reward them for achievements in service excellence.

FROM PULSE TO EDGE

The success stories of service-excellent organizations do not tell you *how* to achieve a sustainable competitive advantage as a quality service provider. Organizations are demanding methodology to go with the philosophy. That is what the EDGE process is, the practical arm of REACH. It looks like this:

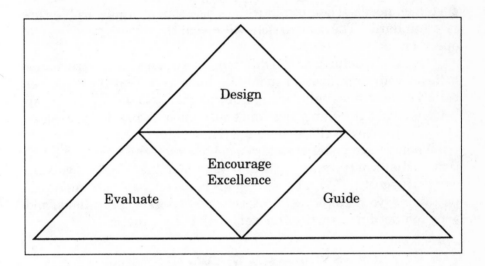

The service EDGE is an interactive and flexible process geared toward encouraging management and staff to take an active part in creating and maintaining a service culture, internally and externally.

EDGE employs the best practices I've discovered in my work with clients and my review of service quality literature. Many of these ideas lie buried in a jungle of seminar and business-book rhetoric, or have been presented in a tangle of complicated steps.

I wanted you to avoid that mistake. So I have taken what I have learned and packaged it in a format that is as short and simple as its acronym is easy to remember: EDGE.

Below, I will briefly introduce the concept; after that, one chapter will be devoted to each stage in the process.

The EDGE process asks, then answers, four questions:

1) Where are we now? — Evaluate
2) Where do we want to be? — Design

3) How do we get there? — Guide

4) How do we stay on top? — Encourage Excellence

Where Are We Now?

This first step is to learn from the best practices of others. You perform an internal and external review of the organization so as to compare your current performance against internal and external customer needs. Then compare this assessment to desirable service standards. The comparison will reveal the service gaps in your operations.

"Gaps" are defined as the difference between what the customer believes your organization should be doing and what the customer believes you are actually doing. For instance, you'll often see a gap between what the employees think that the organization is capable of doing and how well the organization is doing it.

When you consider standards, ask yourself the following questions: What are the standards that your customers believe you are currently meeting? What are the gaps between your customer's expectations, your employees' (internal customers) expectations, and your competitors practices as well as the best practices?

Where Should We Be?

Step two. Ask yourself, I know where I am today, now where do I want to be on this date five years from now, 10 years from now? How do I go about getting there?

The service gaps are reviewed to determine what has caused them. The existing service delivery chain is mapped, service relationships between departments determined, gaps highlighted, and cost-of-service impact analyses performed.

Most of the analysis is done through workshops. The goal of workshops is to find a way to close gaps. Employee groups prepare reports recommending improvements to the service-delivery chain for management approval. Upon approval, these improvements are ranked in order of importance and assembled into a company-wide service implementation plan.

How Do We Get There?

Step three. Here we put the plan into action. Quality teams are assembled. Training is developed and delivered. Performance measures are put in place. Communication processes are stream-lined. The goal is to ensure that a climate of change is felt through-out the organization.

How Do We Stay on Top?

The integration of service excellence in an organization is complete when it results in lasting improvements to the business process.

To make it last, to have the sense that service excellence breathes through the organization, excellence should be rewarded; quality teams should meet regularly; and mechanisms should be put in place to continuously read the market, to keep up with continu-ously changing customer needs.

Let's look at the EDGE process step by step.

C H A P T E R

4

THE EVALUATION PHASE

(Starting the engine and taking hold of the wheel)

Management doesn't pay salaries. They just handle the money. Customers pay salaries.

— Henry Ford

WHERE ARE WE NOW?

Evaluation is step one of the T.Q.S. process. It is the diagnostic step. The Evaluation process goes like this.

The organization reviews its current service performance. Then it determines its internal and external customer needs and contrasts them against its current service performance.

These comparisons will reveal gaps or discrepancies in service delivery. The organization then draws a picture, or map, of those gaps to determine where changes need to be made.

The shape those changes will take will be made clear when the organization "benchmarks" its business against others.

Benchmarking is simply a way of measuring one's own service practices against standards practised by leaders within and outside of your industry segment. It gives you a standard by which to establish superiority in your market.

Benchmarking forms the foundation of all future service planning activities. Your aim is to transfer benchmarked practices to your organization.

The evaluation process must be designed to highlight both areas of current service excellence and areas of service needing improvement. Your efforts should be designed to reveal

- the underlying values expected by customers of the organization, the process by which customers arrive at these values, and their attitudes toward them;
- the relative importance of various aspects of service delivery;
- customer trade-off decisions with respect to service;
- current strengths and weaknesses of service to customers;
- the organization's perception of what service values are important to the customer;
- gaps between service providers and service receivers, through service mapping;
- what needs to be done to close those gaps and achieve an ideal of service.

Put all of the above together and you will see how your organization measures up to agreed-upon industry standards and get a picture of your company, as a service organization, by department or tier.

Here's how we start drawing that picture.

SELF-ASSESSMENT

To begin the service journey, an organization must look at itself.

The goal of self-assessment is to provide an objective analysis of the organization's service-delivery process. This means looking at yourself and your organization honestly — without prejudice and without politically eyeing personal advantage within the company.

The questions below, which you can score by any method you choose, are ones you might use to assess your organization's service status.

After you have answered them yourself, let your senior staff try them.

Planning

- Is customer service part of the basic corporate planning procedure?
- Who is responsible for service in the organization?
- Is service a large or small part of your strategic plans? Your operating plans? Where does it rank?

- Describe the service vision of your organization.
- To what degree have your managers and employees bought-in to service? Has it been easy or difficult?
- What concrete steps have you taken to streamline production and administration for service?
- Do you review the service strategies yourself? The service plans of the competition? How often? What specifically do you look for?
- Is service part of performance appraisal?
- Do you have formal procedures for continuous improvement?

Service Significance

Describe how you have told the members of your organization that customer service takes precedence over cost concerns, sales volume, and so on.

- How much time is set aside for staff service-improvement training?
- In meetings at all levels, how much time is spent discussing service issues? Is it first on the agenda? Last? Give examples of issues recently discussed.
- At busy times, is the level of customer service maintained? Give examples of when it is and when it is not.
- How many times have you cancelled a service meeting or dropped it from the agenda because of more pressing matters?
- How much money do you spend on service?
- Do you spend extra to make sure service stays at its current level?
- Do you advertise service as one benefit of doing business with your company? The only benefit?

Supporting Service

- How much of your work time is spent on service matters?
- Do staff see you involved in service improvement? Give examples.
- By what means do you communicate your expectations for quality service?
- How have you instilled a mood of excitement about service in your organization? Do you see it in front-line employees? Management? How is it demonstrated?
- How have you gone about changing internal procedures to improve service?
- Do you support employees who "bend the rules?"

Employee Participation

- How many people are involved in establishing a service culture?
- Do employees have the power to make decisions beyond their assigned job functions?
- What have you done to break down interdepartmental barriers?
- Do you have service quality teams? Are you on one? Have you led one? How often do you attend team meetings?
- Do you ask your managers for suggestions to improve service? How do you do this?
- Have you redesigned the workplace to ease service delivery? How?
- Do you ask your employees for suggestions to improve service?
- How many suggestions from all levels have you had? How many have you implemented?
- How many people in your organization have received training in service? Describe the training.
- Describe the training you and your managers have given or received in the last year.
- Do front-line people contribute to the hiring process?

Results and Recognition

- Do you measure service quality?
- What are the results?
- What have you personally done to ensure bad service is not given?
- Do you have a regular reward system in place? What are the criteria for giving rewards?
- How many incentive rewards have you personally given out in the past year? How many have your subordinates given?
- How do you communicate to other members of the organization the value of such rewards? Letters of praise in newsletters, employee-of-the-month awards, extra vacation time?
- Does management compensation depend on customer satisfaction?

Customers

- Do you have a written service strategy?
- Do you put customer needs ahead of all else?

- How often have you personally met with external customers to discuss the quality of your products and services?
- How often have you personally met with internal customers to discuss their needs as employees?
- What have you done with the information you learned from these meetings?
- Have you attempted to measure internal or external customer satisfaction? Perceived quality?
- Have you asked customers how they came to choose your product? Because someone else's was worse? Because yours was better?
- Do you use and promote a customer bill of rights and/or a service guarantee?

These are questions you could ask yourself. But this is not all you need to do.

PASSING THE BUCK

Managers, deep down, do not like to admit it, but they, the employees, and the customers are inextricably linked.

Oh come on, managers say, of course I admit that. In fact, I want to encourage that relationship.

Many managers don't like to admit the existence of this relationship because it prevents them from shifting blame on to someone else when something goes wrong.

But the blame often rests with management, and there are some sobering numbers to prove it. Juran puts the figure at 80 per cent, Deming at 85 percent — that is, the percentage of times that management is responsible for quality problems in an organization.

But management doesn't see it this way. A survey in California asked managers, "Who is responsible for quality of product?"

The answers were as follows: the worker, 55 per cent; supervisor, 25 per cent; engineers and designers, 12 per cent; management, 8 per cent.

In Japan, if a worker makes a grievous error and is forced to resign, his or her superiors often do the same. In North America, if an employee makes an error, all too often only the employee takes the blame.

This bad managerial habit must be eliminated for gaps to be found in an organization, and for the whole service enterprise to succeed. There is nothing to be gained when managers try to "hide" gaps to protect their skin. The cost is service success.

EMPLOYEES ARE CUSTOMERS
AND CUSTOMERS ARE EMPLOYEES

Employees uncover gaps. The TARP research has shown that front-line staff can predict with 90 per cent accuracy when, and about what things, customers will complain. Indeed, customers and front-line staff will often say the same thing about a service problem (a billing inconvenience, for example).

The gap between a customer and front-line staff usually means there is also another gap somewhere else up the line — in management.

If the employee dislikes his or her job, feels there are double standards in the organization, or is grumpy because there is too much needless paperwork, the customer will notice. Such attitudes begin in management, and the customer will inevitably conclude that employee behavior indicates management's attitude toward the customer. Management attitudes are always passed on to the customer.

So when evaluating your organization, asking about one group helps you find out about the other two. By talking to employees, one can discover employee and management attitudes toward customers. By talking to customers, one can discover their attitudes toward employees and management. A climate of open discussion must be encouraged so that the three-way relationship is fostered, not damaged.

Manpower's research is both formal and informal. On the informal side, it is just plain listening. "You have to do a lot of listening," says Manpower's Mitchell Fromstein. "That helps you find out your customer's changing needs or the elements on which he or she judges quality. It's a cumulative set of observations that you must make."

SO REMEMBER...

Talk to employees.

Many executives say, "We should talk to the staff," but they never do.

Employees know the small but very significant day-to-day details of your operation. They can best assess how to improve the part of the organization in which they work. After all, employees are your customers, too. And they are the link in the chain between you (management) and the external customer.

By talking with your staff, you receive imaginative ideas on how to solve problems. The staff often knows best. Here's an example.

THE SERVICE QUALITY TO THE ULTIMATE CUSTOMER IS NO BETTER THAN THE POOREST SERVICE WITHIN THE CHAIN.

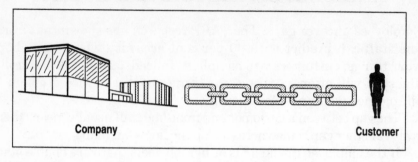

Company   Customer

We are all familiar with the old service dilemma about answering the telephone. Should the receptionist process as many calls as possible without keeping anyone waiting, at the risk of not giving them sufficient attention; or should the receptionist give each caller sufficient time so as to address his or her needs, at the risk of annoying other callers by putting them on hold?

Who is the best person to ask about solving this problem?

The receptionist, of course.

AND REMEMBER...

Talk to customers. This might seem obvious, but you'd be surprised how often companies don't do it, or do it in a haphazard way.

In a well-known case, a soft-drink company judged the market to be changing from sugar-flavored soft drinks to those flavored with artificial sweeteners. So it introduced an artificially sweetened drink to the market. They supported the drink with a massive advertising campaign.

The new drink failed miserably. Customers hated it. The company received over 60,000 written complaints a day. Two months later, it put the original soft drink back on the market. The lesson here is obvious. It does not matter what you think the customer wants. What matters is what they actually want.

WHAT THE CUSTOMER WANTS

Business travellers and the travel industry are at odds. Business travellers want one thing, the travel industry thinks they want something else.

A 1990 *Wall Street Journal* study showed that the travel industry regularly offers services that business travellers don't want. An Opinion Research Corporation survey tells the same tale. It found a large gap between the services frequent travellers say are important and the services airlines and hotels think travellers think are important.

AIRLINE INDUSTRY

Service	Importance	Performance	Gap
On-time arrival	89%	39%	-50%
Check-in procedures	75%	53%	-22%
Checked baggage delivery	75%	31%	-44%
Pre-assigned seating	75%	65%	-10%
Cares about the customer	75%	40%	-35%
Clean, attractive cabins	60%	49%	-11%
Carry-on room	59%	33%	-26%
Friendly & efficient in-flight service	56%	48%	-8%
Quality frequent flyer program	35%	23%	-12%
Quality in-flight food service	31%	21%	-10%

HOTEL INDUSTRY

Service	Importance	Performance	Gap
Billing accuracy	91%	83%	-8%
Efficient check-in	80%	55%	-25%
Reliable message & wake-up service	79%	76%	-3%
Cares about the customer	77%	54%	-23%
Competitive room rates	72%	52%	-20%
Reasonable charge for in-room phone	72%	37%	-35%
Express check-out	68%	63%	-5%
Quality frequent traveler program	41%	34%	-7%
Multiple dining & lounge facilities	36%	54%	+18%
Late evening room service	24%	38%	+14%

* Percentages indicate those who gave a rating of 8, 9, or 10 on a 1 to 10 scale.
** Negative gap indicates service delivery is not meeting importance. Positive gap shows delivery exceeds importance or delivers more of a specific item than is required.

On the chart, "importance" means importance to the customer; "performance" means how well that service is being performed.

In an airline industry, for example, friendly and efficient in-flight service has a narrow gap (-8 per cent). This tells me that airlines do what a lot of companies do: they think customer service is important only at the point where front-line staff meets the customer.

But in-flight service is low on the customer's priority list (56 per cent). On-time arrival, swift check-in procedures and pre-assigned seating — all high on the customer importance list — are (judging by performance level) not high on the airlines' list.

Customers appreciate billing accuracy in hotels. And the hotel industry knows it, as we can see from the small gap of 8 per cent. But a selection of dining and lounge facilities and late evening room service, both low on the customer's priority list, are being delivered by the hotel industry in spades. They are providing services that customers don't want or need.

KNOW WHAT YOU WANT TO KNOW

The most common way to clarify customer needs involves conducting a general survey of current customers, asking them about their expectations of you. This is a big waste of time.

General surveys give you general information. You don't want general information. It is important to tailor your survey to specific customers in order to get specific answers to specific questions.

Florida Power & Light conducts very precise surveys. It claims it can point to customer preferences on a neighborhood-by-neighborhood basis. FP & L President, Robert Tallon, told QE (*The Quality Executive*) that "people who live in the suburbs are likely to be concerned about reliability — power outages, things like that. Older people living on retirement savings in condos near the beach are likely to be concerned about price. People who live near nuclear facilities may be concerned about safety. The point is that knowing the concerns of people in particular geographic settings allows us to address their concerns in a direct, targeted way."

What you survey must also be tied to your service goals.

Federal Express does this very well. Customer satisfaction surveys remain for them the barometer of business performance.

They want to achieve 100 per cent customer satisfaction. Not 97 or 99, but 100 per cent. And they evaluate themselves with this standard in mind. They survey internal and external customers: everything from shippers to consigners to customers who drop off packages in drop-boxes. Some customers are surveyed every three months.

What is more interesting, however, is the way Federal Express sets its evaluation criteria.

In the '80s, Federal Express asked customers to rate their level of satisfaction with the company on a scale of 0 to 100. In 1990, the company changed to a five-point scale, reasoning it would be easier for the customer to answer and for Federal Express to interpret — and because it better fit the company's corporate philosophy. More than anything, Federal Express wants to know how many of its customers are "completely satisfied." Under the old system, they might have arrived at figures of 84 per cent "completely satisfied" and 15 per cent "somewhat satisfied." Add these two figures and the company looks pretty good. Who'd want to improve on 99 per cent?

Now they use "completely satisfied" alone (high score on a scale of up to 5). Federal Express simply asks the customer, "Are you completely satisfied with our service, yes or no?" If the company gets a result of 85 per cent, it knows it has a way to go yet.

By aligning the survey correctly, Federal Express mentally orients itself toward 100 per cent customer satisfaction, not something just a little bit less.

Bob MacGregor, Vice-President of Total Quality & Breakthrough Management at Campbell Soup, stresses the same point when talking about achieving a visionary breakthrough to better performance:

"You are more likely to do uncharacteristic things if you are truly committed to something that you don't know how to achieve. Your mind is then open and is constantly sorting everything that comes at it to achieve this extraordinary vision. If you are shooting for 50 per cent, your mind is open to 50 per cent kinds of ideas; if you're shooting for 5 per cent, your mind is open to 5 per cent kinds of ideas."

SURVEYING

Don't think you are in an organization that is unsuited to doing this kind of thing. A town in California with population of 77,000 surveys its citizen-customers once a year to find out their views on each municipal department.

In Madison, Wisconsin, the police department sends out a custom survey to persons from every thirty-fifth case; they handle about 3,000 cases a year. After charting the results for three years and making appropriate changes to the way it does business, the department has noticed the line on the chart that represents customer satisfaction moving steadily upward.

The object of surveying is to get as much information as you can, from wherever you can. The more the better.

So sit down with staff over a meal. Or have an outside consultant come in and chat with the staff: employees will speak their minds, knowing their words won't be used against them.

A similar method of surveying that has proven to be very informative is the use of users groups. They have been very popular in the computer hardware and software markets. Users groups are essentially customer-led focus groups. Members sit down together and work through problems they have with that company's product and consequently are able to articulate what they would like to see improved in the product.

Also try direct mail questionnaires to particular market segments. Visit key customers at their workplaces. Set up an 800-line that lets customers phone in their opinions. Have the operators ready with extra questions to ask while the customer is on the line.

Some companies wait for people to call them, while others take the initiative. At a bank in Hawaii, tellers who have a free minute or two during the day telephone long-time customers to ask them how service might be improved.

The American Management Association cautions that not all surveys work. Ineffective surveys include point-of-sale inquiries (I suspect because the customer does not like to be bothered while shopping, or is already in a rush and does not want to be delayed) and questionnaires included with merchandise.

The final thing to remember about surveying is to do it often. Customer views change as often as the seasons. Surveys are not a one-time thing. After all, how else can you determine whether you are improving?

Here's a table of results from Cantel. You can see where Cantel has improved its service delivery over a three-year period and where it still needs to do more work.

CUSTOMER REPORT CARD
HERE'S HOW YOU SCORED

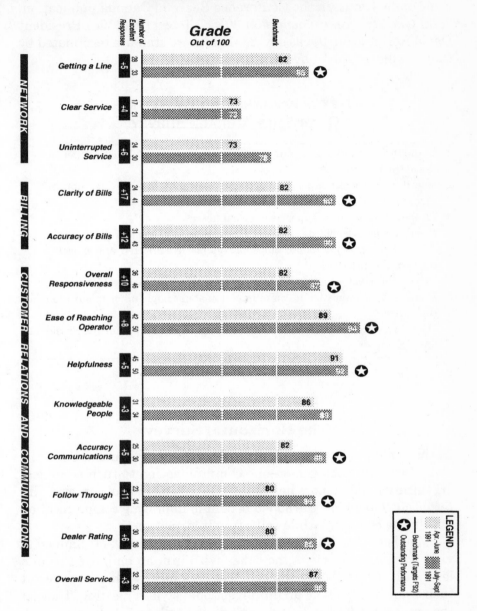

Surveying Employee Morale at Nexus

Nexus Engineering surveys employee morale every three months. To guarantee a pure response, Nexus gets an outside consultant to perform the survey, which is called the Employee Quarterly Morale

Survey. Employees are asked to assess the company as a whole and the performance of their supervisors — and they do not have to put their names on it. In the Conference Board of Canada publication, *Total Quality Management,* #60-90E, October 1990, Vice-President David Rowat is quoted as saying that "more staff are terminated by their employees than by their managers."

NEXUS ENGINEERING EMPLOYEE QUARTERLY MORALE SURVEY

---

1. In the last 3 months, has your morale gone up or down? What happened to cause this?
2. How did your direct supervisor influence your morale in the last quarter?
3. Please list your direct supervisor's strong traits.
4. Please list your direct supervisor's weaknesses.
5. Does your most senior department manager affect your morale? How?
6. What issues, if any, outside your department have affected your morale in the last 3 months?
7. Do you think you could do a better job than what you do now? How?
8. How could we improve our communication about happenings in our group of companies?
9. Do you have something confidential to say that you only want the President and CEO to see?

SOURCE: NEXUS ENGINEERING EMPLOYEE QUARTERLY MORALE SURVEY.

The Horizontal Survey

In the same publication, the President of Avco Financial Services, Don Morrison, uses one-on-one communication to turn a vertical organization into a more horizontal one. His method of surveying internal customers has the added benefit of improving communication within the company while collecting information.

Morrison visits numerous Avco branches. In 1990, he planned to visit 85. On these visits, he takes with him an employee from a level at least one below himself. The two meet with employees at their branch. They hold an unconventional style of meeting. They let the employees set the agenda and do the talking.

An Added Benefit, Just for Asking

Toward the end of a recent business flight, the chief steward knelt down in the aisle beside each customer and asked them if they had enjoyed the flight, if they'd liked the food, if the staff had been helpful, and so on. Many people on the flight were surprised at the airline's interest in their opinions. They were more pleased to have a chance to commend the airline or air some grievances. There was some frank talk. The steward noted their comments in a special book and thanked them all. "Better than just filling out little cards and leaving them in a box," said the fellow behind me. "I liked that." He felt, as a customer, that he had been noticed, and was not just someone handing over money who, once having done so, was forgotten. You can bet he'll be flying that airline again — just because it asked his opinion.

MAPPING THE GAPS

If you plan properly, it's no longer difficult to identify where the service gaps are.

Service mapping does what its name suggests: it maps the service routes of your organization. This is not the same as a map of the paper flow, although it can be.

The object of service mapping is to highlight particular problem areas and identify areas where service standards need to be set (see Chapter 5). A service map can also point to areas where a reward or incentive scheme would be effective.

To maximize the benefit of service mapping, you must first conduct a gap analysis. A well-structured research program will identify customer priorities and your performance relative to their needs. Gaps can be found in many places. Below are a few common ones. (Remember, "customer" refers to both the internal and the external customer."

Gap: *What customers expect from their products versus management perception of those expectations.*

To determine if you have a problem here, you must quantify customer perceptions of your product and your service. And you must determine what management believes to be the customer's view of your products and services.

Gap: *Management perception of what the customer expects versus the translation of that perception into service standards.*

Gap: Similar to the above. *How are management perceptions of the customer translated into service standards? Do the standards suit customer preference?*

Gap: *Service standards versus the service standard that is actually delivered.*

And it is worth watching for a related problem: *Do current standards inhibit employee ability to give service?*

Gap: *What is communicated to the customer through advertising versus what is actually delivered.*

This is the problem of "promising anything." Unrealistic promises quickly alienate customers; they see that your organization "will say anything to get our business." Is the company's vision at odds with its capability to deliver that vision? Is it honestly communicated to the public?

Gap: *What a customer believes he or she will receive from you and what they have received.*

Gap: *The service delivered to the customer versus the way the system was designed to deliver service to the customer.*

These, of course, are not the only gaps, but they are common ones. They give you an idea of where to look for gaps in your service system.

One of the exercises used by employees of Federal Express to analyse the relationship between one operations function and another is to ask three questions:

1) What do you need from me?

2) What do you do with what I give you?

3) What are the gaps between what I give you and what you need?

The answers the company receives help it pinpoint service problems and gives it a clue as to what can be done about them.

Gaps are often hard to see. Like a precipice at night, you can't see it's there. When you have done something in your organization the same way for so long that you take it for granted, you don't see it anymore; you think it is the only way to do things because you've done it that way for so long.

Gaps spot this organizational habit of mind. It is spotting gaps like these, and making changes, that get you on to the road to developing a service culture.

ONTARIO PUBLIC SERVICE (OPS)

The list of gaps above is adapted from the pioneering work of Parasuraman, Zeithaml and Berry at Texas A&M. The Ontario Public Service (OPS), wanting to improve the service given to residents of the province, adapted this conceptual model to study its service delivery systems. In 1992, OPS published a report called *Best Value for Tax Dollars*. The report is a textbook in gap analysis.

A SERVICE QUALITY MODEL

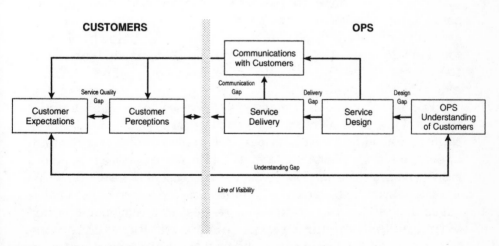

ADAPTED FROM PARASURAMAN, ZEITHAML AND BERRY (1985)

The OPS study found five major gaps in its delivery process. The analysis is generic and applicable both within and outside the public sector. I have therefore taken the liberty of substituting the word "organization" for "OPS." Here are segments of that report with the substitutions.

1) *Service quality:* the gap between customer expectations of service quality and customer perception of the organization's performance.

2) *Understanding:* the gap between customer views of service quality and the organization's views of its service quality.

3) *Design:* the gap between the organization's perception of customer views of service quality and the design of the organization's service-delivery system.

4) *Delivery:* the gap between how the organization's service-delivery systems should operate and how they actually operate.

5) *Communications:* the gap between the service delivered and the level of service being promised to the customer.

After determining these gaps, OPS set out to devise strategies to close them. It considered each strategy in terms of whether customer service would be improved because of the change, the resources required to implement the improvement, the feasibility of the improvement, and the time it would take to see results from the improvement. Here's a brief look at the findings.

Service Quality Gap

The service quality gap is the only one of the five where the external customer comes into direct contact with the organization. Gap research showed that the customer was not receiving the service it expected.

Only one in five respondents said they were getting good value for their dollars. (And it is worth noting that respondents made their observations on a typical service experience, not one that had made them angry.)

The survey ranked 17 elements of service grouped around the themes of timeliness of service, accessibility (for example, number of locations, second-language services), reliability (receiving correct answers to inquiry, consistent information from one employee to another), responsiveness (courtesy, for instance), and cost of transaction.

The respondents ranked receipt of accurate information, knowledgeable staff, and resolution of a request in a reasonable period of time as their top three service preferences. But what the customer thought the organization did well was protect confidentiality, provide convenient locations, and give accurate information. All of this means there were some big gaps somewhere.

As we can see, the biggest gaps were getting what was needed in a reasonable time, receiving a quick response to a request, and finding the right person to deal with the request.

Other results backed this up. Customer satisfaction sank rapidly, by more than half, if a customer had to see four people instead of just one to resolve an inquiry. And the longer a transaction took, the more dissatisfied the customer became.

Understanding Gaps

How did the OPS view the quality of its own services compared to the public's view of the same? This section of the gap analysis

GAPS AND MATCHES ON SERVICE ELEMENTS
Ontario Public, 1991

Element	Difference between importance and performance
Match	
1. My confidentiality was protected	1
Gaps	
2. The office was in a convenient location	13
3. Staff took pride in their work	14
4. The office was designed with my needs in mind	14
5. I got consistent information from different people	14
6. Procedures were easy to understand	15
7. Staff understood my needs fully	15
8. Staff were courteous and helpful	15
9. I got accurate information	16
10. Staff gave direct, straight answers	16
11. Staff communicated clearly, were easy to talk to	16
12. It was easy to get to the right person	17
13. Staff were knowledgeable and competent	17
14. The service was there when I needed it	19
15. I got a quick response to my request	22
16. The service was good value for my tax dollar	23
17. I got what I needed in a reasonable time	23
Average difference	16

asks whether the organization really understands internal and external customer expectations and perceptions of service.

While the results showed that the organization and the customer more or less agreed on issues of external service (services are becoming too complicated, forms are hard to understand, and so on), there was a wide gap between internal service and performance.

Internal customers ranked the information technology infrastructure highest in importance for giving good service to the public. However, internal customers found there was insufficient technical support, too much use of mainframes (which slows response time), and too many contacts required to complete service.

Human resource functions, which ranked second in importance but possessed the widest gap, exhibited similar problems. Human resource services were slow to respond to internal inquiries, were not up to date, and made too many repeat requests for information.

Policy formulation, third-most important, had the second-widest gap. Policy programs have a great impact on service delivery. Among the concerns mentioned by staff were lack of consultation with front-line staff in policy development; delays in finalizing policy followed by a sudden rush to implement it; policy that was frequently out of date; and failure to use plain language.

Design Gap

How did OPS's understanding of its customers compare to the design of its delivery system? In the words of one respondent, "The system is the problem — not the people." System foulups caused external customers to be transferred on the telephone four or five times; one office might take a credit card while its sister office didn't; there were long waits for counter service; the phone lines were always busy; and the rules were too complicated. These are all structural problems.

The survey of internal customer service drew out many of the same frustrations. Describing the bureaucracy, one respondent said, "It's like having to go to three different restaurants for the appetizer, main course and dessert."

The survey highlighted a number of design barriers to service: slow approval processes bound in red tape; slow staff replacement or just plain lack of staff, which led to high workloads; and lack of training, which meant anything from lack of skill requirements for a certain job to inability to use technology.

Importance and Performance Ratings of Eight Internal Services, All OPS, 1991

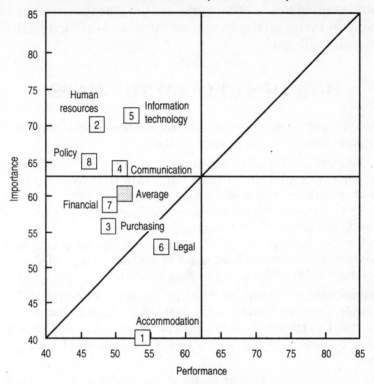

Delivery Gap

The gap between design and delivery had much to do with decentralization of ministries and their ability to formulate policy locally. As a consequence, delivery practices varied from unit to unit. City dwellers, for instance, received better service than rural residents; and the government's stated practice of treating all customers equally regardless of race, age or gender was not always upheld.

Communication Gap

The research found that the public service did not fully communicate the services it had available. Most often, it used "passive" forms of communication; that is, it took the attitude that it is up to the public to find out what information the public service has. While two-thirds of respondents knew of the 1-800 number they could call to get information about government services, only 13 per cent had ever heard of information outlets like the Citizens' Inquiry Bureau.

Internal customer communication was hampered by many of the familiar problems of bureaucracies: the fear that open communication will invite criticism and reprisal; lack of forthrightness; and general bafflegab.

HOW OPS CLOSED THE GAPS

Gap analysis shows an organization what it has to do to improve service delivery, internally and externally.

1) *Service quality*: Improve timeliness, which means reducing the number of persons a customer must talk to resolve an inquiry, and standardize response time for specific services; improve access to the organization, using everything from extended office hours to adoption of clear language in forms; improve telephone services, including expanded central inquiry bureaus; and resolve complaints at the first point of contact. (Many of these suggestions are integrated in the four categories below.)

2) *Understanding*: Bring internal and external customers closer together, through focus groups and the like, to measure what is important to the customer; offer consistent advice at decentralized units; and increase awareness of importance of internal service.

3) *Design*: Use process-improvement methodology; realign management and policy toward service improvement; redeploy resources in service areas that customers rank as important; speed staff replacement; and increase front-line staff.

4) *Delivery*: Improve morale through demonstrated management action; use customer evaluations in performance review; reward service quality; and cross-train staff.

5) *Communication*: Use "active" forms of communication; separate quick service for routine matters from more customized service for complex matters.

This service gap analysis is all fine and good, but which organizations do it best and how can I learn from them? The answer comes through benchmarking.

BENCHMARKING

Very simply, to benchmark, you look outside your organization at what other companies are doing in a particular service area. Just because you handle invoicing very well inside your *industry* (let's say it is the computer industry) doesn't mean you create the best invoices, the most consumer-readable invoices, in business.

Your quality service designer might look for example, at how somebody in the retail industry creates and processes their invoices, to see if they have a better practice than what you currently have in your computer business.

Benchmarking goes outside the organization to look at what other organizations are doing and to establish the best practice. But more importantly, it looks at what those organizations have done to achieve best-of-class recognition.

Now an important distinction.

What I have described above is different from what has been erroneously called benchmarking, which is merely setting a standard and comparing yourself against it.

This kind of comparison — setting a measure or index on the basis of an ideal suited to your own organization — is *internal*. For excellence in service, you need the best *external* measurement you can find.

Benchmarking in its proper sense means measuring yourself against best practices *anywhere*.

The internal approach (also called a "baseline") has two dangers. One, you base your measurement on yourself. This means you can become no better than yourself. It is like trying to understand your own mind with your own mind.

Two, internal benchmarks run into the problem of, or provide an escape hatch for, managers who set standards that can't be reached. Benchmarking outside your organization prevents you from being able to say, after a standard has not been reached, "It can't be done. This standard is impossible." The fact remains that somewhere, outside your organization, outside your industry, there is someone providing an aspect of service in the best known way. And it can be found.

How Do You Go About Benchmarking?

There are a number of ways to benchmark. Surveys and gap analysis will have already told you where you need improvement. They tell you where you are now. Benchmarking will help you establish where you want to be tomorrow.

The simplest way to benchmark is to first establish what aspects of your service delivery need to be improved.

Then you establish a team to develop the questions that you want answered in order to identify what constitutes best practices.

Then you identify the organizations that you believe exhibit those best practices.

Then you go out and talk to them.

And they will talk to you, because you offer them a win-win deal — "I'll share my research with you, and you share with me what you believe are best practices and how you went about developing them." This trade does not threaten either company's market because you come from outside the other's industry.

General Electric and Xerox, for example, scour the planet for companies that are better than they are at some aspect of business, then ask to pick their brains.

Xerox learned the importance of benchmarking the hard way. Michel Desjardins, Manager of Strategic Marketing Projects at Xerox says competitive benchmarking helped convince the company it needed to change, determined what needed to be changed, and developed a picture of how the company wanted to look after it had changed.

"In the late 1970s, says Desjardins," we started to use competitive benchmarking to take a good hard look at our Japanese competition. We were jolted to find that their U.S. selling prices approximated what it was costing us to make a comparable product."

"We incorrectly assumed that low cost meant low quality. We also believed — erroneously — that they [the Japanese] could not possibly be making money. These products were indeed profitable. That woke us up in a hurry, and we aggressively went to work closing the gaps.

"We needed to make a 16 to 18 per cent annual rate of [productivity] improvement to catch the Japanese in any reasonable time frame. This finding caused us to conclude that a fundamental change in the way we did business was absolutely essential."

The list of companies Xerox benchmarked sets an impressive standard. For billing and collection, Xerox turned to American Express; research and development, AT&T; distribution, Hershey Foods; employee suggestions, Milliken Carpet; policy implementation, Texas Instruments.

A company that possessed all the attributes of these business leaders would be a powerful organization indeed. That is what Xerox wants to be.

Benchmarking Emphasis

Companies benchmark many areas of their business, as we can see from the above, but the most important may be customer satisfaction. Among Baldrige Award hopefuls, it certainly carries the most weight: 300 of a possible 1,000 points of the Baldrige scoring system are for customer service. (See Chapter 7 for discussion of the Baldrige Award.)

The PIMS database can give a company a series of "strategic look-alikes" that do not come from its industry. Suitable look-alikes can be selected if you know your competitive position (relative quality, actual and relative market share); market, customer and distribution characteristics; and production style (management structure, type of production process, working capital and so on).

Before you begin benchmarking, it is essential to understand your own organization first. There is little point in barging in the door of a strategic look-alike and asking, "How do *you* satisfy the customer?"

Instead, prepare a map of your organization, take it to the other company and compare it with their map. You are basically asking them, "Here's what I do. What do you do?" Seeing another's operation can be sobering; it can hammer home the fact that you need to change your organization.

This is all very general, so let's look at a couple of industries.

Amdahl on Benchmarking

Amdahl benchmarks in the following way (this is from its *Quality Handbook*):

1) Determine which aspects or attributes of your process and product should be benchmarked. An examination of your customer requirements can be useful, since those requirements ultimately define how the customer differentiates you from the competition. Even if you have no competition, your customer requirements identify what is most important to your customers.

   For example, if your customer wants your output faster than you are currently able to produce it, you might benchmark the cycle time of your process to see how it might be done more quickly.

   Some frequently benchmarked attributes are cost, process cycle time, product performance and functionality, reliability, resource requirements, etc.

   It is important to make a distinction between process and product benchmarks. For example, you might discover that while your product is better than any other, there may be better ways to produce it.

2) Identify the appropriate product, process, or organization against which you will benchmark. For our final products and services

sold to external customers, we generally want to benchmark against our best competitor. However, to compare business processes or output for our internal customers, we have a much wider set of companies against which to benchmark. In these cases, we prefer to benchmark against recognized leaders for each type of process.

For example, L.L. Bean is a recognized leader in warehousing and logistics, and American Express is a recognized leader in customer services related to billing. Benchmarking against these leaders allows us to learn from the very best.

3) Identify the most effective method or tool for benchmarking. There are a variety of ways to gather benchmark information; the best way depends on the product or process being studied.

4) Measure the performance of the benchmark company for the selected product or process attribute, using the tool(s) you have selected. Whenever possible, determine how the company's results were achieved.

5) Translate the benchmark performance measurements into competitive requirements for your process and output.

THE BIG CHANGE AT AIR CANADA

Ten years ago, British Airways (BA) was delivering a product with essentially the same hard specifications it has now — many of the same routes, on modern aircraft, with highly qualified employees. But customers still dubbed BA "bloody awful."

"Certainly, the management at the airline wasn't delivering a bad product on purpose," says James C. Tennant, Executive Vice-President, Human Resources and Total Quality Management, Air Canada. "All those people, many of whom are still with the airline today, haven't suddenly become quality managers — they always were. But one important aspect of their management has changed. Now, they allow their customers to define what quality is.

"It is not difficult to see how the move toward quality changed their business. BA is now one of the world's most profitable airlines. And they got that way by giving customers the service they want. The quality of the planes hasn't changed. Neither have the qualifications of their employees changed.

"But the investment BA made in listening to their customers has. They have 100 researchers who conduct 250,000 interviews in 60 airports around the world each year. And in the course of this research, BA's customers have told them exactly what was lacking in their product — those soft qualities that are so hard to define."

Factoring the customer into the business equation makes determining a product's hard specifications that much more difficult. For example, take seat pitch — the distance between each row of seats on an aircraft. Tennant says that Air Canada has had to search out the middle ground between the company's need to make a profit and the desire to please the customer. "Of course, in our experience, customers say that there can never be enough leg room on an aircraft. But we won't stay in business very long if we can fit only 100 passengers on a 747. So we need to compromise with the customer."

HARD AND SOFT

Hard specifications, like seat pitch, can be determined relatively easily from surveys. So they are easy to measure and prioritize.

The other kind of specifications, the soft ones, are much harder to determine and prioritize. Like friendliness, for example. Air Canada research indicated that in-flight employees needed to be friendlier to passengers. Tennant admits that this is a bit of a grey area. "You can't develop a set of specifications to designate how an employee is to be friendly. Some of it comes naturally, but much of it comes with reinforcement from the corporate culture."

"We have had examples where we have failed on the hard specifications of quality but where the soft side has carried us through unscathed." Tennant uses the example of a flight to London that experienced a lengthy delay for repairs. "Rather than taking the traditional route of providing meal vouchers, one of our people there chartered a bus and took the whole group on a tour of a game farm near the city.

"It is heartening for a customer to see an employee doing everything but cartwheels to provide a quality product. And in the end, that is just as important as the hard specifications."

Tennant stresses that hard and soft qualities must be woven together. One cannot have one without the other and hope the quality initiative will succeed.

Tennant's little story is a microcosm of the overall evaluation process.

He has spotted the gaps, seen what someone else has done in the same situation, and filled the gap, always bearing in mind that resolution of service problems comes from, in his words, "reinforcement from the corporate culture."

American Express has been a service leader for a long time. It knows the importance of research.

"It is critical to our business to know what level of service our customers want and expect," says Vice-President of Operations Betty Daruwala. "And we need to know what our employees think about their jobs and the company. Only then can we retain customers and staff. Systematic research helps us to understand our market's expectations. Of course, research is not a one-time process. To be effective, research must be conducted regularly, so that benchmarks can be established and improved upon. Research takes the guesswork out of our business strategies."

Here's how they do it.

RESEARCH AT AMERICAN EXPRESS

Since 1979, American Express has used sophisticated tracking mechanisms to measure some 30 internal processes. It expanded its horizons. It wanted to improve service in areas that have the greatest impact on customer satisfaction. Specifically, it set out to determine what triggers loyalty and card retention and what aspects of service improve profitability.

Amex felt it needed to ask its customers how *they* felt about its service delivery. What did *they* want Amex to do better? Was Amex meeting or exceeding their expectations? What should Amex service standards be? And what was the payback of good service delivery to the bottom line?

So, in 1986, Amex launched its cardmember satisfaction surveys.

The operations, marketing, market research and quality assurance departments worked with TARP consultants to design the surveys. The first survey was a general one that asked questions about the customer's experiences with Amex. Subsequent qualitative and quantitative research and focus group discussion, however, made Amex realize that the questionnaires had to be more specific to be of any use.

"So we put together five transaction-based questionnaires," says Daruwala. "They are mailed to cardmembers who have recently done a transaction with Amex. Ideally, the questionnaires are mailed within two weeks of contact while the experience is still fresh in the cardmember's mind."

The five transactions (we might also call them moments of truth or points of contact) are

1) *billing inquiry:* where the cardmember recently received a reply to a billing inquiry or request for a copy of his or her statement;

2) *telephone inquiry:* where the cardmember recently contacted the telephone service centre to request information or initiate a billing inquiry;

3) *card replacement* where a card was issued by regular mail, courier or at a travel office anywhere in the world;

4) *authorization inquiry:* where a cardmember had recently been called to the phone to speak to an authorizer while using the card anywhere in the world;

5) *dunning:* which went to customers who were dunned by letter or telephone for overdue balances.

The surveys have been distributed in 14 countries and in eight languages, with an average response rate of 38 per cent. Portions of these studies are to be found in Appendix IV. Some countries run the surveys each year. Others run them in alternate years, thus giving time for the phases of the improvement program to become better established. Formalized continuous tracking also allows Amex to remain sensitive to customer trends and to see how its service initiative is progressing.

Findings

By way of example, here's what Amex found.

The billing inquiry survey revealed that fair resolution of an inquiry gave the greatest customer satisfaction. Satisfaction decreased as the length of time it took to resolve the inquiry increased, even though Amex had already placed a temporary credit on the account. The survey also revealed that customers expected status updates on their inquiry. Amex responded to the survey results by making plans to reduce resolution time and to give updates.

From the telephone inquiry survey, Amex learned that transferring the customer to a second representative caused the greatest dissatisfaction. Amex now attempts to have calls completed at the first point of customer contact.

Talking to Employees

"The success of Amex depends on its employees — on their values and their commitment to our values," says Daruwala in no uncertain terms. In 1990, Amex researched employees at all levels worldwide. Employees were asked their opinion of the principles that guide business at Amex, on what needed to change at the company, and how Amex could become the best place to work.

Amex conducted written surveys and one-on-one interviews with 10 per cent of the employees, chosen at random, in each country. The response rate averaged 85 per cent. Employees were asked to comment on the importance of nine aspects of the company:

1) the mission of American Express;

2) the work itself that employees do;

3) their satisfaction with their work;

4) opportunities for development;

5) the values of American Express;

6) the climate within the company;

7) leadership at various levels;

8) communication; and

9) compensation, rewards and recognition.

Employees were also asked to rate Amex's performance in terms of these nine business aspects. There was also space for comments, which many employees offered.

Results were then compared to the results from other countries and regions. Each aspect of business was placed under the heading "Things we do well" or "High need for changes."

Each country published its survey results in employee newsletters. Human resource departments followed up by conducting focus groups within each department to acquire a more in-depth understanding of the needed changes. Suggestions were gathered. Management and associate teams devised plans to make the changes.

The survey process is ongoing at Amex. "A worldwide values 're-survey' is scheduled for August [1992]," says Daruwala, "so we will be able to gauge our progress toward becoming the best place to work. As with the results of the customer satisfaction surveys, the employee-values survey results are included in our management goals. We want to ensure continuous improvement in customer and employee satisfaction."

Research at Coca-Cola

Coca-Cola goes about research the same way, although it uses different terms.

"Simply making the statement 'customer service is important and that we must ensure customer satisfaction' doesn't make it happen," says George Gourlay, Vice-President and Director of Corporate Manufacturing Operations, in the Fall 1991 issue of the

ICSA Journal. "Goals must be set, benchmarks established, communication and quality measurement systems established, tools and training provided."

Coke's first step is to find out what its customers want. That means it must

1) identify areas for opportunity versus customer expectations and benchmarks;

2) establish a priority list of customer requirement and expectations;

3) determine the current customer satisfaction level in terms of the requirements list;

4) establish customer satisfaction benchmarks and Coca-Cola Company performance goals; and

5) establish key leverage points and performance measurement criteria to measure performance objectively against goals and customer expectations.

"While we may set what appear to be adequate service standards," says Gourley, "only the customer knows what is needed. It's easy to set our standards for the customer or to set performance measurement criteria that are not important to the customer. But that deludes us into believing that we are providing excellent service, only to find out later that we are not. So, it is essential that we agree with our customers in advance exactly what is important to them."

Coke's customer service standards, outlined in its customer service statement, are nothing if not thorough:

1) We ensure absolute continuity of supply of product and service.

2) We understand our customer needs and satisfy their expectations through regular contact and communication.

3) We respond to all customer queries and complaints within 24 hours.

4) Our delivery time is flexible and is set in accordance with customer requirements. We "make to order" whenever possible.

5) We minimize the cost of delivery through effective route scheduling and negotiation with carriers.

Coca-Cola has put in place specific performance measurement criteria to track company performance against its customers' expectations. Says Gourlay, "with established requirements, we can constantly monitor our performance and ensure that we continuously improve."

ONE FINANCIAL INSTITUTION'S SERVICE STORY

One of the country's largest financial institutions, which prefers to downplay its external communication regarding its commitment to quality service researches service in a number of ways. It first looks at the big picture through strategic research; then it seeks out customer needs at the local level with tactical research.

In this organization's view, the first step in understanding how research contributes to the quality improvement effort is to have a solid grasp of the criteria involved. Good research must be clearly focused on the customer. It must provide value by being specific and actionable. What good is research if it doesn't lead to behavior change?

Good research coincides with a company's business plans. It doesn't sail off on its own. It's solidly anchored to the goals of management. And it actively supports the basic strategic thrusts of the business.

For this financial institution, the research goal is to understand

➤ what its customers expect;

➤ what it is doing to meet their needs; and

➤ how it is doing versus the competition.

It feels that knowing how it fares against the competition is extremely important in the banking business. The institution's research found that its average customer deals with two to three other financial institutions. That means it has to constantly outperform its competitors. To do this, it must first know how it stacks up in the marketplace. This is where strategic research comes in.

Strategic Research

Strategic research focuses on aspects of banking operations from a bank-wide perspective. For instance, core business groups — corporate and retail — sponsor annual studies. What the organization learns from these ongoing studies enables each core group to formulate strategy, start up new delivery mechanisms, initiate product development, and identify improvements required in quality service.

At regular intervals, it also conducts comprehensive staff opinion surveys which include several questions specifically related to service delivery. "We ask our staff to evaluate management's commitment to customer service. We also ask about our processes and the extent to which they are conducive to providing quality service."

This financial institution also surveys shareholders annually. It believes shareholders give good feedback because they are customers as well as shareholders.

Image Studies and Tactical Research

Each year the bank does what it calls an image study. This study tracks customer and non-customer perception of the bank in terms of financial stability, products, service quality and prices. "We want to know how Canadians perceive us in general."

The bank must understand the different needs of the many and varied communities in which it operates. So it uses tactical research to understand the expectations of customers at the local level.

"We wanted to get closer to our customers — to create an environment that would make it easier for our people to put the customer first. To do this, we began decentralizing authority back to the grassroots. It just didn't make sense to have someone in a field headquarters department make decisions that affected how a branch operated hundreds of miles away."

Focus Groups

On the retail side, they have well over 100 area management teams across the country. They have responsibility for anywhere between three and 10 branches and they are physically located in their market — close to their customers and their staff. The area managers are expected to identify and pro-actively respond to the particular needs of their customers.

To help area managers with the process, the bank uses focus groups as a means of research. For example, if the bank wanted to improve its quality of service in an area with a high population of senior citizens, the branch would hold a number of focus groups with them. At these sessions, the bank would want to find out

➤ what kinds of services seniors want;

➤ which aspects of service were most important to them;

➤ what they did not like about the service they were receiving at present.

The bank would also hold focus groups with staff known for offering seniors a particularly high level of service. The findings from the various focus groups would then be used to help structure a seniors centre or similar delivery mechanism.

Service Excellence

Another key initiative of the bank, based on extensive surveying, is its Service Excellence Program. The program begins with a survey that invites input from customers at the branch level. The goal of this survey is to

➤ provide local branch staff and area management with immediate feedback on how well they are meeting the needs of their customers;

➤ help identify where the bank needs to take specific action to improve; and

➤ recognize individuals and branch teams who clearly demonstrate the very highest service standards.

Input into the survey from the front line is crucial. Its success has proven that research must always be the first step in any local quality improvement effort.

Tactical research can also be done in less formal ways. Area managers are expected to get out of the office and talk to customers and staff. They are expected to get to know personally their business and consumer customers.

By becoming actively involved in their community and by participating in local chambers of commerce and other groups, the area managers are able to obtain valuable insights. Some of the best feedback they receive is through these informal channels. Meeting one-on-one with customers means they get clear, unfiltered feedback. They have an opportunity to probe and hear not only the words, but the message.

When the bank actively generates research at the local level and gives managers considerable autonomy to act on their findings, area managers can do much to improve service quality. Sometimes, the best way to find out what a customer is thinking is by simply picking up the phone and calling him or her. Contacting a customer following the sale of a product, after transferring their account, or when a new service has been put in their business can be enlightening. Not only does it allow the bank to ensure the client is satisfied, it gives the organization an opportunity to take corrective action if required. In our fast-paced world, sometimes we forget how valuable a personal touch can be to our businesses.

Taking Suggestions

You'd think the above collection of research methods was pretty complete, but there's more.

For example, there is a Staff Suggestion Program. Through it you can encourage staff to suggest ways to improve how you do business. One financial institution expects to receive in excess of 10,000 suggestions this year, and many of these will focus on customer service. These are logged and tracked.

The bank also analyses customer complaints. There was a time when a customer complaint was looked upon as a nuisance. This attitude has certainly changed. Today, they are called "customer concerns" and everyone realizes the true value of this kind of feedback.

To make sure it receives customer input, the Royal Bank has produced two brochures: "How To Take Action When Things Go Wrong" and "Straight Talk about Making a Complaint at Royal Bank." The second of these pamphlets outlines the steps customers can take to obtain redress, including writing the President of the bank or the Superintendent of Financial Institutions.

One month after a complaint has been resolved, the bank surveys the client. Specifically, it asks them to evaluate

➤ the bank's responsiveness;

➤ the bank's understanding of the issue; and

➤ the client's satisfaction with the solution.

The bank has found this feedback helps it keep in touch with customers' expectations and improves its concern-handling process.

The bank also uses 1-800 numbers to keep up with the customer. Each month, Customer Information Phone Centres handle over 30,000 inquiries about subjects ranging from interest rates to the location of the nearest branch. And they often receive calls that identify a service defect or poor communication between bank and customer.

Getting Out of the Office

Today, account mangers go to their clients. They visit their place of business, and frequently they are accompanied by an officer responsible for the business's day-to-day transaction requirements. They learn first-hand what our customers expect, both from the business owner and the people who do the job.

Next to your customers, front-line staff are the best source of information. They know what the customers want. They can tell you what to do to improve your quality of service.

Surveying Never Stops

A survey conducted by the Canadian Bankers' Association revealed that 3 per cent of bank customers will change financial institutions this year. On the surface, it may not appear significant that 3 per cent of customers leave. But for one financial institution it means they will lose 225,000 customers. At an average profit of $80 per annum, this 3 per cent becomes $18 million walking out the door. That is a figure that will get anyone's attention.

Customer expectations are ever-increasing and ever-changing. What was considered good service yesterday may be only mediocre tomorrow. The onus will be on the providers of the service to find out what customers expect.

Customers are beginning to say "enough!" to traditional research methods. Clearly, we will need to find new and innovative ways of determining and anticipating our customers' expectations. The best companies will do this. Now, more than ever, we need to find out what our customers expect, how well we are doing, and where we can do better. Research is only a first step. But it's an essential one if we are to ensure that we deliver world-class quality in the '90s, and beyond.

CHECKLIST

1) Have you identified your current service standards?

2) Have you compared your performance against these standards through internal and external research?

3) Have you surveyed internal and external customers through
   - mail questionnaires
   - direct mail
   - internal climate surveys
   - suggestion programs
   - focus groups
   - customer panels
   - quality circles

4) Have you evaluated your performance relative to the competition through competitive intelligence and market research?

5) Have you used benchmarking to identify best practices and to set new goals?

6) Do your research methods allow you to qualitatively track customer trends and shifts, as well as rank priorities? Do they allow you to evaluate management commitment to the service process and spot potential middle-management impediments?

7) Do these research methods include rating scales and priority rankings?

8) Have you formalized the research process to ensure that it will be continuous?

9) Have you identified your internal and external service gaps?

C H A P T E R

5

THE DESIGN PHASE
(Choosing the best road)

When we want to take a journey, the first thing we normally do is decide where we will go. The same is true when designing a customer service program.

— *Marva McArthur, Investors Fiduciary Trust Co.*

Where are we going? Who's driving? Have we brought everything we need? Is the car in good shape?

Most of all, when we get there ...

WHERE SHOULD WE BE?

Now that you have thoroughly researched yourself and your service delivery, assessed your market in service terms, and discovered what must change in your organization to put a quality service program in place, the next step is to design a service strategy.

A service strategy must be at one with the overall objectives of the organization and, moreover, it must complement the strategic direction of the organization.

I can't overstate how important correct design and correct implementation is to the success of a service strategy. Neither can the President of Campbell soup, Dave Clark:

"We're all reading the same information, we're observing the same phenomena, we're exposed to the same market forces. We all tend to use almost identical strategies, and yet there are some very different results. Some strategies are very successful, some are less so, some are much less so. Why is that?

"It's not because the strategies are that different; it's the implementation of the strategy that counts. This is particularly true when it comes to total quality. There must be a gazillion consultants, academics, practitioners, all of whom pursue essentially the same total quality approach to their business. However, there is wide variance in effectiveness of the outcome, and the only conclusion you can come to is that it's not the framework, but how well it gets implemented. That's what makes the difference."

So to start making a difference, decide where you want to be and how you want your employees to be five years from now. The design phase answers this question: How would you want the processes of your organization to look if all of your problems were solved? What would the standards be?

The design phase reinforces service priorities, gives shape to the best way to achieve an organization-wide buy-in, and puts them together into a service strategy.

OPERATIONAL CHANGE

When it comes to designing a program, five operational areas may see change.

1) *Organizational structure:* There may be changes in the reporting relationship, number of levels of management, and scope of managerial responsibility.

2) *Policy and procedures:* Superior service delivery will necessitate changes to many policies and procedures that conflict with one another, that have an operational rather than a service focus, that are counter-productive, or that are generally inefficient. New standards will be created.

3) *Personnel practice:* The notion of achievable superior service will be woven into the personnel fabric of the entire organization through employee selection procedures, orientation, training, performance review, promotion guidelines and compensation plans.

4) *Facilities and systems:* There may be changes in, for example, the organization's billing system, the structure of its computer network, or even its front-desk layout.

5) *Process flow:* There will be less emphasis within the organization on jobs as functions and less vertical decision-making, but more cross-functional work and horizontal decision-making.

These changes will be framed within a strategic service vision. Bear in mind that a service plan that is a product of the T.Q.S. process should not be seen as a replacement for existing strategic planning exercises.

Of course, I can't tell you what your service strategy should be. Everyone is different. But I can give you a framework for designing a service strategy. And I can show you the pitfalls many organizations stumble into, the things they forget. To start, here's ...

A Key Fact to Remember

When developing a service strategy remember this: It is not enough to match the competition, you will have to out-think them.

Business today is like being stuck in traffic. Everybody is going the same way, and to the same place; consequently, no one goes anywhere. In technical terms, this is the problem of insufficient differentiation.

When you have determined the attributes of your competition and have determined your customers' needs, you must do more than merely close the gap between the two.

Closing this gap will, of course, increase your competitive advantage. Unfortunately, it will also reduce your differentiation. In other words, you merely imitate the competition. And worse, because you are doing what they have done, you become dependent on what they do, instead of striking out on your own to provide something no one else provides. You must abandon the old attitude of "If it ain't broke, don't fix it."

This way of doing business has been called catch-up. Catching up to the competition is not the object of T.Q.S.

The catch-up approach is a product-based approach; you do as the competition does. You don't want to do that. You want to move ahead of them. That means taking a quality-added approach — putting out a product equal to that of anyone else in the market, and making it better by delivering it with a unique level of service.

The best way to look for the means to move ahead is to find a space where a customer need is not being met — and that need, as study after study has shown, is service.

The owner of a supermarket chain described service differentiation in more down-to-earth terms. He told *Family Business* (April

1990) that "a can of peas is a can of peas on anybody's shelf. The difference is how the customers feel about the place while they're buying those peas."

Remember also that, as you increase your relative perceived quality, that of your competition declines. And this can snowball. The gap between you and them can widen and widen.

WHERE DOES DESIGN BEGIN?

Now we come to the design phase.

Take the mission statement down off the wall and knock the dust off it. It's probably been up there so long that no one notices it among the calendars and year-old memos, and no one understands what it means anymore.

A mission statement isn't much use to anyone if it's out of date and irrelevant to current concerns and if it does not have a service strategy built into it. It must be made visible again to all employees. And that service strategy needs clear goals, goals unequivocally stated, and it needs to be precise. Goals, priorities and a sense of commitment must breathe through it.

And it must have goals that you intend to follow through on — there is little to be gained from creating a service strategy just because it is the thing to do.

An important step in the service journey is the revision of the mission statement to include a quality service statement, and to make sure the customer and the employee-as-customer appear in it.

The Quality Service strategy is the sum of your commitment to the service project; this sense of mission must be translated to the employees. Otherwise, they'll think it's just another thing to cover space on the wall of the receiving bay.

"Many of you said it best when you pointed out that we can't *implement* values; we have to *behave* in a way that will show we understand and believe in them," says Dennis Caplice, Deputy Minister of the Ontario Ministry of Government Services. "Our principles aren't a menu we use to choose what appeals to us. Rather, they form a coherent framework that we will try to live by every day, and some days we will be more successful than others. The key is to keep trying."

The Quality Service strategy is a serious statement of intent — that is, it is not a vague, feel-good set of slogans. Vague statements yield no results. After all, how can you measure what you can't understand? Ron Weiner of Weiner Consulting Services in Woodridge, Illinois, says in the *ICSA Journal* that way back when he was a customer service manager, he devised a report to measure performance that was actually part of the mission statement.

SERVICE LEVEL REPORT

Activity	Goal	Actual Performance
Order Entry	Same Day	95% Same Day 5% Next Day
Quote Response	Within 24 Hours	98% Within 24 Hours 2% Within 48 Hours
Shipping Performance	All Within 24 Hours	100% Within 24 Hours
Providing Technical Response	Same Day	85% Same Day 10% Next Day 5% Over 48 Hours

Weiner's reporting chart makes sure mission statements are specific and their goals are attainable and, therefore, measurable. Further, he recommends that all levels of the organization pitch in on the mission statement's development; otherwise, personnel who haven't had a hand in shaping it think they aren't part of the mission and that they exist just to take orders. If the Quality Service statement says "98 per cent of all products will be in stock at all times," that had better be agreed to by those responsible for making it happen.

The Quality Service strategy must differentiate you from your competitors. So must your ...

CUSTOMER BILL OF RIGHTS

A customer bill of rights is exactly that. It tells the customers what they can expect every time they do business with you. It guarantees service. It tells customers what you will do to meet their expectations.

The customer bill of rights must raise the value of your company in customers' eyes. And you must be able to deliver what it promises.

A customer bill of rights is a set of standards. Therefore, it can help you measure performance (for more on this subject, see the discussion under the heading "Service Guarantees," in Chapter 8). If your bill of rights says "the customer will receive a response to an inquiry within 24 hours," you can measure your performance to see if you are meeting that standard. It is also important to have an internal bill of rights to measure internal service performance.

The example below, from Liptons International, meets these requirements. Both it and the accompanying Quality Service statement for American Express suggest to the customer — this is what we want to be famous for.

Customer
Service Pledge

I Pledge

To greet all customers as guests and
invite them back.

To acknowledge verbally all
customers throughout the store wherever
eye contact is made.

To personally follow through
when a customer asks for assistance until
their requests are satisfied.

To remember customers are the people
that make it possible to pay my salary.

To call customers when I have something
important to say.

To provide every customer with a unique
shopping experience.

EMPLOYEE PERCEPTION EQUALS CUSTOMER PERCEPTION

The mission statement is an important document. It tells employees whether or not you are serious. Employees want to know that their contribution will be valued and that what they do is important.

Everything you do in your day-to-day business activities communicates your attitude about service, about the customer, about the employee. And what you do can inadvertently work against the professed aims of your mission statement. Who gets promoted, who gets which parking space, the state of the lunchroom...all these little things say something to others about your attitude toward them. Other examples:

A head office memo is circulated saying superior service performance will be rewarded, but employees see that good performance and bad performance are rewarded equally at promotion time.

Or, management calls for ideas from the front line, but the ideas are never seen or heard from again; the employee never hears if they were accepted or rejected.

Employees are easily put off by this kind of behavior. They begin to act contrary to desired goals and values. Why? Because they don't know what the real values are or no longer believe in the stated values because they ring hollow.

Can you blame them?

The mission statement must be consistent, it must be followed, and it must come from the top. A service culture must be total, or it's not a service culture but a rag-bag of ideas and slogans that sound good but mean nothing.

And this affects the customer. They get inconsistent service. They get uncaring service. Because that is what the organization is — inconsistent, uncaring. That is how it acts internally. Everything an organization does internally reflects its appearance externally.

PLAN TO HIRE THE RIGHT PEOPLE

One more thing. Work into the service strategy a plan to hire people who are oriented toward the kind of service you wish to give. Robert DeMone, President of Canadian Pacific Hotels & Resorts, sees the importance of hiring service-minded people clearly.

"You have to start with people who are service-minded people. There is no point in hiring square pegs and trying to fit them into round holes. You've got to hire those capable of being service-oriented. With outside experts, we have developed a screening technique for identifying round pegs to fit the round holes.

"As far as I'm concerned, you've got to have people who are service-oriented by nature and who have an inclination to make the service industry their chosen career. And coupled with that, I happen to believe that every single solitary person born on this earth has a unique talent and a unique ability to contribute to an enterprise. And I think it's up to those who are leaders in their companies and industries to provide a work environment that brings forth that talent that is latent in every person."

THE SERVICE STRATEGY
BLUEPRINT: DRAW IT

This may seem obvious. But too often 'design' means little more than introducing a new slogan, like "the Customer is Always Right," or handing out little plaques to stick on your desk that say "Commitment is Job 1."

These verbal, feel-good approaches inevitably go haywire. Everybody starts to do their own thing. Everybody tries to row in the direction they think is best, and the boat goes round and round in a wonky circle.

A blueprint gets the sense of culture down on paper. By blueprint, I mean the service map and the Quality Service strategy. A blueprint gives you the total picture of your service aims. Everyone looks at the same drawing. It cannot be misinterpreted. Writing it down helps you to shape the service direction you wish to take and to make sure everyone goes in that direction.

Front-line employees are often victims of bad service design. Often a service problem on the front-line originates in management and the program they have designed. It surfaces only at the end of the process, at the worst moment —when dealing with a customer. It's like discovering, when you sit down to eat, that you forgot to put salt in your porridge. Only when you take the first spoonful do you discover your mistake. It's a mistake that can't be rectified until next time. And in today's world of tight competition and choosy customers, there may be no next time.

Putting the service strategy down on paper allows the organization to play-test it. To try it out. Hear the staff's opinions. The customer's. If problems crop up, they can be corrected — before the system is in place. The worst thing one can do is to say, "I want a service culture," then leave it to the employees to implement as they see fit — because that will leave you with an erratic approach to service that will hamper your ability to shift with changing market conditions. Leave nothing to chance.

The blueprint of your service strategy is a roadmap. Never leave home without it.

THE NEXT ELEMENT OF THE DESIGN PHASE

Senior service executives were asked in a 1988 study to identify what part of their company was responsible for customer satisfaction. Amazingly, most said operations or marketing. Administration (which usually includes the human resources department) ranked third.

Over half the respondents did not even mention administration in connection with customer satisfaction. Most respondents were senior vice-presidents; few CEOs completed the survey (despite being part of administration), which goes to show that customer satisfaction is not thought to be important at the top level of management.

Now consider this:

Success magazine asked J.W. Marriott Jr., CEO of the Marriott hotel chain, how he went about assessing his company's service practices. His answer should sit on the desk of all executives.

"First, get out of the office.

"Second, don't just visit — ask questions all day. Ask your employees about their jobs. What are their frustrations in dealing with their customers and their bosses? Do they have the right setup? Do they have enough authority — do they have to defer decisions to their boss's boss?

"Third, respond to their problems. You have to take some action on what they tell you, and get back to them. Otherwise, they'll assume you didn't really care about what they said, and they won't tell you anything again.

"Most important, set the example for service. I recently met a man who'd just bought a car. He got a call from the president of the dealership asking how the car was working out. The man said, 'Fine, I think. But it's my wife who drives it.' So the president said, 'Tell me where I can call to ask her.' And he followed up with the man's wife. That's how you keep customers."

There are many things implied in this short quote, all of which are essential to the design of a service plan: the shortened distance between the CEO and front-line staff; the need for management to listen to employees and customers; and the need for commitment at the top. Marriott, in short, seeks to overcome internal barriers to quality service by putting his hand in.

At Federal Express, some 40,000 people are in regular contact with the customer. This stems from the company philosophy. Federal Express wants to keep the distance between management and front-line staff as short as possible, so that ideas can easily and quickly find their way to the right person at the top. It has a shallow hierarchy that puts the customer at the top, at the widest part of the inverted pyramid, and the CEO at the bottom.

Also, note how few levels the pyramid has. As I mentioned in Chapter 1, the more levels of decision-making there are in an organization, the slower the organization's response time when responding to customer needs.

MAINTAINING A "FLAT" ORGANIZATIONAL HIERARCHY.

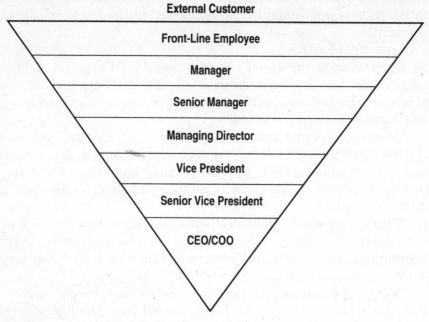

SOURCE: BLUEPRINTS FOR SERVICE QUALITY: THE FEDERAL EXPRESS APPROACH, AMA MEMBERSHIP PUBLICATIONS DIVISION

XEROX — A CUSTOMER-DRIVEN ORGANIZATION

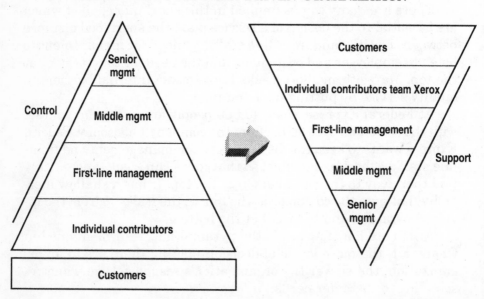

SOURCE: USED WITH THE PERMISSION OF XEROX CANADA LTD.

RIVALRY

Internal rivalry is a chronic problem in hierarchical organizations. It is an impediment to flattening the hierarchy and improving communication, both of which need to be accomplished for the service process to succeed. By using a service process rather than a program, you will foster co-operation rather than competition in the organization. A service process allows you to satisfy the internal customer and, at the same time, satisfy the external customer. To put it another way, individual success means company success: individual success does not mean the kind of success that comes at the expense of someone or some other department within the company (this can be the case, for example, in a rivalry between ambitious managers of complementary departments). The functional approach to serving the customer (internally or externally) tends to "silo" departments, which causes bitterness and competitiveness among departments.

Adversarial relationships plague western business. Many companies that build complex machinery (cars, say) buy parts from contractors; contractors bid to supply the parts; the company pits them against each other to bring down the price.

The Japanese do it differently. They have one regular supplier. And they set up an agreement with the supplier so that it supplies the part when it is needed at a set price; that part then goes directly to the production line. This method eliminates storage costs, saves time, and sets up a close non-competitive relationship between supplier and company. This is, of course, an external relationship, but it is easy to see how this kind of relationship could exist between internal departments as well.

SILOS

Many employees would rather operate in their own silos.

Related to the problem of rivalry is the problem of silos. Many organizations are filled with silos.

An organization has many departments. Often, each department takes the attitude that, once a job has passed through it and on to the next, "It's their problem now, not mine."

For example, the cashier at a hotel balances the till at the end of the day, then passes it on to the accounting department. The cashier's job is to make sure that the till balances. But at a hotel filled with silos, the cashier will let accounting figure out whether the till is balanced: "My job is to collect money, not balance the books," the cashier says.

Obviously, in this hotel internal processes would be slow and inefficient. In many large organizations, a department will throw things over the wall into somebody else's silo, and that other person will throw it into someone else's silo, and so on.

This is why you see many organizations fighting themselves when designing a quality service initiative. They have looked at service delivery, changed it, discovered that their level of customer satisfaction is the same as ever, and now wonder, "Why aren't we able to develop a service culture. Why can't we create better service?"

The reason is that they have not helped the people in the service chain realize that they are part of that chain.

I've found many organizations to be cluttered with silos. Siloing is a structural problem. Silo walls must be broken down to make the service venture succeed. After breaking them down, the organization must replace them with a structure that makes people feel that they are part of a team and that everything they do affects the total service-delivery process.

The crux of the problem is that the people in the information systems department don't realize that they help the customer service person at the other end of the organization to do his or her job. They see their role in the company in isolation; they don't see that they have the same impact on service as do those at the front line. They don't feel that they are part of the company: they feel that they are part of the information systems department. The information systems department is their silo.

Once that service strategy is developed, the next step is to help employees realize that they are part of a total chain, in that they are an integral part of strategy and that what they do affects others. Therefore, they have to understand what the others do. The service mapping process achieves this goal.

SERVICE MAPPING

Mapping the service chain works like this. Make a chart for each type of customer transaction. Note the customer and which front-line staff member deals with the customer. This interaction is called a "point of contact."

Then note the points of contact and personnel not seen by the customer. These could be a number of different people and/or job functions: computer support, the billing office, a manager, a supervisor, and so on. These are the internal points of contact.

Next, note the internal points of contact between management at all levels.

When you're done, you will be able to

➤ describe the service-delivery process;

➤ identify redundancies and cost inefficiencies;

➤ understand how to break down silos;

➤ train employees in the functions of other departments; and

➤ establish interdepartmental standards.

Mapping: The Process

Here's how the mapping process works in detail. There are eight steps to the process. Before you proceed to Step One, you must form cross-functional teams with personnel from every department that, in one way or another, is involved in the process under review (More about teams later in this chapter).

Step One: Identify the service deliverable that you would like to achieve, for example, accurate and timely, bills or invoices. Document answers to the following questions: What is to be delivered and by whom? What makes the delivered service successful? What impediments are there to this success? What are the existing service standards and performance measurement criteria for this process?

If the group cannot answer any of these questions, that indicates "red flags" where corrective action must be taken. The team's most common difficulty will be identifying who the customer is and what is needed to satisfy the customer.

Steps Two and Three: Identify all points of contact without regard for the department or division involved, or the sequence of activities. Team members may have to speak to other departments to make sure no steps in the sequence are left out. Note whether the activity is direct or indirect.

As an example, suppose there is a process to send a welcome package to a new customer. It is more than a matter of just sending the package off in the mail. You want to know about the process. Who gets involved? What are the activities involved? Which departments are involved in the delivery in some capacity. Is a given activity direct or indirect? A direct activity means that you go from step A to step B, then to step C after you finish B. An indirect activity is something that supports the A-B-C sequence, like the telephone system or the back-up computer system.

Remember, the mapping process does not simply map paper flow. Rather, it maps job functions.

COMPANY "X"

Service Deliverable: Provide Client Information Package to a New/Prospective Client

Department(s)	Activity/Contact Point	Direct/Indirect
Voice Communication	Phone call from client	Indirect
Retail Sales	Client account opened	Direct
Computer Sales	Program utilized	Indirect
Network	Computer system back-up	Indirect
Computer Operation	Letters printed	Direct
Mail Room	Package mailed	Direct
Administration	Confirmation received and filed	Direct
Marketing	Inserts created	Indirect
Graphics	Art produced for package	Indirect
Marketing	Inserts changed as required	Indirect
Human Resources	Materials translated	Indirect
Printing	Printing/reprinting	Indirect
Purchasing	Materials purchasing/ contracting	Indirect

Place each activity into one of the four categories (I for Initiation, P for Processing, E for Execution and F for Follow-up) on the chart for Step Three. (You will probably see that category F is rather empty.)

Step Four: Draw a map or flow chart of the delivery process. Keep the number of symbols to a minimum for clarity.

CLIENT INFORMATION PACKAGE

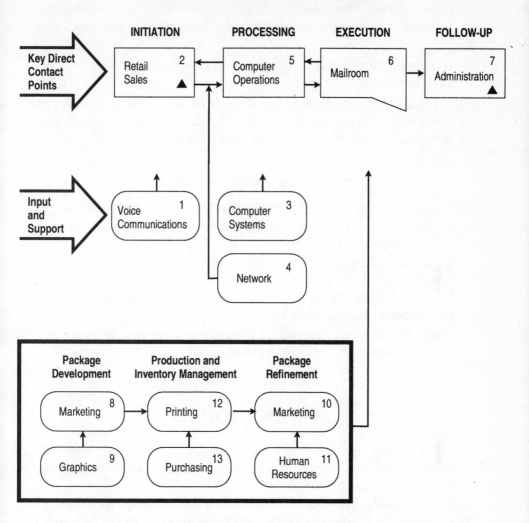

Step Five: On the map, identify service redundancies and needless effort. Redraw the map to eliminate these things.

Step Six: Review each point of contact or "hand-off" between department or function. Identify areas of improvement. Prioritize them (see below for more on prioritizing). Set standards for these improvements. Set performance measures and a timetable for implementation of changes.

Note: Setting standards related directly to empowerment. You can't just say to somebody, "You are charged with the responsibility, don't worry, you're empowered. You can make that decision." The person has to know what the standard is, and what the allowable deviations are, to be able to exercise the power he or she has been given.

Step Seven: Implement improvements in order of priority. Begin performance measurement.

Step Eight: Step Eight repeats Step One. The service process is ongoing, continuous improvement. As the new service-delivery process takes hold, begin the mapping process anew.

What You Have Learned

The service mapping process will have taught its participants

➤ appreciation of the work done by other departments (in this way, it breaks down silos);

➤ a way of looking at their work as part of a continuum rather than simply as "my job";

➤ meaningful standards — standards that have been set by the participants themselves; and

➤ about the service culture and the co-operative role each person plays in the service-delivery chain.

WORKSHOPS

The first step to breaking down silos involves getting people from different departments together and involving them in the design of a service organization.

Conducting workshops is the first step in building quality service teams. Workshops perform the additional function of breaking down internal barriers to service by bringing together people who work at different points in the service chain.

Through functional and cross-functional workshops, employee groups review and redesign the service-delivery process in the areas in which you have determined improvement opportunities exist. Study the service maps you have made and the business cases you have gathered from the benchmarking process. Brainstorm to solve problems: Who internally is not being served? Have the necessary people been trained to support this service function? Does job evaluation cover service roles? And so on.

PLAYING CATCH

The Japanese use a brainstorming technique that is like playing catch.

One person throws out an idea, no matter how outrageous or un-workable. Somebody else "catches" it. Even if the idea sounds daft, that person doesn't throw it away (it would be a dull way to play catch). Instead, that person takes it, turns it over, improves it, adds to it, sub-tracts from it, then tosses it to someone else, who does the same.

The idea gets tossed around the team and comes back to the person who started it. It comes back far different from how it began. But it has now become a rough idea of a way to improve some aspect of company service. The idea has been scrutinized by all whom it di-rectly affects. You can now start throwing this nascent idea around again, or pass it to a focus group or team who will be responsible for getting it ready to be implemented by the company.

Playing "catch" can lead to some surprising results.

Shaping a Change

Having caught the ball, you must next sit down and work out how to put it in place.

IBM Canada, when redesigning job functions, for example, asks these essential questions, the answers to which shape the redesigned job:

➤ Which service encounters are handled by a particular job?

➤ During a certain service encounter, what other jobs or depart-ments come into play?

- ➤ What level of customer expectations relate to those other levels?
- ➤ What are the findings of customer research with respect to this particular service encounter?
- ➤ What is the quality of job performance in terms of customer satisfaction?
- ➤ What does the person need to know to satisfactorily complete this service encounter?
- ➤ How many other people are needed to complete this service encounter?
- ➤ How can that number be reduced to as few as possible?
- ➤ How does the person need to be empowered to raise the customer satisfaction to a suitable level?
- ➤ What is the optimal workplace design for this job — consider furniture, computer access, procedures, and so on — with respect to realigning it toward a service culture?

PRIORITIZE

You now have a small pile of ideas to improve service in your company. You probably can't implement them all at once. So the next step is to prioritize. Determine the projects that can begin right away and the ones that can wait. Set a time frame for each.

At this point, everyone asks, "How do we prioritize?" The answer is easy.

Begin with the things the customer thinks are most important. It's the old Swiss cheese approach: look for the biggest holes. You should already know what the customer thinks is important from your surveys and evaluation.

A popular method of prioritizing, used by Federal Express among others, is the Pareto Chart. The Pareto principle (developed by an Italian sociologist and economist of that name) states that 20 per cent of the population owns 80 per cent of the wealth. This ratio, Pareto later discovered, could be applied elsewhere. It is now widely used in business.

A graph of employee absenteeism, for example, might have a dozen categories of reasons why employees miss work. Application of the Pareto principle will show that three or four of those categories will account for 80 per cent of the reasons for employee absenteeism. Applying the principle helps to isolate the main problems from trivial or less important ones (problems that, even if solved, will not greatly change the organization in proportion to the effort involved).

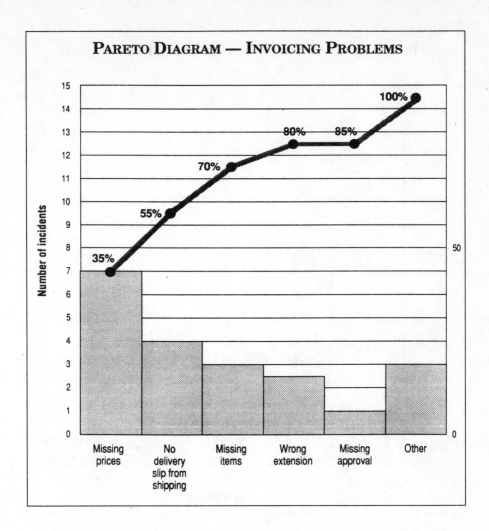

PARETO DIAGRAM — INVOICING PROBLEMS

Number of incidents

35% 55% 70% 80% 85% 100%

Missing prices | No delivery slip from shipping | Missing items | Wrong extension | Missing approval | Other

Another good method for determining priorities is the histogram, which highlights patterns and variations in a process (for example, the number of telephone calls per minute versus the number of seconds taken to respond).

Federal Express also uses a "weighting" system to prioritize service delivery problems. It uses an ongoing program to monitor what it calls Service Quality Indicators (SQIs). SQIs are indicators of bad service — lost packages, reopened complaints, missing proofs of delivery, and so on. From studies of its organization, Federal Express has isolated 12 SQIs, each of which has been assigned a "weight" corresponding to its importance to the customer. The "heavier" the weight, the greater the impact that indicator has on customer satisfaction. A customer will be less dissatisfied with a

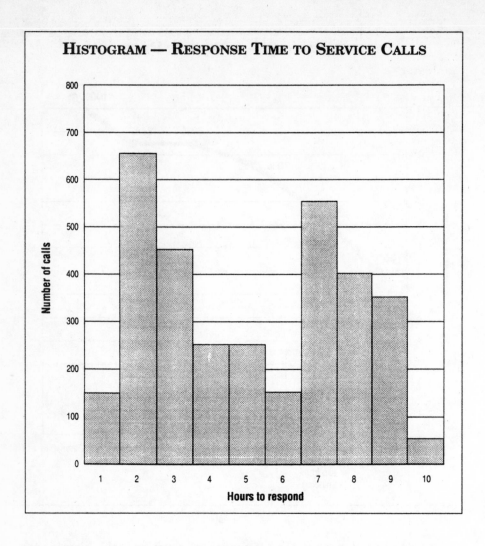

HISTOGRAM — RESPONSE TIME TO SERVICE CALLS

Number of calls (y-axis: 0, 100, 200, 300, 400, 500, 600, 700, 800)

Hours to respond (x-axis: 1, 2, 3, 4, 5, 6, 7, 8, 9, 10)

package delivered late (1 point) than with one that is lost (10 points). The SQI system represents how Federal Express prioritized what needed to be changed in its service-delivery system.

Federal Express implemented SQIs in 1988. The company's goal is to reduce its "failure points" by 90 percent by 1993. Failure points are calculated by multiplying the SQI weight by the number of occurrences of that SQI. (As an aside, the company's goal of reducing failure points gets tougher each year because of increased sales volume, the outgrowth of a successful service system.)

And, as Federal Express sees how well it is reducing failure point percentages from year to year in various parts of its business, it can pinpoint where on its service map it needs to improve or put more emphasis.

FEDERAL EXPRESS SERVICE QUALITY INDICATORS (SQI)

Indicator	Weight
Abandoned Calls	1
Complaints Reopened	5
Damaged Packages	10
International	1
Invoice Adjustments Requested	1
Lost Packages	10
Missed Pick-ups	10
Missing Proofs of Delivery	1
Overgoods (Lost and Found)	5
Right Day Late Deliveries	1
Traces	1
Wrong Day Late Deliveries	5

DETERMINATION OF PRIORITIES AT FLORIDA POWER & LIGHT

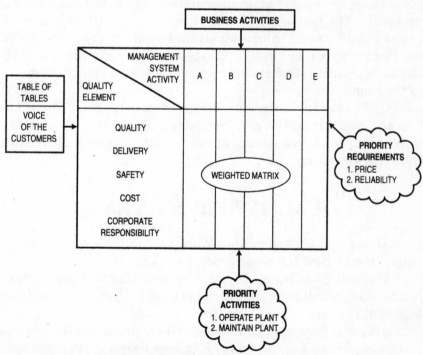

SOURCE: FLORIDA POWER & LIGHT, FROM CUSTOMER SATISFACTION THROUGH QUALITY, CONFERENCE BOARD OF CANADA REPORT 74-91-E OCTOBER 1991

WORK-OUT

General Electric employs 298,000 people, the population of a small city. In the late '80s, GE went through sweeping structural changes, trimming staff and flattening their cake-like hierarchy. That didn't seem to do enough. Chairman John F. Welch Jr. wanted more. He wanted a cultural change. And he got it.

In early 1989, GE began a program called Work-Out. In an interview with *Fortune* magazine (August 12, 1991), Welch likened the process to a New England town meeting. It works like this:

Between 40 and 100 staffers from all levels meet in a conference centre. A senior manager whips up an agenda on the spot, then leaves the room. The staff breaks into teams to work on different parts of the agenda for a day and a half. On the final day, staff and the manager meet again to go over what each team discovered and to weigh the proposed solutions.

The manager, who has no idea what has been discussed at team meetings, takes his place at the front of the auditorium. Each team makes its proposals. The manager can do one of three things: say yes, say no, or request more information. There are often over 100 proposals. The manager, with the heat on and with only a minute or so to decide, must think quickly and act decisively; and it would not do to give a lot of no's or maybe's in front of a big crowd. The manager cannot be overruled by his or her superiors, who may be in the room at the time.

This form of high-pressure listening introduces employee ideas into the workplace. GE has discovered that many of these ideas have led to great cost saving at many plants, as well as increased worker satisfaction.

QUALITY SERVICE TEAMS

Workshops and programs like Work-Out involve quality service teams. Here's how the team process works.

Campbell Soup takes a typical approach to teamwork. Theirs is a method worth learning from, because it shows how teamwork begins at the top.

Campbell creates teams to work on problematic business processes. Each team consists of members from various functions to ensure that there are representatives present from all aspects of the process under review.

Each team has a facilitator who has been trained thoroughly in the problem-solving techniques and process redesign. That person leads the team through the problem-solving process.

There is no one in charge of processes because processes, by definition, cut across functions and departments. So every team has a team leader. The team leader is the "owner" of the process and usually has a work-connected interest in the process. Every process is assigned an owner from the management committee at the vice-presidential level. That person is charged with removing impediments and providing resources to the team to achieve what it has been designated to achieve.

The other person at the team meeting is the coach. The coach has been trained in what Campbell's calls "breakthrough thinking." Among other ideas, breakthrough thinking stresses that work is a conversation, and that if you change the conversation — improve the way people communicate — you change the work.

The coach makes sure that the team converses openly and is working toward a breakthrough, not just incremental improvement. If conversation falters, the coach guides the team back out of the ruts that teams inevitably fall into, such as the tendency to feel they are victims of outside forces and wanting to throw up their hands and say "we can't do anything." The coach leads the team members away from such self-defeating attitudes, reminding them that they can make something happen through teamwork.

How do you pick team leaders? According to Campbell Soup's Vice-President of Quality and Breakthrough Management, Bob MacGregor, "You look into your organization and you find those core people who really make things happen. They are recognized by the people to whom they report and their peers as being people who really know what's going on, and they're making the sucker hum, making the work go forward.

"We made a complete list of these people, gathered the owners together and let the owners choose up, as in baseball, which people they wanted on their team. We also made some general rules. Every team has a person from the Information Services Department to ensure that ongoing work in that area isn't compromised. And, of course, we made sure that each team has a functional representative from each point that the process crosses, so that we can start to knock down the barriers and find out how the process really works."

Teams and Management Structure

Teamwork requires that everyone, from management to workers, eliminate the barriers so often caused by organizational strata. When restructuring your organization to facilitate teamwork, it is especially important that executives do not put barriers around themselves, because that will encourage barriers to be formed elsewhere throughout the company.

Above, we saw how Campbell's structured the teamwork process to avoid building new barriers from the ones that have been torn down. NCR does it this way:

It has a "champion" in each of five divisions: Finance & Administration, Systems Engineering, Field Engineering (which gets two), Imaging Systems and System Media.

A champion is an ISO (International Standards Organization) 9000 champion. He/she will be *the* guru (in the words of Ron James, Manager, Quality Assurance) of each division. Each champion is given the responsibility for implementing the ISO 9000 quality system in his or her division.

Below the champions are sub-champions, who are in charge of key areas within each of the divisions.

Below each of the sub-champions are process owners, like at Campbell Soup. The process owner owns the process and establishes a team made up of personnel from relevant departments.

Time Frames

Teams at Amdahl meet every two to three weeks for about three hours and, in each of those meetings, participants commit to taking an action before the next meeting. Operations Vice-President Cam Bright says participants commit themselves to three or four hours of work over the next two weeks.

Why so short a time? Bright says his firm is not interested in taking the "home run" or, in his words, "Big Bang," approach to service improvement. He says that by hitting one single after another, even on larger processes, "you can make some pretty significant progress in two to four months."

Importance of Workshops and Teams

Dave Clark of Campbell Soup is a champion of the team concept. He knows what teams can do.

"The source of power comes from an individual's willingness to take responsibility for something. That's what gives you power. The minute that you give up responsibility, or you say that is somebody else's job, you are less powerful, and in some cases powerless. So, while the ultimate source for power lies within, in a team context, one of the benefits of team membership is that the members can help empower each other.

"We all falter, we all give up at times, though we don't intend to give up our sense of responsibility. In an effective team, when one of the members or some of the members begin to behave in that fashion or act that way, others can help empower them. Now, that's not a question of just saying, 'Go forth and do good.'

"In fact, far from being the powerless victims that we all too often think of ourselves as, we are in fact the masters, ultimately the only masters, of our fate."

MacGregor, in describing how the teams work, agrees with his superior.

"We tell everyone that we're interested in finding out the problems with the process; not the problems with function A, or the problems with person A who works in function A. We want to focus attention in a non-personal way on the process. What happens very soon is that people get off the idea that they personally are being inspected. It frees them up to tell the truth.

"One of the great things is that they learn how the other function lives, what it's like in the real world for the other function, what it means when a function doesn't hand over the output properly to another function. It's a new experience for a lot of people. A lot of these people have never met people from other functions; they've just heard stories about how the functions operate."

Teams and the Middle Manager

Building self-managed or cross-functional teams is not easy.

Rosabeth Moss Kanter, in a *Harvard Business Review* survey on world business leadership ("The Boundaries of Business," May-June, 1991), noted that non-managers work better in teams than managers do. On the other hand, managers possess more cross-functional knowledge than non-managers. And, while managers are better apprised of strategic information, they tend to reserve this information for themselves.

To me, these observations sound a warning. If employee teams are not privy to strategic information, their ability to solve problems in the best interest of the organization will be severely limited. What direction should we take? ask team members. Lack of knowledge restricts their ability to initiate improvement projects.

The conclusion to draw is that managers must learn more about team skills and co-operation, while employees must learn more about strategic aims.

It is, of course, not easy to teach decision-making to people who have never had to make a decision. Nor is it easy to teach managers who always make decisions to let go of the decision-making reins.

Teams take over many responsibilities that have previously belonged to management: production targets, the hiring and training of new staff, even performance appraisal. But the manager should not be left standing on the highway looking for a lift at this stage. It is the manager's job to make sure the team works as a team, to guide the team, and to lend his or her expertise in areas that are still unfamiliar to team members.

The middle manager is like the typical baseball manager. He may not have been much of a player himself. But that is not his job. He lets the players do the playing. He just makes sure the engine keeps running, building momentum. The middle manager's job is to instil in self-managed teams a new way of thinking, a new way of looking at the way the company does business.

1) Do management and all parties involved in implementation understand the service gaps in the organization?

2) Have you defined the service strategy that will fill these gaps?

3) Have you mapped the service-delivery process and involved a cross-function of management in this process?

4) Did the maps identify
   - revised qualitative and quantitative standards?
   - service redundancies?
   - operations that can be streamlined?

5) Have you established service-improvement priorities (in light of a cost-benefit analysis)? Does this require an organizational change or change in policies and procedures?

6) Have you developed a Quality Service mission statement and a Customer Bill of Rights?

7) Have you established standards and a performance-measurement process that will assess the above?

8) Have you defined the employees' role in the service strategy?

9) Have you set up support mechanisms like
   - suggestion programs?
   - recognition programs?
   - training and orientation programs?

10) Have you communicated the aims of the strategy to everyone in the organization?

CHAPTER 6

THE GUIDANCE PHASE
(Avoiding the potholes and detours)

You cannot travel on the path until you have become the Path itself.

— Gautama Buddha

HOW DO WE GET THERE?

You have now determined your current level of service and formulated a service strategy.

Diagnosis and planning, by themselves, do not lead to improvement. Managers and staff must now correctly implement their strategy to create an environment of Total Quality Service. That means doing three things: communicating your aims to the employee, empowering the employee, and training the employee. Do all three and you build ...

MOMENTUM

We've all played a favorite sport and had that heady feeling of having the momentum in our favor. We say the tide is with us. We feel power, and what once required strength now seems to take no effort at all.

In the business world, momentum is no different. The hardest part of building momentum is just plain getting it started. Once it gets started, it builds, feeds on itself, and snowballs so fast that you may reach your goal well ahead of schedule.

To build momentum, one must move forward quickly. Once you have made your service evaluations and set up a service plan, get at it. Put the plan into practice. Hand responsibility to the employees. Train them in what they need to know. The ball will start rolling and it will go faster and faster. Soon, everyone will be keen to push.

KEEPING THE BALL ROLLING

It is obvious that T.Q.S. cannot be trained into people. The sense of a service culture develops within employees on their own or in groups, as they change the way they do their jobs through discussion and constructive assistance.

Staff groups, or teams, will naturally flounder a bit. The idea of a service culture is new to them. And changing old ways may be difficult at first.

But fumbling is a good sign; it means they are learning. What is important is ensuring that the learning process does not go stale or get bogged down. Management must stick with it. Managers must work with employees, must get their hands dirty. If begun properly, the process ceases to be just another feel-good training exercise and becomes instead a forum for constructive organizational change.

IMPLEMENTATION

Implementation is motivation.

Gone is the day when waving a big bonus cheque at the employee was enough to inspire him or her to do better. Employees want more from their company than just money.

Good managers realize that the long-term future of the company depends upon the employee. Employees are only as good as their supervisors; so supervisors must treat the employee as they would any external customer.

Listen if the employee says there is something inefficient about the way things are done.

Support the employee; you want the employee to do things right. And support cross-functional teams and quality service councils for they will be making the concrete changes to the organization.

Praise genuinely. Reward genuinely. Forget those tired and meaningless forms of rote recognition — a stock memo sent around congratulating everyone on how well they are doing — which seems to go out every four months or so, as if on a schedule. The employee doesn't believe the words on that memo. When the employee doesn't believe you, your service journey will end.

Redesign the workplace with employee input. Leave your door open. Move the noisy printers and copiers to a place where employees will not be interrupted. A good working environment will not only make the employee enjoy coming to work, but also allow him or her to concentrate better. The work environment can actually create the cultural behavior you want.

Motivate your employees by acting on their ideas and giving credit for them. If a suggestion didn't work out, there must be a reason. There may be a hint of the real solution to a problem in the rejected suggestion; perhaps the suggestion just needs a little refinement. Where employees feel they have contributed successfully, where their voices have been heard, you have motivation ... and continued motivation. The ball keeps rolling.

Implementation Is Like Riding a Bike

Management should always be on hand to give assistance. To make sure teams function smoothly. To encourage suggestions. To listen to suggestions. James Tennant, Executive Vice-President, Human Resources and Total Quality Management, Air Canada says, "It's a bit like ensuring that the training wheels are on the bicycle while basic skills like pedalling and steering are acquired. We have to build up confidence in our employee's capability of handling the new role. We need to be comfortable that our employees can do their job so management won't get nervous and try to snatch back control at any moment."

Integrating Change

Employees don't mind technological change. It's changing their relationship to their co-workers that they find difficult.

Employees become set in their ways. They know and understand the relationship they have with the person who is their supervisor, because that person is the *supervisor*. They have a different relationship with those whom they work beside, or with those in another department. But when a supervisor, for example, becomes a co-worker, the transition is difficult. Both sides find it hard to adjust to the new relationship.

To make the transition easy, managers should put away the production schedules and the performance reviews and concentrate on the "gap" between manager and subordinate. This gap is just like the one between front-line employee and customer. Manager and employee are, after all, each other's customers.

The results of an American study conducted in the late 1940s still hold true today. It examined the relationship between change in the workplace and participation.

Three groups of operators on a factory floor were instructed to change the way they did their work.

Group One was called into a room and told what changes were going to be made. The members of this group returned to their jobs to make the changes. Group Two, on the other hand, was gathered together with management; they all sat down and hashed out among themselves how best to alter the working methods. Everyone put in their two cents.

(There was also a third group, a control group, for which no changes took place.)

The production of each group was monitored for a month. In Group One, production fell off by a third. There was hostility between workers and supervisors. Grievances were filed. In Group Two, output fell at first, then zoomed upward to exceed its previous rate. There was much co-operation.

The lessons of this study are far-reaching. Participation and change are not tricks to con people into "wanting" to do as they are told, the study concluded. Yet this is often the perception employees receive. Customers think the same about insincere advertising.

From the employees' point of view, the assumptions made in Group One were that management did not believe that they knew or understood their own jobs, that they did not contribute to the company, and that the way they were doing things was wrong. Small wonder they resisted change.

People who work closely together trade ideas and fiddle with the way they do things to make their work go better. They have the liberty to do so. They know their work intimately. But when change is seen as something coming from outside, they resist it. They accept only that change that comes from inside. It is important to understand this social aspect of change: it succeeds only if it is the product of give and take, not command.

Most managers do not know about the social furnace on the shop floor from which ideas and innovations rise. Whenever management trivializes, or outright ignores, workplace social arrangements, it disrespects the employee's skill at his or her job.

Managers often don't know any better. They are victims of their own designs. It is easy to see why CEOs have such difficulty; organizations are so big, the skills so diverse — there are accountants, machinists, data processors, computer analysts, shippers — that CEOs have only superficial knowledge of any one skill. In short, the typically hierarchical structure of a North American company makes management ignorant.

RESISTANCE

Resistance: managers can see only their own little world, the scope of their own job; they tend not to think of others; they are blinded by their own ideas and the need to make a name for themselves or their plan. They are so in love with the perfection of their idea that they don't want anyone to change it: they just know it will work; and they can't understand other people who don't think the same way.

The employee's resistance to change should not be seen as something to overcome, but as a warning signal that something in the organization needs to be adjusted. According to the author of the above factory study, Paul Lawrence, "Participation will never work so long as it is treated as a device to get somebody else to do what you want him to. Real participation is based on respect."

Why This Is Important

TARP studies have shown that employees who lack the authority to solve problems are more prone to frustration and burnout than those who have such powers.

Employees like to help customers, and it frustrates them to have to say no to a customer because the company emphasizes production over service. For instance, the employee agrees with the customer that the customer is in the right about, say, a refund of merchandise, but lacks the means to redress the problem without having to get higher approval. The study found that only 15 per cent of banks, for example, gave tellers the power to adjust an account for sums over $20.

When the employee can't contribute, or feels his or her contribution has not been recognized, he or she becomes dissatisfied. The employee loses interest in work, let alone the will to try new things. The employee looks elsewhere to find the satisfaction of commitment.

"Most people have to find encouragement outside work," says Dave Clark, President of Campbell Soup. "They become Brownie leaders, or they participate in local politics, or they have a gang they hang around with at the local pub because they are important to that gang. They find a sense of importance and satisfaction.

"I am determined that they should find that same sense of importance and contribution and satisfaction in their work environment. I mean, why can't they? It's not their fault. It tends to be the fault of the organization, and the system, and the beliefs that we get trapped in."

POWER

To employees, power is always seen to rest with those at the top. This very notion discourages commitment.

Power means having a say. The employee knows this; having worked for so long without a say, the employee grows into the belief that he or she will be "managed" just like anyone or anything else in the company.

I want executives to get away from this notion. To see what I mean, think of power not in manager-employee terms, but in customer service terms.

The employee is an internal customer. Suppose you are selling the customer a pair of shoes. Would you let a customer across the counter know that you have power and he or she does not? That if they don't like the shoes, tough luck? Of course not. This is the kind of thinking executives must abandon.

You must not exercise your power on the employee any more than you would on a customer standing on the other side of the counter. It's that simple.

This is the basic concept one must understand when we talk of empowerment.

"If managers see power as a zero-sum game in which someone else's having more means that they must have less," says John Young, Senior Vice-President of Human Resources at Four Seasons Hotels, "then they will hold on to their share of it desperately — while simultaneously making others feel impotent and useless.

"If, on the other hand, managers see power as something everyone has and something that can be enhanced by pooling it, then they will seek to involve others in their thinking and decision-making — while simultaneously recognizing others are important and useful contributors."

Whenever the organization feels an expressed need to demonstrate its power over an employee, the employee understandably concludes that he or she must be working at odds with the organization.

There will be no commitment to a service culture from the employee in such an atmosphere. In fact, the opposite will happen. Commitment will be an empty word on a mission statement nobody reads.

Commitment originates from the following: employees want to get something out of their work; those desires must be the very ones management wants for the organization.

Remember, the employee, as customer, is always right.

What Would You Change If You Had the Authority To Do So?

The chance to be CEO for a day. Now there's a challenge. Many employees would jump at it, because they know things about the organization no one else knows.

Employees have an intimate understanding of the things they work with so closely, day in and day out. Employees can solve in a minute what managers can take months of analysing to figure out.

Many managers think (erroneously) that handing employees decision-making power means that they will lose their own. Today, this is especially true of middle managers, whose role is being squeezed out by tough economic times.

Yet the truth is that managers who fear loss of power *will* be phased out.

"Managers who are frightened of making mistakes and are unwilling to tackle responsibility for the actions of others, others whom they have not directly controlled, will not empower those people," says Jeffrey Gandz, business professor at the University of Western Ontario. "Managers who limit their empowerment only to those employees whom they know they can trust — usually as a result of past experience — will not empower sufficient numbers of people to make a difference."

Gun-shy managers choke off, rather than open up, opportunities for an organization to achieve Total Quality Service. A manager who, deep down, does not believe that employees will work for the good of the company's shared vision will throttle the company's growth.

Bottlenecking

"The image many of us have of strong, positive management, even leadership, is one of forceful exercise of hierarchical power — the power of position —in very traditional, top-down ways," says James Tennant of Air Canada.

Tennant cites David Nadler, the President of the Delta Consulting Group, who says the traditional manager lives by quality-hostile assumptions like the following: "The manager's job is to think; the worker's job is to do ... We're smarter than the customers ... Senior management needs to pay attention to strategy, not operations."

Many managers still rely on traditional forms of profit or performance measurement, which are often not directly relevant to a customer-driven organization. Nor do such managers have the daily contact with customers that would allow them to appreciate the pressing need for change.

"Small wonder that middle management often has the greatest difficulty in recognizing the need for change," says Tennant. "They are not used to a new process where decisions emanate from customers rather than themselves, where they must listen to their subordinates as attentively as they listen to their superiors."

While management often believes employees are resistant to the changes required to make a company more responsive to customer needs, it is hard to see why. Employees working on the front line, who deal with customers every day, are more aware than managers of what changes are required to achieve quality.

"Employees work directly with the customers and the end product they receive. While managers may have to wait days or weeks to obtain a computer printout that will tell them how well their company is performing, employees get an instant and accurate response directly from the customer."

Tennant feels it is important to understand how the front-line employee's role within the service industry has changed. In the past, management determined what the customer wanted and how those wants would be delivered. But companies that embrace Total Quality Service as a goal make sure that the front-line employee is equipped to tap into customer wants and needs.

"In our model of total quality, every person in the company is required to make a paradigm shift — to see their business in different terms. And along with this shift, we are required to change processes and attitudes.

"One of the most difficult barriers to overcome in the early days when a company embarks on a pursuit of quality is the problem of mixed messages. These can come from a number of sources, but they are most likely to stem from inexperience with the new management requirements and a few management holdouts who insist on retaining the old processes to achieve new goals.

"This is where strong leadership comes in. It is difficult to convince employees of the desired result if management is divided on the means of achieving their goal."

GET OFF THE SOAPBOX

Here's Robert DeMone, President of Canadian Pacific Hotels & Resorts, on how and how not to get the most out of your employees:

"To foster an environment that brings forth the best in everyone, avoid telling people what to do, and encourage people to do what the job requires. Two very different things, I believe.

"It's very different to stand up on a pedestal and tell people what to do, as opposed to telling people what the end result will be — consistent service excellence.

"You don't get people to provide consistent service excellence by standing on a soapbox and telling them what to do. You tell them what you want done, and their natural talents will, if they are properly selected and trained, get the job done."

EMPOWERMENT: BECOME A PLAYER-COACH

Campbell's Dave Clark has an interesting story about a middle manager.

"I can remember one middle manager in one of our plants coming up to me after I'd done an orientation session on empowerment. He said to me, 'Dave, I've worked for 20 years to get myself into a position to be able to direct people, to manage, to give orders, and now you're telling me that I can't do that. *Why* should I do this?'

"My answer to him was, 'because you will find it one thousand times more satisfactory to be a coach than to be a boss; you will find that the boss relationship invariably breeds resistance because it is a top dog/underdog relationship, and that the underdog always resents it, and the underdog always gets even.'

"He and I talked a bit about how he had a lot of what he thought was formal power and about how, in fact, the people underneath him could at any point completely subvert anything he ordered them to do.

"I said, 'Wouldn't it be so much more meaningful to you to be in a relationship with those whom you currently boss where, instead of them resenting and resisting you, they view you as a resource, as a helper, as somebody who is on their side, and who is helping them to do something they very much want to do?'

"I happened to know that this fellow coached kids' hockey; and I said, 'I've seen you (because we have a kids' hockey program here), I've seen you at work as a coach in that hockey school and those kids love you. Why can't it be like that with your fellow workers; why can't they love you too. Wouldn't that make you feel better?'

"He thought about that. He's still with us, so I guess he must have decided ...."

Stand to the Side and Let the Team Play the Game

Management's role in creating a service culture is to get the ball rolling, then step aside to let others do their bit, while running alongside to make sure the ball doesn't roll off the road.

Managers must let employees straighten out a problem and let them have a hand in shaping its resolution, rather than force employees to do what management thinks is right, no questions asked.

This way of thinking eliminates employee suspicion that all the fancy talk coming from management about empowerment is a con. Management must approach a project in this way if the employee's natural resistance to change, and to management ideas, is to be overcome.

Winning baseball managers know that they can't use their regular nine players day in and day out and let the back-ups grow mould on the bench. A winner motivates his team by giving everyone work. Everyone gets to contribute their bit, and so feels needed and appreciated. The manager's greatest contribution is to direct traffic, making sure it keeps flowing.

Empowerment Defined

The well-known anecdote about a man checking into a hotel is worth repeating.

The front desk clerk is wearing a button that says "Yes, I Can." The man asks if she could give him one. She says, "No, I can't."

Then she says, "It's management policy to wear the button. I'm sorry, but we don't have any extras."

She couldn't do what the company wanted her to do.

She couldn't do what the customer wanted her to do.

She lacked empowerment.

There is a big gap here that needs closing. The woman behind the desk has responsibility, but no authority. Responsibility without authority makes empowerment powerless. This is why the issue of service standards must be addressed in the design phase. The employee must know the service standards of the organization *and* know the allowable deviations from those standards. You say to the employee, "You have the power to do this; this is the standard we expect as circumstances permit."

In other words, encourage employees *not* to be slaves to the letter of the law.

For example, your restaurant has a standard whereby the customer must receive his or her meal within 15 minutes of ordering. "The guideline says 15 minutes," the waiter thinks. The waiter meets that standard, but senses that the customer feels the service has been a bit slow. "Do I give the customer a free dessert anyway?"

The unempowered waiter wouldn't know what to do in this situation, and probably would err on the side of the 15-minute rule and not give the free dessert.

The empowered waiter would see that the customer is a bit annoyed and would exercise his or her own judgment. Thinking of the customer first, and not the rules first, he or she would give the customer the dessert. This employee has no fear of being punished for bending the rules to please the customer. Empowerment means being able to satisfy the customer.

Another Definition

This comes from J.W. Marriott, CEO of the Marriott hotel chain:

"By empowerment, we mean the process of extending to the associate closest to the customer the resources, education and authority to create extraordinary service while preserving profitability.

"Empowered associates are able to make the decisions and take the initiative that will continuously improve the level of Marriott service in the eyes of both our guests and our fellow associates. In short, our associates must be empowered to do whatever it takes to create satisfied customers by

➤ meeting or exceeding the standards set by Marriott;
➤ going above and beyond the call of duty;
➤ preventing future failures; and
➤ creating service enhancements.

"But doing 'whatever it takes' is not a realistic way of doing business unless we first take steps to prepare ourselves and the organization to operate in this more flexible way.

"The first step is to remove the barriers that people feel are in the way of their doing 'whatever it takes' to satisfy the customers. The most powerful barrier to being comfortable in exercising your empowerment is not having a clear, realistic understanding of the boundaries of your authority."

Two Steps

There are two steps to empowerment.

The *second* step is to involve employees in changes to the workplace, to listen to them, to seek their opinions on ways to improve operations, and to keep them informed. That is the second step. And it will all go to waste without the first step: You must trust the employees. And that means handing them genuine decision-making authority.

Empowerment and Expectations at Four Seasons

You may wonder why so many examples are taken from the hospitality industry. It is my belief that that industry, possibly because of competition and the need for differentiation, has made some important changes in order to gain a strategic advantage. Perhaps no one organization has done more to advance the practice of empowerment than Four Seasons Hotels.

John Young of Four Seasons says there is a temptation to equate empowerment with freedom of action. This is dangerous. "As Teddy Roosevelt put it, 'Order without liberty is oppressive, but liberty without order is chaos. Order without liberty and liberty without order are equally destructive.'"

Four Seasons defines empowerment in two ways:

1) Empowerment is a condition or state of mind in which employees feel freed from unnecessary restrictions on their ability to take action in the interests of customer satisfaction.

2) Empowerment is a process through which managers and employees, individually and collectively, attempt consciously and continuously to make progress toward that condition.

Young likes to stress that empowerment arises only from within an integrated process. Many managers, however, develop a program with a beginning and an end that lets them control the process. "They are missing the point," says Young.

"You don't generate empowerment through the implementation of a program designed, implemented and monitored by management, from the outside. Rather, management behavior and involvement is intrinsic. If the process doesn't achieve the desired results, management can't simply blame the failure on lack of employee interest or effort, and wash its hands of responsibility." Because management is an integral part of the process, management must continually review its own role and the degree to which that role is adding to or detracting from achievement of the desired results.

"Creating expectations is a delicate balancing act. Like a manager told a new employee, 'Integrity and wisdom are essential to success. By integrity, I mean that when you promise a customer something, keep that promise even if you lose money.' 'What is wisdom?,' the new man asked. 'Don't make such idiotic promises,' the manager stated."

Young uses this anecdote to illustrate the mental block that many managers have about corporate values. In North America, the dominant philosophy of business holds that shareholders' interests come first. "In this view, shareholders contract, through their managers, to pay employees a specified wage for work narrowly defined. So management has set up elaborate controls to protect the shareholders, which has led, of course, to unions that protect the workers from management. But we can't expect employees to go all out for a company that puts its shareholders' interest first. Return on equity is not a purpose that stirs an employee's soul."

At Four Seasons, every executive from the chairperson down has to be a role model. It is important to get employees at every level of the company to believe that management means what it says. And it's more than management and staff just uttering the company credo. "It can only be done the way doctors learn through interning; the way top craftsmen learn through apprenticeship; the way children learn from their parents through personal example and experience."

When a company sells on value rather than price, it needs employees who understand value, and are willing and able to deliver it. And this is tricky.

Quality people are not made on an assembly line.

Four Seasons supplies an expensive luxury product, but the company can't check its quality before it's sold. While you can check a Rolls Royce or a bottle of Chivas Regal before it leaves the plant, a hotel's product exists only at the moment of delivery. "The only control we have over how a doorman greets a guest, or how a busboy responds to a request, is through the mindset of these employees. Our service quality depends entirely on the self-discipline and empathy of our employees."

Young knows that employees don't want to be controlled. If Four Seasons wants committed employees, it must liberate and empower them; it must hand responsibility and authority to them. All Four Seasons employees know that company service standards must be met or exceeded and that, in many difficult situations, they will have to rely on the resources of their own judgment. Yet they assume the responsibility with confidence, because they know that customer satisfaction is a priority at the company. "We trust them to use common sense and they give us trust in return."

And Four Season executives want to hear what employees have to say. They use a method like the Work-Out program at General Electric, discussed in Chapter 5.

"Every department in each hotel elects a non-supervisory representative, and they all meet as a group every month with the general manager, alone. They exchange ideas, kudos and criticism, and the general manager has to tell them 1) 'I'll do this or correct that,' or 2) 'I'll look into this and report back next meeting,' or 3) 'I won't do that, and here's why.' And everyone understands that any retaliation against a representative for speaking out is grounds for dismissal."

Make Roles, Not Jobs

The ideal employee is one who does not see his or her job as a set of fixed tasks, but rather someone who sees what they do as a role, a role that is part of a larger process in which they work toward some objective, using whatever skills are necessary to accomplish that objective.

The notion of a "job" dates back to production-oriented thinking. My concern is customer service, which requires thinking in terms of processes and relationships.

Under production-thinking, managers try to improve performance by raising the number of parts a worker makes per minute. Under relationship-thinking, the idea is to consider what is being made in terms of what the customer wants.

Give Employees Cross-Knowledge

Turning a job into a role means giving employees cross-knowledge. Sales staff, for example, should know how to handle a billing problem, though it is not a primary part of their job. Accounts receivable clerks should know how to handle a sales inquiry, though it is not part of their job.

At the Royal Garden Hotel in Hong Kong, concierges spend time in the telephone department and in the laundry room; department heads learn something different every day: one day, it might be a turndown inspection; the next, a check of bars. The employee thus learns to see the hotel as a whole, rather than from the blinkered standpoint of their particular job.

A staff member's knowledge of others' jobs, while not as thorough as that of the people who regularly do the other jobs, cuts down on division of function in the workplace. Cross-knowledge brings people from disparate parts of the organization closer together. Silos disappear. And the employee gains a more comprehensive view of his or her job and where it fits into the company's scheme of things.

And, often, employees learn to fix a problem themselves. With that ability, their self-esteem increases, which means they are more inclined to commit themselves to organizational goals.

Conversely, when work and workers are divided and isolated, the worker doesn't know what impact his or her job has on the rest of the organization. It also precludes the emotion generated by exchanging ideas, and therefore undermines commitment.

Not Too Much at First

A word of warning. Empowerment has to be kept within reason. People like responsibility, but not too much at first.

The First National Bank of Chicago found that tellers became unsure of themselves when they were given the power to handle large sums of money. The bank quickly changed its policy. Tellers were given lower sums to start with, then moved on to the greater responsibility of higher sums when they became more comfortable with the process.

THE NEW TRAINING

Gone are the days when executives could see employees as raw material — raw material purchased at the lowest price, in the way you might buy a piece of new equipment. As I mentioned in Chapter 1, business in the '90s has shifted away from production of newer and better products to the ability to produce quality products cheaply. Success now depends on process improvement in quality and in service.

This shift from production-thinking to process-thinking means companies have less need for the "ideas people" who dream up newfangled products and the semi-skilled workers who push buttons to pump them out; now, companies have more need for people with the skills to operate sophisticated technology. Companies need to improve their processes continuously, and the only way to do that is to ask the people operating the equipment how it can be done better.

If companies put in new processes, the employees will have to learn them. Proper training is needed. Otherwise, if the employees take longer to learn how to use these new skills than do the employees at the competition because there has been insufficient low-end training, the cost of the new processes to your company will be higher than the cost to your competitors. The end result will be that poorly trained employees will drag down the profit margin, with the predictable dire consequences.

Training is Empowerment

You can give an employee the power to make decisions, but the employee won't make any, or will make poor ones, if he or she has not been trained to do so.

Basic training includes not just technical upgrading, but negotiation skills, group brainstorming skills, and decision-making skills.

Most employees are used to just doing a job; in the workplace, they have never been called on to use skills they may use in their daily life. The organization must tap into these resources.

With training, employees learn to take pride in their role in the company. Many managers already have pride, but they forget that employees do not possess this attitude because they have always lacked the means to gain it.

At a typical Japanese company, it is not surprising to find as much as 12 per cent of total salary cost put into training. In the United States, it is a measly 1.4 per cent; in France, 2 per cent. A mid-sized Canadian company will devote only $100 to $250 per employee to training! Companies that have no qualms about investing large amounts of money in equipment maintenance balk at doing the same for good employees.

Four Seasons on Training

"People ask us, 'How do you find employees like these? What is your secret in training them?'

"The truth of the matter," says John Young, "is that these are ordinary people who feel free and encouraged to do extraordinary things. And there is no great training secret. What we do have is an attitude that focuses on the needs of others, rather than on one's own needs. And that attitude is created and sustained by an environment in which many components work together and build on one another." By that, he means a service culture.

Empowerment at Four Seasons begins with the kind of people it hires. "We don't want people to think serving others is demeaning — we want people with high self-esteem, not people who say in a crisis, 'That's not my job,' but people who say, 'How can I help?' Not people who answer a guest by saying, 'I don't know,' but people who say 'I'll find out.' We want people who feel good enough about themselves that they can focus their attention on the needs of others."

Four Seasons looks, for the most part, at the character and personality of a candidate, rather than the person's technical expertise. It believes that staff can be taught technical skills, but that no amount of effort on the company's part will change the person's character and personality. Training cannot change the fundamental nature of a person.

"Admittedly, it's harder to hire by subjective judgment than on hard data. For the Four Seasons Chicago, we screened 15,500 applicants for 545 jobs. All the potential prospects were screened four or five times, the last time by the general manager personally."

It is a long and expensive procedure, Young admits, but it pays off in high employee retention and productivity. "If you hire well, you seldom have to fire. And it sends a morale-boosting message to all employees, long-term and new, that we recognize from the beginning how important they are."

Four Seasons uses the hiring process to introduce employees to its service culture. Four Seasons hopes potential employees, by the end of their interview, will already understand one of its key principles: "It's okay to err in favor of the guest."

The question is "You can bring in motivated people, you can bring in people who understand the culture, but how can you keep them motivated?" Four Seasons knows, of course, that you can't.

"As managers, we can pressure people but we can't really motivate them; we can't make people want to work. But we can create a climate in which they feel encouraged to contribute and rewarded for doing so, and from which they can derive stimulation and satisfaction.

"In this climate, people drive themselves much more effectively than managers ever could. And we are exceptionally careful about who gets to be a general manager. Not only do they go through multiple interviews, they also undergo a full psychological-developmental assessment. Over 90 per cent are internal promotions, so they're already familiar with our values and culture."

Cutting Turnover

A contented workforce sticks around. It has been and always will be, regardless of recessionary influences or growth in our markets, increasingly difficult to find good skilled workers in today's labor market. There is a skill, not people, shortage. This is very important to remember when creating a service culture.

Offering employees a good benefits package (flex-hours, dental coverage, and so on) is a good start, of course, but an organization cannot depend on that alone to keep employees around. The employee may be lured by a better package from another firm. There is high competition for labor, as we all know. If a good benefits package is the best your company can offer an employee, you'll keep that person around only until they find something better.

This is why an organization must develop a "culture," or mood, or atmosphere that makes the employee think that *this* is the place to work. Remember, incentives cannot be seen as motivators in themselves.

Training As Hiring

Canadian Pacific Hotels trains by hiring the right people first, because it saves the company a lot of work later.

Traditional job interviews that stress credentials and work background have acquired a notorious reputation for unreliability when it comes to selecting ideal service-position candidates. So CP devised an interview process that instead emphasizes service-interest.

Out went questions like, "Are you a perfectionist?" and "Tell me about yourself?" and in came questions like, "How would you make a guest come back again?" and "Do you use more soap than most people?"

The kind of answer CP receives to the first of these new questions immediately indicates whether the person is concerned about giving good customer service. To the second, the ideal chambermaid or cleaner would answer yes.

Carolyn Clark, Vice-President of Human Resources, says the company asks such an apparently odd question to discover people who love to clean. Since adopting the new interview procedures, turnover among chambermaids has dropped by 60 per cent.

HIRING TIPS

Clark has taken an approach to hiring that shows good business sense.

Many businesses today still hire low-skilled, easily replaced people to handle front-line service duties. I never cease to wonder at this. Why put so little effort into hiring front-line staff when they handle the most important job in the organization — dealing with the external customer? There is always a gap here; companies always want to close it, yet they often make it wider by paying insufficient attention to the kind of people they hire for this role.

Hiring service-minded people can start the service journey off with a bang. Of course, it is not easy to get the right people. There are always "other" circumstances.

Robert W. Rogers, CEO of Development Dimensions International in Bridgeville, Pennsylvania, says companies would do well to make their hiring processes better suited to their needs.

Too often, companies make poor decisions because they are under pressure to fill a position, because the skills needed for the job are not clearly understood by the interviewer, because interviewers use different yardsticks to assess candidates, or because interviewers overemphasize certain qualities in a candidate at the expense of other qualities.

There are two kinds of skills, Rogers says: trainable (equipment operation, sales techniques, for example) and non-trainable (motivation).

In an interview, it is easy to see if the candidate possesses the trainable skills. Whether the candidate has the second kind, however, is much more difficult to determine. But for the service organization, these non-trainable skills may be the most important.

As a human resources manager, your main concern is whether the candidate will fit your organization. So, you should ask questions that bring out the candidate's normal behavior, as CP has done. Rather than give the old "interrogation" interview (the person being interviewed will inevitably be self-conscious), try to make the candidate relax. Make the interview a conversation; don't use it as a means to test the candidate's self-esteem.

Rogers lists seven things to look for in a behavior-based interview. Is the candidate

1) a good communicator?

2) sensitive to customers?

3) able to act decisively on customer needs or complaints?

4) energetic and responsive to the customer?

5) able to derive satisfaction from helping the customer?

6) able to be fair and to remain calm when dealing with irate customers?

7) a person with high personal standards of customer service?

Reimer's Videos

"I saw an article in *The Globe & Mail* with the headline 'Economic Performance Linked to Training,'" says John Perry, Vice-President of Training and Quality at Reimer Express, one of the first organizations to receive the Canadian Award for Business Excellence. "Why do we even need to study if economic performance and training are linked? They are like turkey with turkey dressing — inseparable."

Perry believes that continuous improvement comes only through education and training. For instance, Reimer's in-house magazine, *Expressions*, has a regular section on quality. Freight handlers — the local city drivers and people who work on Reimer's freight docks — meet every two months with local supervisors to go over quality issues.

Reimer also uses videos. Videos are central to the quality-training process. Reimer is certainly a leader in thorough use of videos as a communication tool.

"Our Quality Office has developed some of the most extensive videotape training in our industry. Its whole purpose is to make sure that all employees, from day one, fully understand job requirements and methods by which they can work on continuous improvement."

Perry will go around with his video camera interviewing Reimer staff about quality, or taping the Quality Management Team in action. The video will be viewed in various offices.

Reimer uses video even in the hiring process. "As part of the interviewing process, potential employees view a video tape which provides information on Reimer's company philosophy and its quality standards. It also covers what the organization expects from the employee and what the employee should expect from the organization."

After the candidate has viewed the video, he or she has the option of accepting or turning down the position. After watching the video, the candidate knows exactly what he or she can expect.

COMMUNICATE!

John Young speaks for all successful service managers when he says, "We can never take it for granted that our aims are understood. A survey of Fortune 500 executives four months ago found that 82 per cent of executives believed their aims were understood by everyone. A survey of their employees found that two-thirds thought their goals were unclear.

"*Fortune* magazine reported recently that a majority of companies won't take surveys because they don't want to hear unpleasant news.

"Last year, a Louis Harris poll of office workers and managers found a growing gap between what employees really want and what top management thinks they want. Management thinks they want job security more than anything else. The poll found they want, first, more respect. Second, higher standards of management ethics. Third, more recognition for what they contribute. And, fourth, more communication.

At Reimer Express, the company motto stresses communication, but perhaps from a different perspective.

OUR MOTTO
FreightFlow is our Business

OUR VERSE
Do Not Let Any Unwholesome
Talk Come Out of Your Mouth,
But Only What Is Helpful for
Building Others Up According
to Their Needs, That It May
Benefit Those Who Listen.

Ephesians 4:29

OUR MISSION
To Be The Very Best at
What We Do, Through
our Commitment to Quality.

How Amdahl Communicates

Cam Bright, Vice-President of Operations, approached the question of communication at Amdahl by looking in the dictionary first. His review of both a dictionary and a thesaurus yielded these definitions and synonyms for "communication":

➤ information exchange
➤ technique for expressing ideas effectively
➤ personal rapport
➤ a message
➤ transfer of plans and ideas

To put my own words around these definitions, communication must

➤ be based on mutual respect and trust;
➤ be built on both form and substance;
➤ include commitment; and
➤ be part of a shared vision.

There are many ways to communicate the quality message. Some will be subtle, almost subliminal, says Bright, while others will be much more direct and forceful. All should support and reinforce each other to avoid mixed messages.

"I don't believe that any company can claim either effective communication or a genuine focus on quality and quality service unless both are embedded in the culture of the company, woven into the very fabric of the enterprise."

Amdahl has quite a variety of communication techniques. "Communication education" starts on day one.

The first day on the job, new employees are told about Amdahl's values, Amdahl's commitment to quality, its views about people, its management style, and the importance of customer service and customer satisfaction. They are given a booklet that provides not only Amdahl's quality objective, but also a dictionary of quality terms to ensure that everybody speaks the same language. (Parts of this dictionary are found in the Glossary.)

A plaque displaying Amdahl's values can be found in every Amdahl office around the world.

New employees often hear about Amdahl's corporate values even earlier. Service values are discussed during the hiring interview. Bright is pleased to see that employees frequently refer to Amdahl values in conversation, memos, performance reviews and, sometimes, in a question about something they've seen or heard that conflicts with some aspect of company values. "Whatever the reason, we hear enough references to know that our employees know and understand our values and are very loyal to them."

The Amdahl quality objective, like its values statement, is described at the outset of an employee's career with the company and reinforced frequently. One practice is to distribute copies of the statement on small cards for the employee to carry in his or her wallet. The employee can then show it to, and discuss it with, a customer or prospect.

Bright says that this happens so often that many Amdahl managers give out these cards to customers almost as often as they give out business cards.

> **❝** To have our customers and prospects agree that we meet or exceed their expectations and are superior to the competition in everything we do. **❞**

Of all the things the quality objective communicates, says Bright, the message contained in the last four words is the most important. The words 'in everything we do' clearly communicates that quality and customer satisfaction is everyone's job and everyone's commitment to those goals is critical to our differentiation in the eyes of our customers.

Lunch with Ron

Once every month or so, a notice is posted on bulletin boards at Amdahl, inviting employees from all levels to join President Ron Smith and up to a dozen other employees for an informal communication session over lunch. Attendance is voluntary.

Attendees are free to ask questions about any aspect of the business. Smith frequently discusses company plans and results, strategic direction, the rationale for major decisions that directly affect the employees, and customer service.

Smith strongly believes that getting people to follow a vision does not come from the organization but from leadership, and that people will follow a leader if there is mutual respect, if they believe the leader is on the right path, and if they see an opportunity for self-improvement.

"Lunch with Ron," says Bright, "is one way for an Amdahl employee to participate equally and freely in a spontaneous discussion about the business and to make personal judgments about the quality of leadership."

Also, consider the highly successful Amdahl television network, known as ATN.

Amdahl offices throughout North America and Western Europe are linked via satellite to a television studio located in Amdahl's corporate offices in Sunnyvale, California. Viewers tune in to hear directly from senior corporate executives about many Amdahl business issues and activities. Some broadcasts are restricted to managers; most are available to all staff.

"Most are taped for showing at employee meetings to those who were unable to attend the live broadcast," says Bright. "All of the broadcasts are interactive, with audience participation via on-air telephone calls."

ATN broadcasts are intended primarily for Amdahl employees, but customers have been invited on several occasions to hear new product announcements, or to share their Amdahl product and service experiences with corporate executives.

"ATN has proven to be an extraordinarily effective means of communication. The President of the corporation consistently meets his stated goal of open, candid dialogue, and he gives his personal assurance that no question is off-limits and that no employee need be intimidated or will be seen as having asked what are sometimes called career-limiting or career-threatening questions."

SPEED

In Chapter 1, I discussed customer complaints. The studies discussed showed some awe-inspiring figures of money wasted and business lost.

Empowered personnel can bring those numbers down. An empowered employee will solve a customer's problem quickly, if not instantly; the customer thus stays with the company, and perhaps will be even more loyal than before.

An unempowered employee in the same situation will say, "I have to get the manager," or "I need the manager's signature." There is a long delay. The customer, tapping his foot, tired of waiting for redress, plans not to come back again.

Cake-like hierarchical organizational structures make empowerment impossible, as I have said. Speed of response to a customer request depends on empowerment of the employee. Speed of response is a key differentiator. If the employee has to pass a request through many levels, for even the simplest thing (for example a refund on merchandise), the customer will have to wait. Many levels slow communication. Many levels slow delivery. Slow delivery raises costs.

When employees are well-trained and possess decision-making powers as well as negotiation, communication and group-process skills, they reduce costs while providing better service. The company benefits. The employee benefits. And the company should share the accrued benefits with the employee. This is the subject of the next chapter.

CHECKLIST

1) Do you have an implementation plan to integrate the change in service culture?

2) Does the plan include
   - hiring standards for all levels of management — front line, middle and senior management?
   - training guidelines for team building, communication, empowerment, encouraging ideas, and learning the principles of T.Q.S.?

3) Have you set up specialized training for all levels? Are there programs to train the trainers?

4) Do you encourage and facilitate communication on progress within the organization? Has a structure been developed to support continuous improvement through the use, for example, of
   - suggestion programs,
   - rewards/awards as positive reinforcement?

5) Are service guarantees being considered?

CHAPTER

7

ENCOURAGING EXCELLENCE
(Staying on course and not running out of gas)

Some want success. Others must have it. Must. *They are not merely interested, they are* passionate. *They are not merely motivated, they are* possessed. *And those are the people who succeed.*

— *Business Week*

HOW DO WE STAY ON TOP?

It is one thing to put a service quality organization in place, another to keep it going.

Having undertaken steps to improve service, empower its employees, and satisfy the customer, a top-flight organization wanting to stay that way must measure its efforts and reward those who have made the service culture initiative succeed.

Service performance measurement is, essentially, feedback. Feedback will tell you if you are falling short of, meeting, or exceeding your service standards. This is especially important in light of the fact that service standards set today may not meet the customer needs of tomorrow.

Steady feedback and regular reassessment ensures that Total Quality Service remains self-sustaining.

There are many feedback techniques available: surveys, suggestion boxes, field tests, 1-800 lines, customer panels and employee-customer focus groups. These techniques produce usable information on a regular basis.

I have discussed many of these techniques in earlier chapters, so I won't repeat them here. The techniques I want to emphasize in this chapter are award systems and suggestion systems. But first ...

DON'T ENCOURAGE SUCCESS

Here are some thoughts on success.

Success for an individual or a company depends on what others think of them. Consequently, success is perishable.

Excellence, on the other hand, is dependable and lasting because it depends only on the self.

You never see people from companies that seek excellence hanging their heads after an expensive marketing gaffe, or groaning and pointing fingers at some larger cause beyond their control, like "market forces." They never do this because their minds are focused on improvement, almost as if they don't care about the outside world.

Those obsessed with success, with achieving a recognized status or standard, see quality and service performance through the eyes of other companies. They consequently become cripplingly dependent on the vision of those other companies.

Excellence sustains itself; nothing seems to get in its way. Whereas excellence nourishes whomever pursues it, success — where success means to remain successful in others eyes — drains those who pursue it. Indeed, success resents real excellence; but companies concerned with excellence are impressed when they see it in others, and they want to learn how that company does it so they can be that way too.

Excellence, not success, is at the heart of Total Quality Service. Bear the distinction in mind when planning employee reward and suggestion systems. After all, the achievement of excellence is your reason for empowering the employee in the first place.

ROTE RESPONSE

Like excellence and success, there is love of learning and love of good grades.

Too many organizations confuse encouraging excellence with waving carrots in front of employees, hoping to exhort them to do better. To employees, this is a way of saying, "You should pursue good grades, not learning."

Success masked as excellence can be seen in many service initiatives.

Think of how many restaurants you have been to over the years that insist on having the waiter come around and introduce himself or herself. Although it is management policy, an attempt by the restaurant to emphasize the personal attention they are giving the customer, not all customers like waiter-introductions. Many find it intrusive during an intimate dinner or business lunch. Waiter-introductions are another example of management trying to please the customer without actually thinking of the customer first.

The same goes for smile training, which is treated with scepticism by many service thinkers, for good reason. So often, smiling at the customer is a directive from management, which makes the employee feel pressured. Employees resent it. And customers sense that resentment.

The practices above derive from the quick-fix notion of quality service. I want to get away from that. In a service culture built on excellence, a smile will come naturally. In one built on success, it will be forced and unnatural. Empowerment allows the employee to act more naturally and more practically when handling whatever curve day-to-day business serves up.

"Success thinkers" feel that handing out rewards for good service might give employees the wrong impression. They fear employees will perceive quality service as some sort of extra beyond their normal workload. Employees may even see it as a burden, a way of buying them off to get them to work harder.

The root of this fear lies in the incentive schemes themselves. The schemes have the wrong focus. They reward productivity (couriers, for example, who deliver more packages on time than before) rather than the quality of service. Followers of such schemes erroneously understand superior service delivery only in terms of productivity. For example, consider the thorny old problem of handling phone calls — don't look for volume of calls processed; look for how well the person on the other end of the line was served.

TRUST AND RECOGNITION
AT FOUR SEASONS

"I know only two ways to win trust: earn it and give it," says John Young, Senior Vice-President of Human Resources at Four Seasons Hotels & Resorts. "I think too many managers fear they'll lose control if they trust the employees to manage themselves. They'd sooner try to robotize employees through rules: 'Answer the phone by the third ring,' 'smile twice a minute.' They limit personal service to a routine — and distinctive service, by definition, can never be routine.

"Employees want their contributions recognized. Employees want to know that what they're doing is useful and meaningful. Plato called a man 'a being in search of meaning.' Our work defines our self-image. Accomplishment gives us pride, along with enthusiasm and assurance — motivation to live up to our self-image.

"We activate these emotions only when we give employees feedback: appreciation, praise, recognition. Our hotel general managers make it a point to pass along, personally, all guest commendations on service. Every hotel has employee-of-the-month and employee-of-the-year awards. Employee performance, like a marriage, deteriorates when we take it for granted."

THINK ABOUT THE FUTURE

In the last few years, United States Automobile Insurance (USAI) has reduced its turnover rate to 7 per cent from 40 per cent and has seen its property and casualty division reduce its customer loss rate to a measly 2 per cent in an industry in which 10 per cent is the norm.

Part of the reason for the improvement is a system for measuring performance that does not over emphasize productivity (number of phone calls per hour, say) at the expense of quality (the quality of service of those calls).

USAI is thinking ahead. By the turn of the century, most lower level employees now working across North America will be seeking middle or high management positions. Naturally, you will want to keep them around because they know so much about the organization and how it runs.

In the future, there will also be fewer people available to fill front-line entry-level positions than there are now. This means companies, in order to keep these people, will have to empower current front-line employees and pay and reward them accordingly.

"The way to get people to do better work, to do more work, is to give them authority," observes Bob Stone, U.S. Deputy Assistant Secretary of Defense. "That encourages them to respond with enthusiasm. It puts them in charge of their world. People like to be in charge of their world."

Empowerment means giving authority — it means putting people in charge. But a company giving authority to its employees without also recognizing the value of a job well done, and honoring it, makes the act of giving authority pointless. After all, if you were the employee, why would you bother using your authority if no one seems to give a hoot what you do?

THE RECOGNITION GAP

Employee performance objectives and award/reward schemes influence customer satisfaction. Simply put, employees will not treat the customer well unless they themselves are treated in a like manner by management.

Says John Young of Four Seasons, "Performance sets an example; employees are boss-watchers. We can't get quality in a company until its management, as a whole, shows that quality is a priority. We can't create a sense of togetherness by practising class distinctions with private dining rooms, reserved parking, off-limits executive suites. Leadership, like excellence, is attitude in action.

"It's no longer, 'Do as I say.' It's 'Do as I do.' We don't need psychologists to explain the old kick-the-cat syndrome: people will treat others as they themselves have been treated. So if we expect employees to show concern for our customers, we have to show concern for our employees."

RECOGNITION IS COMMUNICATION

At Four Seasons, says Young, the company communicates through praise and recognition. "People who go the extra mile win employee-of-the-month and employee-of-the-year awards. And these are very public awards."

Four Seasons does everything from forwarding to the general manager letters from guests commending employees to instituting profit-sharing plans that recognize good performance.

"Good performance that's rewarded is likely to be repeated.

Good performance that isn't will likely deteriorate. Everybody wants recognition.

"We deliberately circulate stories of exceptional front-line service, stories that feed and strengthen our service culture. And no matter how busy we are, we observe the social niceties, like retirement and holiday parties. They also strengthen the culture, the sense of belonging, the sense of pride."

What Young is saying, in short is "spread the word."

Make known the successes you've had in making changes to the way you do business, but don't be afraid to admit failures and what you have learned from them. Communication builds momentum.

Recognize employees and managers in some tangible way for their contribution to service improvement.

Mention how they have made empowerment work and how they have made it a reality for others. Because ...

People concerned with success are jealous of others.

People concerned with excellence want to see others have it, too, and to learn from others.

Spread the word, and make those words count by ...

GIVING REWARDS THAT COUNT

When executives think of rewards, they most often think of money. This is by no means the only possible form of recognition. And it may not be the best form in all circumstances. (Note that a reward is generally monetary or tangible, while an award symbolic, like a plaque.)

A 1988 survey by the American Productivity and Quality Center found that the primary employee motivator was a good old slap on the back for a job well done. Also ranking high were "challenging work" and "knowing that what you said or did counted." Monetary rewards ranked further down the list.

At Reimer Express, the most desired award is non-monetary.

"We do not believe in bells and whistles," says John Perry, Vice-President of Training and Quality. "We believe in establishing team targets and recognizing quality performance. The highest award at Reimer Express for quality is our QA, or Quality Award.

It works like this. Each Reimer Express business unit has a set of measurable objectives, which are audited for QA awards. When a business unit wins a QA, the President and some of the executive staff visit the location for the award ceremony. The business unit receives a beautiful hand-made plaque. Then comes a day-long celebration. "QA days at terminals are very exciting — a celebration for quality achievement.

"While the QA award is a team prize, we recognize individual quality achievers. Employees decide who should receive a Quality Achiever award within their own work group."

PRE-AWARD AND POST-AWARD SYSTEMS

There are a number of things to bear in mind when considering a recognition system. Jerry McAdams, Vice-President of Performance Improvement Systems at Martiz Inc., says executives should first distinguish between performance improvement plans and recognition plans.

Performance improvement awards are based on determination of what needs to be improved, then measurement to see whether improvement has been made. Employees are rewarded for reaching that goal. I call these "pre-awards."

Recognition plans are "after-the-fact" or "post-awards." According to McAdams, these awards raise awareness about the program they honor, hold up the winner as a role model, and encourage recipients to remain with the organization.

WHICH SYSTEM TO USE WHEN?

There are good reasons for using non-monetary awards. Your organization may already have a cash incentive award plan in place and may not want to monkey with it. You certainly don't want to replace it, if it is cash-based. Employees won't like it.

A non-monetary plan to award service excellence can be set up in addition to the current cash-based plan. Non-monetary plans have the advantage of allowing you to target awards for specific service projects and — this is very important — call attention to their importance.

Cash awards can, of course, be easily tied to service quality team work. For instance, a cash award can be given to team members who come up with a cost-saving process. They can receive a predetermined percentage of the cost saving to the company as a reward. This truly lets employees know that you are listening to them and are willing to act on their suggestions.

Rewards are essential to the suggestion process (discussed below). However, companies who take employee suggestions, implement them, pocket the proceeds and recognize employees with feeble compensation afterward, will guarantee that no suggestions will come from employees again.

Non-monetary awards (as opposed to cash awards) have a visible aspect. Like trophies, they can be seen as symbols of achievement. Winners proudly display them. People will see those trophies as a reminder of something they might like to achieve, too.

Cash awards suit performance-driven job functions, like sales, line-work or management. Non-monetary awards, on the other hand, suit employees whose performance is not directly measurable in terms of sales or revenue, like shippers, accounts receivable clerks, and so on.

Be careful not to award prizes only to top employees. Setting a preset goal that everyone has a chance of reaching tends to reward only the few who achieve it. Giving these awards retains the best employees but does little to keep the rest.

This is not to say everyone in the organization should get a prize, which would make a mockery of a recognition program; however, award systems must be designed so that all workers have a chance to be honored. If not, teamwork will fall apart as individuals pursue personal goals. Nor will there be a focus on service and working together on service. Employees will be out for themselves. They will compete rather than co-operate with each other.

Here's an example. A company that sold ski equipment, ski accessories and ski clothing gave cash incentives to its salespeople based on equipment sales. The incentive worked too well.

Sales on skis increased; sales on clothing took a dive. Salespeople couldn't be bothered with the clothing section, which became quite messy over the course of a typical day as customers looked at items then just tossed them back on the shelf. The problem was that salespeople were too busy competing among themselves for equipment sales to bother tidying up the (highly visible) clothing section.

The better way to reward service is to set goals for all teams and departments. That way, rewards are spread out around the company and everyone has a chance at winning them without being in competition with others. Awards should emphasize achievement by groups rather than achievement by individuals. After all, Total Quality Service involves everyone in the organization, not just the stars.

POINT SYSTEMS FOR AWARDS

"One of the problems with the quality award system we implemented a couple of years ago," says Ron James of NCR, "was that, after a while in a small location, you suddenly find that everybody in the location has a quality award.

"It's fine [to hand out an award] in a large organization, where you could start identifying people that have made a significant contribution, but in a smaller organization, we're talking about five, seven, ten people. A quality award very quickly doesn't carry any weight because it has become a habit."

One possible solution to James's problem is to give employees points. If they have made a suggestion, or if they have performed exemplary service, give them points. They can accumulate points and, at some future date, cash in those points for a reward — say a seminar, or a stereo system. What's more, with this method the worker can win more than once. And it encourages employee longevity and a continuous desire to contribute.

The Body Shop, the adventurous cosmetics firm, gives employees points on a five-point scale — one point for "a job well done," five for "unbelievable" performance. The program is called "Bravo!" Employees recommend their peers, although management can do it too. Speed of recognition is important at the Body Shop. Management asks employees to call them right away with a recommendation, so that a letter can be sent to the employee within three days. Management also decides how many Bravo! points the person will receive. These points go into a bank. They can be redeemed for various rewards. When an employee reaches the 60-point level, he or she can redeem the points for an airline ticket or a pedigree kitten or puppy.

TYPES OF NON-MONETARY AWARDS

McAdams lists five types of non-monetary awards:

1) *Social reinforcement:* The good old pat on the back. This should be used anyway. It costs nothing and it means a lot. Use in conjunction with other types below.

2) *Merchandise awards:* Awards should be objects of significant value, like a television set, stereo system or set of luggage. There should also be a selection from which to choose. A winner may not want a TV if he or she already owns two. So provide a catalogue of anywhere from 10 to 200 award items. McAdams suggests

that an individual award should be worth over 2 per cent of the employee's annual salary.

A merchandise award can be given as a one-time award or after an employee has earned enough service points to claim it. Service points are a handy measure of performance. Employees receive points every time they perform exceptional service. (These point races are worth charting. It keeps everyone in the game.) Employees can use their points right away or wait until they have accumulated a large number of points to gain a larger prize.

And a note about quality service in award giving. If an employee selects a prize, make sure he or she receives it right away. Good service should be practised at all times in the organization, even when giving awards. Be quick to recognize service excellence.

3) *Travel:* Give points or single awards for travel. And not just for individuals, either. For departments or teams, too. There is nothing like a well-earned week-long trip to Hawaii to bring a department or team even closer together.

Trips can be expensive. Often, the problem is that an unrealistically large number of points needs to be accumulated to qualify. So don't make your point total so high that people are discouraged by the sheer time it would take to win.

The New Orleans Hilton has an Employee-of-the-Year, Supervisor-of-the-Year, Department Head-of-the-Year and even Employee-of-the-Decade. These are real company-wide morale boosters. Winners get 12 nights at a Hilton in Hawaii, round-trip air tickets, two weeks off with pay, $1,000 cash, and $1,000 in clothes.

CP Hotels does something similar. Each year, each hotel picks an Employee-of-the-Year from all the Employee-of-the-Month winners and flies them to be feted at the Royal York Hotel in Toronto. The big winner receives 1,000 CP shares, a trip to Hollywood for the entire family, and $500 spending money.

4) *Symbolic:* Symbolic awards can be very high-profile awards. Some companies award rings or watches for high service achievement. Symbolic awards perform the dual function of emphasizing how important service is to the company by holding up the winner as a role model for others and giving that person well-deserved recognition.

Pins and T-shirts are two common awards; desk plaques are permanent reminders to the winner and to others who see it of the company's commitment to service excellence.

5) *Time off:* Time off is similar to travel. Like travel awards, time off gives hard working, committed workers well-deserved time to be with their families. The usual practice is to bank points; the days off earned can be added to the employee's regular vacation allotment.

A WAY TO AWARD MANAGERS

At IBM, managers now have a customer satisfaction bonus clause tied to their salaries — 15 per cent of their salaries, in fact. They receive the money if customer surveys report that IBM is matching the competition. They may get a bonus if service exceeds expectations.

It's the same at Thermo King, a 1990 Baldrige Award finalist. The company puts service into the job descriptions of senior managers; managers have a set minimum number of times they must contact external customers, a non-bottom-line goal for which they are held accountable.

RECOGNITION BRINGS SUGGESTIONS

"To make the staff feel important, we let them see positive guest comments," Heinrich Kapfenberger, General Manager of the Royal Garden Hotel Hong Kong, told *Innkeeping World*: "I let them come up with ideas rather than say 'This is how I want it.' I never shut people down; even if an employee comes up with an idea which is unacceptable to me, I let them know how much I appreciate their suggestion, but then explain why — at least for the time being — we have to look for another solution. I try to keep them coming back with ideas."

SUGGESTIONS: KEEP THEM COMING

Suggestions are communication. Employees feel they are part of the organization when the suggestions they make are considered seriously by the organization. They feel the job they do is important to the company.

There is always a better way to do a job. A formal suggestion system provides employees with a means of communicating with decision-makers on ideas of how to do something better — ideas that the senior management, being so far removed from the front line, may never come up with.

Employees feel they are part of the organization when their suggestions are considered seriously.

Creating a formal system of encouraging and implementing employee suggestions knits together all of the service themes I have talked about so far in this book.

Commitment, leadership, involvement, design, teamwork: each facet of the Total Quality Service process is reflected in the mirror of the suggestion process. Suggestion systems are the most important concept of Total Quality Service.

I don't find it surprising that employee suggestions are being seen as more and more necessary to the way North Americans do business. There is now a national organization in the United States solely concerned with implementation of formalized suggestion systems.

The National Association of Suggestion Systems has over 1,000 members. It estimated that, in 1990, employee suggestions saved its members over $2.3 billion. There can be little doubt about the importance of suggestions in service improvement. Just consider the history of Toyota.

Toyota began its suggestion system in 1951. The first year generated 789 suggestions, which came from 8 per cent of the staff; 23 per cent of suggestions were implemented, an average of 0.1

suggestion per employee. (It is depressing to note that, today, U.S. companies average 0.14 suggestions per employee — about the level that the Japanese had attained 30 years ago!)

The number of suggestions at Toyota rose slowly but steadily over the years. It was not until 1972 that they surpassed the 100,000 suggestion mark. That year, Toyota had over 168,000 suggestions. It is interesting to consider why that year saw such a jump in suggestions. The oil crisis was at its peak and the car industry was taking a beating. Car companies had to do something to change the kind of cars they made.

In 1986, Toyota received 2.6 million suggestions, which translated into 47.7 suggestions per employee; 95 per cent of employees contributed ideas, and 96 per cent of those ideas were implemented.

The latter is also a telling statistic. Toyota has a policy of responding to employee suggestions within 24 hours and rewarding employees for good ideas. Although I have no way of proving it, I suspect that this high percentage reflects employee willingness to pitch-in to the quality initiative because employees have seen that their ideas will be seriously considered by senior management. The suggestion system has started the ball rolling. Whereas, initially, only a few suggestions were offered and fewer were implemented, now everyone puts forward ideas and most are implemented. Toyota employees really must be working together to accomplish those kinds of numbers. (See Appendix VI for the Toyota Employee Suggestion Program form.)

STAR

STAR stands for "Suggestions That Receive Results," the plan to make full use of innovative service thinking at B.C. Telephone. Employees receive cash awards for ideas that result in cost saving or revenue increases. Each award is up to 10 per cent of the estimated first year's saving or benefit, to a maximum of $20,000. Over 4,700 suggestions have been submitted since the program began; 296 of those have been adopted, saving the company in excess of $5.2 million; awards have totalled over $270,000.

Suggestions As Culture

Dave Clark of Campbell Soup envisions a time when suggestions will be so integral to the way his company does business that employees won't even see them as something out of the ordinary.

"My vision of the future is that employees wouldn't have to suggest, they would just make it happen. 'Suggestions' almost suggests to me that there is still a hierarchy at work, and you've got to get permission from higher-ups in order to do good. Now my idea is a bit idealistic, but I think it's a very inspiring vision of the future; a company where there is no suggestion program because the employees don't have to suggest; if they've got a good idea, they just go out and make it happen.

"My experience has been, and you can talk to some of the people in our plants who are much more knowledgeable in a hands-on fashion about this than I — my experience has been that when you allow people to take real responsibility for what it is that they do, they cannot help but respond by offering up improvements."

A SUGGESTION SYSTEM

Every aspect of the organization should be open to improvement. The billing procedure. Where the photocopiers are located. A faster way to pack boxes on the line. Frequency of meetings. You name it. And let the employees know that anything can be changed for the better.

The first step in a formalized suggestion system is to submit a suggestion in writing to management. The submission should be on a multi-part form expressly used for suggestions. The suggester should describe the new operation in detail, list the shortcomings of the old method and, if possible, give hard evidence of time and/or cost saving. The suggester should keep one part of the form as a "receipt."

Submissions should be forwarded to a central bureau that handles suggestions rather than to department heads in order to avoid having the suggestion disappear into a superior's file, never to be seen again.

A central bureau forwards the submission to a management committee or team who assesses it. Ideally, the committee should be cross-functional, or at least have a representative from each department.

The committee promises to report back to the employee with a decision after a fixed period. They must keep that promise. Whether the decision is yes or no, the suggester should be told the reasons for the decision. Unless it is impractical to do so, this should be done face-to-face with the suggester; it lets him or her know why a decision (and the decision is often difficult) was made. This practice is a good one. It obliges management to be honest about its aims and it lets the employee know how important suggestions are to the organization.

The committee should break suggestions into categories like time saving, cost reduction, safety, service improvement, working environment and employee facilities, then prioritize them. It should assess the cost of a suggestion to the company, examine its feasibility, determine whether it is an actual improvement to operations and whether it can be combined with other suggestions, and establish a time frame for implementation.

The Royal Bank, for example, uses three parameters to assess suggestions: relative value to the company, in terms of number of people the suggestion will affect and the frequency of occurrence of the problem that the suggestion has been put forward to resolve; duration of the solution; and effectiveness of the solution.

The Royal Bank also decides how an award for an implemented suggestion should be divided if the suggestion came from more than one person or from a team. This must be done in accordance with income tax regulations. The Royal Bank has another good practice to avoid misunderstandings that multiple suggestions inevitably cause. It recommends the suggesters decide, before they submit the suggestion, how any award will be distributed.

During the committee decision-making process, note should be made of the employee who made the suggestion. The suggester can receive points for a suggestion and additional points if the suggestion is approved. Or he or she can receive a percentage of the amount the suggestion saved or otherwise benefited the company over time.

At Credit Union Central of Ontario, all suggestions are recorded in the employee's file (not the suggestions themselves, but the fact that the employee made one) and are considered during the employee's performance review.

Suggestions should also be tracked. Keep an eye out for those parts of the organization where suggestions are constantly being made. It may be time to overhaul that part of your operation completely.

The success of a suggestion program depends on management's willingness to listen. As in any other aspect of building a service culture, commitment begins at the top.

THE SCOPE OF SUGGESTIONS

For Employees

A system must offer the employees a genuine opportunity to suggest improvements and receive due recognition for their efforts. Employees should receive training on how to present suggestions that cut costs, change operations or save work-time. Supervisors and team leaders should show employees how to review their own operations.

For Supervisors

Same as above, with these additions. Suggestions must solve unit problems. Supervisors must encourage suggestions from subordinates and help them prepare suggestions for submission. Supervisors must be held accountable for implementing good suggestions. They should be rewarded for bringing forward suggestions from their area.

For Senior Managers

Same as both of the above, with these additions. Senior management, foremost, must encourage suggestions and must act on them. Prompt action on suggestions sends a signal from the top that management cares about employee involvement. Senior management must also lead the way in seeing that implemented service suggestions are recognized, and recognized quickly.

SUGGESTION BOXES

Suggestion boxes have developed a reputation for being dust-covered gripe boxes that are never cleaned out. But they work if you attend to them.

For a start, tell employees to use the box and show them that you are using it by responding quickly to their suggestions — within two weeks, for example. If you take much longer, employees lose faith that you are listening to them. Offer a prize for suggestion-givers each month. Make everyone who submits a suggestion eligible for a draw for a dinner for two or a small bonus cheque (on top of any award you may give for implementing the suggestion). Also, it never hurts to set some rules to avoid conflict if more than one person submits the same suggestion.

CONTINUOUS IMPROVEMENT

Suggestions are the core of continuous improvement. To know how and where you need to improve, you need to measure your service performance.

Every service activity you do should point in only one direction; continuous improvement of your company as a service organization. Continuous improvement is the hub of the wheel of Total Quality Service. It makes the wheel roll. Continuous improvement should be the company's way of life. Says Cam Bright of Amdahl, "The day we believe that anything we do can't be done better is the day that we start to decline."

Bright admits that a company must be pragmatic and business-like, that it must pay attention to the shareholders and the bottom line. "But never, ever allow any of those to become reasons why we can't afford any more quality."

Continuous improvement means sitting down and talking to the customer, regularly. "One of the things that we ask the customer to tell us about is, 'How well do we understand your needs?' " But Amdahl also asks the customer to tell it how important certain services are, "because the customer may be incredibly satisfied with something that isn't very important to them."

Bright says that Amdahl uses the phrase "process improvement" much more often than the word "quality." "Process improvement is the road to quality. Continuous improvement is the name of the model, but what we're improving are processes. 'Improvement' is a word we use more than 'quality.' Quality is what comes from that."

Continuous improvement also means being on guard. The business climate changes as fast as the weather. A service process that works today might be useless tomorrow. So companies must be in a state of perpetual readiness to change the way they deliver service. And that means measure, measure, and measure again.

PERFORMANCE MEASUREMENT

I have talked about this earlier, but it is worth reiterating. Performance measurement is ongoing. It completes the service loop of Evaluation, Design, Guidance, Encouragement and back to Evaluation again.

You will remember that in the Evaluation phase, you measured many aspects of your organization. Evaluation and measurement do not stop there. One must assess and reassess. Assess and reassess everything.

Quality councils and quality teams must meet regularly. They must monitor service gaps; seek out best practices; track customer trends; reassess and upgrade the training program if necessary; and modify hiring practices to fit changing customer and organization needs. Remember, the name of the game is continuous improvement.

IF YOU CAN'T MEASURE IT, YOU CAN'T IMPROVE IT

"Measurement is a key ingredient for us in service quality," says John Perry of Reimer Express. Reimer regularly measures non-conformance and related costs, as well as external and internal customer perception. It does a quality survey of external customers and, each year, sends out an extensive questionnaire to its employees to measure how they perceive quality in the company. The results are charted and discussed before the Quality Steering Committee. Reimer understands that it is important to communicate what it has learned, so the results are made available to all employees across the country. We have only two things to worry about — our employees and our customers." Reimer has established standards for every highway on which it operates and relentlessly works on service improvement. "To do this, we have to measure. We know where we stand on performance, and that's one of the reasons why we were the first truck-transportation company in North America to offer an 'on time or free' guarantee. That's where quality and marketing come together. It's not possible to gain market share if you can't produce the goods. It's easy to make promises about service and quality. What matters is performance. What matters are results."

WORDS TO THE WISE

One has to be careful when assessing employee performance on the basis of a statistical standard. Your organization might be operating at 100 per cent efficiency, but your customers may still be complaining.

Consider the experience of an insurance company. It mails out customer claim checks within two weeks. Over the years, this has become the standard. No one sees the need to improve. The company feels it is operating at peak efficiency.

There are two problems here. One, the organization is measuring productivity, not customer wishes. Two, it is measuring against existing practices, not desired practices.

It's just like the old telephone problem, where receptionists who must handle a certain number of calls per hour or answer them in a certain period of time are simply too busy to solve each customer's problem properly.

What must be measured are service processes, not standards based solely on the quality of the task done. Track service problems without regard to task. Survey the customer, not the staff, to see if service is improving.

MEASURE WHAT'S IMPORTANT

I said above that performance measurement is not a means to slap yourself on the back. Often, companies measure things that are not worth measuring. One should measure only those aspects of the business that are important to your customer and those things that you can change.

Also, don't measure too much; you're not going to take action on anything if you do.

When you do measure, the results of your measurement should raise customers' expectations. You raise their awareness. And you commit yourself to meeting that expectation. After all, you've asked them for input and they expect you to do something about it. Don't try to raise expectations in an area that you can't do anything about, either. Customers are very sensitive to false promises.

DOING THINGS OVER

The other key aspect of performance measurement is tracking the number of service actions that have to be done again. Says John Perry of Reimer Express, "Conformance cost is simply the cost to do things right, such as the cost of our training. In a service business, the biggest opportunity for lowering controllable cost is a reduction in non-conformance. I like to call it 'hassle' costs.

"The cost of doing things over or just plain wrong is expensive. We established a measurement system that is reviewed by the steering committee. It helps us keep track of improvements and highlights the need for action.

"As we reduce 'hassle' in work, we naturally lower non-productive time. It is an absolute fact that when quality goes up, costs go down. The traditional 'fix it' attitude about quality does not work. It never did."

EXAMPLES OF PERFORMANCE MEASUREMENT

Below are methods of performance measurement used by service-leading companies.

Tracking Service Quality at Federal Express

Federal Express has developed an on-line package-tracking system that benefits customers and staff alike. It brings the two closer together, which is the way it should be in a service-first organization.

The computer system, called COSMOS IIB, can tell a customer where exactly on the planet their package is at that moment. The waybill of each package has a barcode, which is entered into the system each time the package changes hands. The computer records time, date and place entered. The computer can then follow the journey of the package with real-time calculations based on the information entered into it. Obviously, staff can provide maximum service here, because they can tell where a package is, whether it has been delivered, or who signed for it.

FedEx employees can analyse package-handling through computer records. It is an equivalent of my gap analysis. FedEx can analyse flow of packages to see where delivery delays are occurring. The existence of the system demonstrates the importance FedEx places on front-line package-handling and the company's relation to the customer.

First Chicago

The First National Bank of Chicago has measured service quality since 1981. It tracks over 500 customer service processes. Combining customer needs and industry standards, First Chicago draws up charts. Each product area presents these charts at weekly performance meetings with senior management. There are two lines on the chart; the MAP line, for minimum acceptable performance, and the goal line, the level of exceptional performance.

In 1982, the minimum acceptable time it took to perform a money transfer was 15 minutes, even though in reality transfers were taking anywhere from five to 50 minutes. Staff performed at the minimally acceptable level about half the time.

By 1989, not only had staff cut transfer time to 12 minutes or less, they had raised the MAP line to 12 minutes and had inched closer to and finally touched the five-minute standard of exceptional performance.

Performance Measurement Needs Openness

An aerospace firm redesigning aircraft for the U.S. Navy invited representatives of the client to visit the shop floor any time they wanted to check for quality and make any recommendations they felt were needed in the project. Managers discussed with the visitors performance reports not normally shown to outsiders. Supervisors implemented changes suggested by the customer without having to get approval from a higher authority. The result? So many improvements were made that the company, as it neared completion of the project, had reduced the number of worker-hours required to rebuilt an aircraft by 40 per cent of the total originally anticipated. And the quality never faltered.

Customer Cards for Employees

At every hotel in the Hyatt Hotel Corporation, employees fill out an opinion survey to rate the general manager's performance. The news had better be good.

Coca-Cola: Everybody's Customer

When it comes to pleasing the customer and getting information to do that, Coca-Cola is a front-runner. The company does a customer service survey once a year. Also, it meets customers at least once a year. Sometimes every three months. It sends the customer a quality checklist to be filled out and returned with every shipment. Every purchaser is contacted at least once after the sale. Every complaint gets an immediate response.

The company has a performance measurement system, too. Customer surveys are done on a five-point scale. Late shipments and complaints are followed until a resolution is found. Responses to customer requests are measured in hours. It is easy to see why the company does this. Coca-Cola is the archetypal global company. It has customers in 100 countries speaking as many languages. It must have a system that embraces each and every one of its customers.

External Customer Care Council (ECC)

That's the name Bell Cellular gives its program to find ways to make it easier to do business with the company. The ECC produces new ideas to provide service improvements and each department develops its own tactics. Each department has a customer service liaison to ensure the division is properly serving the customer. And it does not stop there. Bell Cellular constantly assesses current and future customer needs and perceptions. There are regular assessments like the 24-hour customer care line, customer out-reach programs, welcome calls and anniversary calls. There's a free direct emergency line to police. The slogan of the program? It makes for a great pun: "Going Above and Beyond the Call."

Go to the Customer

A company that provides temporary office services wanted to better fit its workers to customer requirements. So it contacted 29 of its leading clients and paid them a visit. It sat down with each client and studied the jobs their employees did and how they did them. It asked the clients about what they thought temporary workers were good and not so good at, as well as what skills they needed that the company was not providing. The representatives of the company even did many of the jobs themselves, to learn first-hand.

And the company wanted to know what new skills would be needed in the future. Later, it was able to create a profile of customer needs and, from that profile, develop a program that would help the company identify workers who would best fit its clients' needs. Today, the customers needs are being met.

Visibility Is Service

The city of Portland, Oregon, has put police on bikes not only to make them more manoeuvrable in traffic, but to make them more visible and accessible to members of the public wishing to pass on information or complaints. By so doing, the city has closed the often yawning gap between police and the public at large.

How's Your Stay?

Every month, the CEO of the Atlanticare Medical Center invites 25 patients to dinner in the hospital cafeteria. The meal is on him. And he wants to hear what they have to say. Do they like the food? What about the services the hospital provides?

Number 1

Novotel, the hotel chain, gives its guests a pin that says "Number 1" when they register. They are asked to give it to an employee who gives them exceptional service during their stay. The employees redeem their pin collections later for awards.

Doin' It Right

The general manager of the Sheraton Tel Aviv, Raoul Jacoby, has come up with a novel solution to the problem of employees' natural fear of management.

When he catches employees doing something right, he personally rewards them. He told *Innkeeping World*: "It goes with my basic belief that you can't manage by fear, only by understanding, respect and appreciation."

Secret Shopping

Secret or mystery shoppers are a good measuring tool, because they guarantee independent assessment. There are companies that provide this service at an hourly rate. These "shoppers" are paid to be watchful and super-critical customers. Domino's Pizza is nothing if not loyal to the method. Each year, it pays 10,000 customers to buy pizza just to hear the feedback.

The company buying the service provides the questions. The company asks the secret shopping company to survey its service. It asks questions based on the mission statement or service guarantee — the things for which it wants to be known. The buyer should also let staff know that there will be periodic inspections, and that the inspectors will be looking for particular service-related things.

When the results come in, you should reward employees who did well in areas you want done well. In other words, don't just reward superior service — reward what is done well.

HOW TO WIN THE BALDRIGE AWARD

I think there is nothing that would encourage excellence more than winning the Malcolm Baldrige Award.

Mitchell Fromstein, President of Manpower Temporary Services, says you don't even have to go that far.

He believes that using the Baldrige criteria to measure quality in your organization is incentive enough. "To me, Baldrige is a way of thinking and a way of practising — not just an award."

The Baldrige Award is the American equivalent of the highly coveted Deming Prize. Inaugurated in 1987 under the National Quality Improvement Act, its message is simple: companies had better sharpen up and think about the quality of what they do. The standards are tough. No more than two awards are handed out per year in three categories — manufacturing, service and small business.

The National Institute of Standards and Technology sets the award criteria. Winners are those who score highest on a 1,000-point, seven-category scale. The seven categories are Leadership, Information and Analysis, Strategic Quality Planning, Human Resource Utilization, Quality Assurance, Quality Results and Customer Satisfaction.

Each category has a point value. Customer Satisfaction is the highest at 300 points. Information and Analysis is the lowest at 60 points. The weightings have changed over the years. The Leadership category has decreased from 150 (1988) to 100 (1991). Quality Results has risen from 100 to 180 during the same span.

Curt Reimann, Director of the Baldrige program, said in his keynote address to the 1990 Minnesota Quality Conference that the Baldrige Award aims to

➤ elevate quality standards throughout the United States;

➤ create a quality-excellence standard for the United States to be used in all organizations;

➤ create harmony, communication and consistency; and

➤ foster involvement of people and organizations.

A service journey is a long one; the Baldrige criteria constitute a useful roadmap for shaping a mission statement along service quality lines. A quick analysis of how well your company scores on the Baldrige scale should put to rest any notion that instituting a service culture will be a quick-fix.

As a way of summarizing Total Quality Service, here are the Baldrige criteria one by one. I am indebted to Harvard Business

School professor and former Baldrige judge David Garvin's article on the Baldrige Awards in the *Harvard Business Review*, November-December 1991, for much of the information herein.

Leadership (100 Points)

The traditional senior executive roles of financial planning and setting productivity levels are passed over in favor of activities that foster quality and service in the workplace. Baldrige examiners don't want to know about heroic Rambo-like demonstrations of service commitment; they want to see what executives do day to day to instil service in the company. Do executives sit on teams? Sit down with customers? Work the front line? How often?

One thing Baldrige judges do during their on-site analysis of a company is ask the CEO to flip open his or her daily calendar. The examiners review the CEO's activity during recent months. They seek to find out if the CEO's actually do what they claim to be doing to promote the service culture. At a glance, the judge can see how much time is truly spent on it.

Judges also want to know how well managers understand the lower levels of the company, how they work. They will quiz managers to see how well they understand operations a few levels below their position (Garvin calls this "skip-level communication"). This reveals whether managers are listening to employees and whether the company structure is flattening out to ease communication among levels.

Information and Analysis (70 Points)

Benchmarking and availability of usable quality data are the themes of this category. According to Garvin, many companies benchmark by simply popping over to the Baldrige winner next door to borrow their processes, despite the fact that these companies do well only in some service areas. (Garvin also notes that Baldrige winners tend to be above-average in every category, but do not necessarily stand out in any particular one. Therefore, these companies, by themselves, are poor choices for benchmarking the world standard for some aspect of service.)

Garvin also finds that companies go to competitors without a clear idea of what they want to learn from that company. They seem to hope their visit will magically yield a solution to what ails them. Instead, companies should determine what they need in a particular service area, find the top-notch provider in that area, learn how that company does it, and take this knowledge home to adapt it to their own organization.

Baldrige examiners are also picky about hard data. They want to see that managers use real numbers, not feel-good talk, to improve quality decision-making at their organization. The information must touch on all business areas, everything from the customer right up to the CEO's suite. And the information must be handy. Garvin says customer comments should not be compiled then shoved into some file somewhere, and that detailed operational processes should not rest in a computer program that only a few know how to use.

Strategic Quality Planning (60 Points)

"What we're looking for are two or three specific goals in a one- or two-year period," Garvin reports one examiner saying, "and the fact that the company can tell us, explicitly and specifically, what they are going to improve and why." He gives the example of "cutting telephone waiting time by 50 per cent" as being superior to a promise-all, promise-nothing statement like "becoming the auto industry's supplier of choice." In a strategic business plan, statements like the latter are so vague as to be meaningless. They are not concrete objectives and, consequently, will never be truly achieved. Examiners also look for large-scale changes or, rather, goals that demand the company make large-scale changes, like a reduction in quality errors by 95 per cent within five years.

Human Resource Utilization (150 points)

Empowerment is a vague word to some, vague enough to give the impression that you are giving employees power when you are not. The Baldrige examiners consequently allot a big chunk of their points to this category to see if you are sincere. They want to see quantifiable data that show how your organization is actually using its human resource potential. Examiners look for front-line responsibility — can staffers authorize large-dollar refunds? Can an assembly line worker press the button if he or she thinks something is wrong with the system?

Next, examiners want to know if employees are reprimanded or supported for taking "above and beyond the call" actions. Does your organization have a suggestion system? Are there work teams? Are suggestions implemented? What percentage of those submitted are implemented? How long does it take to get an answer?

Examiners want to know about the training package. I stress "package," because success to Baldrige examiners is more than the right person doing the right job. Does the employee also have knowledge of co-workers' jobs? Decision-making skills? Problem-solving skills? Baldrige examiners get answers to these questions by sitting around and gabbing with employees about their jobs, what they know of the company's aims, how well the place is working, and so on.

Quality Assurance of Products and Services (140 Points)

This is basically the vertical-versus-horizontal problem. Managers have been unwilling to let go of narrow, vertical decision-making. Examiners will want to know how well information flows across company lines and the degree of cross-functionalization in a new procedure. It is one thing to improve core business functions, like sales, but another to improve smaller, ancillary functions, like billing or packaging, that are related to them. In short, examiners ask, "Has the service program been mapped? Have the service gaps been analysed?"

Quality Results (180 Points)

Examiners want to see real numbers on wrong delivery rates or the percentage of returning customers or relative perceived market share. They want to see real, measurable development in areas that will change the bottom line over a number of years. What is the relationship between improved service and customer satisfaction?

Customer Satisfaction (300 Points)

This is the most important of the seven categories. Companies must show that they have used measured customer analysis from a variety of sources — surveys, focus groups, customer cards, and so on. This information should include current as well as lost customers. Information on the latter is particularly telling, for without it, the company often receives a flattering image of its own achievement.

Also important are the steps taken to resolve customer complaints. How long does it take to resolve a complaint? Who has the power to resolve complaints? Are complaints analysed in a way that reveals service weaknesses? Does management regularly sit down with customers to find out what they like and don't like about the company?

WHAT WE'VE LEARNED

A quick survey of your company using the Baldrige criteria should give you some clue of what you have to do in terms of service improvement. And it is not a matter of "me against the rest." Garvin points out that the Baldrige Award has demonstrated an "outpouring of co-operative behavior and a level of corporate sharing seldom seen in this country."

Service in North America has quickly evolved from cheery speeches to actual organization change. Service is being taken seriously. Companies are now more willing to go to other companies to see how they do what they are really good at. Companies are no longer smug or uptight about seeking ideas from others and adapting them. Benchmarking has grown in popularity, which indicates to me that companies are willing to work together to create a better economic environment in North America. In Garvin's words, which seem to wink at the Japanese across the ocean, "To become more competitive, American companies have discovered co-operation."

CHECKLIST

1) Have you measured qualitative and quantitative performance against standards?

2) Do you continue to use internal and external research to
   • monitor best practices?
   • monitor customer and employee satisfaction?

3) Do you continually evaluate service gaps and re-evaluate training and hiring programs in light of changing organizational and customer needs?

4) Have you formed Quality Service teams or Quality Councils?

5) Do you regularly use award/reward programs to recognize continuous improvement and support Total Quality Service?

6) Are there award/reward programs for all levels?

7) Do you have a suggestion system in place?

8) Are you adhering strictly to the hiring practices necessary to support your quality initiative?

CHAPTER 8

Lessons Learned and Not Forgotten
(Some driving tips from the experts)

Failure is success if we learn from it.
— Malcolm Forbes

WHAT WE'VE LEARNED

Implementing a service culture is a tough job. It takes full commitment. It also takes time; I've turned down the opportunity to work with companies the minute I heard them say they wanted a service culture up and running in their organization within six months. An organization must have a good measure of perseverance, because the service journey is a long one, and it will not always be clear sailing.

What separates the service award-winners from the merely good service providers is the ability to make often-dramatic service recoveries. When presented with a service predicament, the winners see it as a test of their service reputation, and they know how to respond. These situations are the big tests of a service culture. On the other hand, the day-to-day tests are customer complaints; here, winning companies again demonstrate their unflappable attitude: they look for complaints. Service recovery and quick complaint-resolution are, for winning companies, proof of their service guarantees.

THE COMPLAINT PARADOX

Florida Power & Light began a quality service improvement program in 1986, after receiving 2,222 complaints about its quality of service the year before. (This made it the poorest-performing utility in the United States, according to the Public Service Commission.)

At the end of 1987, after the program had been in effect for a year, there were only 1,143 complaints; in 1988, the number had dropped to 879, and in 1989, it was only 706.

I mention these figures because they put a company like FP & L in a funny spot. Complaints tell you about customer needs; you want to know about complaints so that you know what's on the customer's mind. Unfortunately, the less you hear, the less you know.

On the other hand, when you receive fewer and fewer complaints over time, you must be doing something right. It's tough to say which position you'd rather be in. A pleasant problem.

Complaints: A Chance To Learn

"WAITER! THERE'S A FLY-BALL IN MY SOUP!"

Complaints are a chance to learn.

Successful companies welcome complaints. Complaints let the company know what its customers don't like. Complaints highlight specific problems at those points of contact that can be mapped.

Complaint analysis is a very useful measuring device. Successful companies track complaints by type (employee attitude, quality of product, speed of delivery, and so on); by frequency; and by department.

Frequent complaints about one section of your operations should warn you that that section needs attention. Complaints draw a picture of the organization from the customer's point of view. Think of them as a barometer of what must change and where changes must be made in the organization.

How To Measure Complaints

Coca-Cola's complaint-assessment practices are exemplary. The company approaches the complaint problem in preventative terms. Each plant has a complaint-handling system developed by its employees. Coke's system works like this:

1) Complaints are logged and numbered for proper follow-up and for inclusion in monthly and weekly reports.
2) An acknowledgment is sent to the customer within 24 hours of receipt.
3) Data are shared among all departments for analysis of likely causes and appropriate corrective action.
4) There is continuous follow-up until the root cause is determined and corrective actions have proven effective.
5) The customer receives a complete report of the root cause and of the actions taken as soon as the investigation is complete, usually within 48 hours.
6) Any process or system improvement is implemented at all locations.

SERVICE RECOVERY

Remember my story in Chapter 1 about the makeshift American Express office that opened up after an earthquake? Amex has developed a reputation for going the extra mile.

An important part of a service culture is providing service under any circumstances. The same goes for service recovery: coping with circumstances that suddenly prevent you from delivering a service you have promised. Success under arduous conditions *proves* that you do have a service culture. Perennial service leaders weather these storms. It is why they stay on top.

A couple of years ago, the Amex office in Hong Kong launched a flower and gift delivery service for gold cardmembers, through a well-established vendor. The service was convenient, and cardmembers loved it.

Expecting an increase in demand as Valentine's Day approached, Amex made sure the vendor had enough capacity to deliver. However, the number of orders far exceeded expectations. The vendor could not cope with the volume of orders. By noon on Valentine's Day, the phone lines were jammed with customers wanting to know where all the flowers had gone?

Amex had a disaster on its hands. It had to do something, and fast.

So it grabbed 15 employees from its customer service department and put them in taxis to deliver flowers. The next day, the general manager signed 300 letters of apology, which were delivered to cardmembers along with boxes of chocolates. "We acknowledged a problem, made an attempt to correct it, and apologized," said Betty Daruwala, Vice-President of Operations. "As a result, we gained goodwill. Not a single cardmember was lost. Of course, we got out of the flower delivery business!"

Toyota turned a potential disaster into a benefit when it discovered, three months after the Lexus LS400 model had been introduced, that all 8,000 of them had to be recalled.

But instead of writing customers to tell them there was something wrong with their cars and asking them to bring the cars in, Toyota phoned each car owner and asked when it could come over and pick it up. In one case, Toyota flew technicians from Detroit to Grand Rapids, Michigan, to repair cars on the spot. (Does this kind of effort pay off? Within a year of the introduction of Lexus, Toyota moved ahead of Mercedes-Benz and BMW in the U.S. luxury car market.)

Service quality gives a company competitive advantage. Regardless of the excellent service a company aims to provide, however, setbacks do occur. That is why every company must have service recovery processes in place.

Service recovery should be an integral part of an organization's culture and customer service strategies, says Daruwala. "Unless good recovery processes exist, customers will rightly assume that the company doesn't care about them, and they will slowly defect to the competition."

The Road to Recovery

Service recovery plans are required in two situations: 1) the one-off cases where major or minor problems occur and the day must be saved; and 2) situations where your customers are slowly defecting, either by reducing their patronage or by moving away from you completely.

One-off cases are unforseen situations, totally beyond company control. Sometimes they are the result of an oversight or a misunderstanding by the customer. Regardless of the reason, if the customer is dissatisfied, you must regain his or her loyalty.

The first step in turning a bad situation into a good one is to acknowledge the problem and apologize sincerely. Next, find solutions to fix the immediate problem. Get the customers involved and give them a fair shake; customers appreciate your concern. Offer them something of value, like a fee rebate, or a gift coupon, or a free dessert, for their trouble. Your actions make the customer realize that they are important to you.

A final step: Make sure you tell all employees who may serve this customer about the problem and your solution. Nothing could be worse than saving a customer, only to have the same mistake happen again because you did not inform everyone who needed to know about it. In Daruwala's words, "Don't add the free dessert to the tab!" To make sure that problems don't recur, Amex puts notes on its computer system, so that all employees who deal with that customer will know what occurred, what recovery methods were used, and what commitments were made.

The service recovery process is often stifled because the customer wishes to speak to a more senior person but cannot. We have all encountered the situation where we have been told the supervisor is "away," is "busy," or "can't change the decision."

Daruwala believes there are three benefits to letting customers speak to more senior personnel.

First, simply speaking to someone at a higher level often diffuses much of the customer's anger, which can be a barrier to satisfying the customer. The customer feels that if senior staff are listening, they must care.

Second, your management can learn about specific customer problems and can take action to prevent recurrence.

Third, handling customer problems is an easy way for management to stay in touch with customer needs. "If your organization does not let customers speak to supervisors and managers, you are losing valuable opportunities to rebuild loyalty."

Two Recovery Experiences at Amex

Daruwala tells two stories, one of a successful recovery, one to file under Lessons Learned.

"Recently, we made a keying error on a payment from a long-tenure customer — instead of keying $2,500, we keyed in $25. Obviously, this error caused the account to age past due, resulting in the customer's receiving collection letters and phone calls. The customer wrote to our president to cancel his account. Immediately, our customer relations staff spoke to the cardmember, apologizing and acknowledging the error. She saved the account and also signed up that company for 1,400 corporate cards."

The second story is about a platinum cardmember (who wasn't a big spender) who one day wanted to buy a $45,000 BMW. Because the purchase was totally out of character, our authorizer asked the cardmember for financial information. The customer was so offended he walked out of the dealership and phoned Amex to demand an explanation.

Amex apologized and explained the circumstances. It regained the customer's goodwill, and asked him to return to the dealership and drive away in his BMW.

A while later, the cardmember was back on the phone, livid — the dealer had refused to accept the transaction. "We had neglected to call and advise the dealer that the charge would be authorized. So the initial service recovery with the cardmember was wasted. Quality control is never more critical than during service recovery."

Recover Your Tracks

Many service problems are not so obvious as the ones above and, without adequate tracking systems, often go undetected.

Service recovery requires an organizational environment within which employees understand the value of retaining customers for a lifetime.

A number of companies that participated in the PULSE survey keep statistics on all service problems, the number of customers saved, and the reasons why customers wouldn't accept a solution. By focusing on customers, and encouraging employees to eliminate the source of complaints, these companies gain loyal customers and motivated staff.

A formal infrastructure goes a long way toward ensuring service recovery. The infrastructure should include a tracking system, a customer service unit, and a quality team.

Begin with a tracking system that calculates the profit lost through customer defections. It's also useful to have means to calculate expected cash flows over a customer's lifetime. No matter how you look at it, once you assign dollars to every customer relationship, you can justify spending money to retain customers who are unhappy.

Track customer complaints over several months, then classify them with the aim of ferreting out the root causes of the problems. Then fix these problems where they begin.

Next, you need to make customer service personnel accessible to your clients.

Amex uses a telephone service center, which receives most of the inquiries. It resolves 95 per cent of the issues on the spot. "We are particularly alert to second requests," says Daruwala. "When customers tell us this is the second time they are contacting us, or the second time a problem has arisen, senior staff resolve the problems immediately."

Amex also has a "save-a-cardmember" unit, which speaks to every customer who wishes to give up his or her membership. Amex wants to understand why the customer wants to leave, and this contact presents an opportunity to reinforce cardholder benefits and clear up any misunderstandings. Daruwala says the save rate is high, because cardmembers value the personalized contact and appreciate the company's desire to retain their membership. "Often the result is that customers upgrade to a premium card product — a true service recovery."

SERVICE GUARANTEES

Companies that make great service recoveries tend to be those with service guarantees. Guarantees make recoveries possible.

Service guarantees are the engines of successful service organizations. Every aspect of the service process — evaluation, design, delivery, continuous improvement — is a part of this engine.

In the definitive article on the subject of service guarantees, "The Power of Unconditional Service Guarantees," *(Harvard Business Review,* July/August, 1988) Christopher W.L. Hart tells about the service guarantee offered by a Miami-based pest control company called "Bug's" Burger Bug Killers (BBBK). Its service guarantee looked at first like a tall order.

BBBK's guarantee includes the proviso that the customer pays only if all pests are eradicated from the premises. If dissatisfied with BBBK's work, the customer receives a refund of up to 12 months of the company's services — and BBBK will pay the extermination fees of a company of the customer's choice for the next year. If the health department closes the customer's facility because of vermin, BBBK will pay all fines, reimburse lost profits, and throw in $5,000 on top.

Again, it's a tall order. But the guarantee has made the company very successful. It charges more than anyone else in the pest control business and it has the greatest market share.

Why is BBBK successful? Its founder designed his company around the service guarantee. He first came up with an unconditional guarantee and then, working backwards, shaped his entire organization in terms of the requirements of the guarantee. In other words, he built his company on the promise of error-free service.

There is good sense in the BBBK approach. Commitment to error-free service, says Hart, forces a company to provide it.

Service guarantees are like mission statements; they are next to useless if they make promises that are too vague or slyly misleading to be fulfilled. Hart gives the example of an airline that guaranteed its customers would make connecting flights provided, of course, there were no delays caused by weather or air-traffic control problems — events out of the airline's control.

This sounds like a good deal, until you learn that these two types of problems cause 95 per cent of all flight delays.

The service guarantee forces you to pay attention to the customer and the customer's service needs, not management's idea of what those needs are.

By its very nature, a service guarantee sets standards that must be met. As Hart points out, if a service guarantee says, to use the Federal Express example, "absolutely, positively by 10:30 a.m.," it does not mean "sometime tomorrow, probably." To Federal Express, this standard can, must, and will be met. And it is specific enough to be measured: either the package is delivered on time or it isn't.

According to Frank O'Connor, Managing Director for Central Region at Federal Express Canada, "All by themselves, our guarantees create a powerful quality goal. And they keep it in front of every FedEx employee, every minute of every day. Those guarantees literally *define* — with every sweep of the second-hand of the clock — what our company *is*. They define Federal Express to our customers. And they define us to ourselves, in ways that nothing else could."

The FedEx guarantee works like this: "We promise to deliver your package by a set time the next day — either 5 p.m., noon, or

10:30 in the morning. And there are no excuses. The weather doesn't matter. Transportation problems at either end don't matter. Traffic volumes don't matter. We will deliver on time, or the customer doesn't pay for the delivery.

"If our delivery is one minute late, the customer doesn't pay. And we have invoices designed to show exactly what time we took the package and what time it was delivered. The customer gets a record of our performance on the bill. And if the performance doesn't meet the promise — there in black and white — the customer doesn't pay."

By having to live by such a standard, employees know what the company expects of them and customers know what they can expect from the company. When Manpower Temporary Services was thinking of dropping its service guarantee, thinking that its customers were all familiar with it and the guarantee had lost its marketing impact, the employees got mad. President Mitchell Fromstein told Hart: "Our employees' reaction was fierce — and it had a lot less to do with marketing than with the pride they take in their work." A guarantee also curbs the habit of many firms — promising anything to get a sale without being able to deliver it. The service guarantee is binding because the customer makes it so.

The Guarantee and the Bottom Line

One of the things I like most about service guarantees is that they encapsulate everything that is important to Total Quality Service. If you are repeatedly making refunds for slow service at your restaurant, for example, you can see right away that a problem exists somewhere in your delivery process. Then, you can sit down and examine your service system to find out the cause of the delay. You can examine weak links in the service-delivery chain. In other words, upholding the guarantee produces measurable data of performance.

Hart also points out that service guarantees have a direct bearing on market share. The purpose of a service guarantee is to foster repeat business. If you live up to your guarantee, customers see that and respect that, and they will buy from you again.

I talked in Chapter 1 about the effect of customer retention on the bottom line. As a recap, consider the results of a TARP survey that asked unhappy customers to decide whether they would buy from a company again.

Among non-complainants who lost $1 to $5, 37 per cent said yes; for those who lost over $100, only 9 per cent said yes. These were the lowest figures among the results. Complainants' figures were much higher. Among complainants who did not have their complaint resolved, 46 per cent of those suffering a minor loss and 19 per cent of those suffering a major loss said yes. For complaints that were resolved quickly, the results were 95 per cent (minor) and 82 per cent (major). So it is clear that if you resolve customers' complaints quickly and satisfactorily, you will not lose them.

It makes sense. The customer feels he or she can trust you; quick resolution encourages loyalty — you treated them well, they appreciated that, and they will enjoy coming back to see you again. And knowing you as a company that has and will come through for them, they feel less risk in buying one of your products. Why take a chance on someone else?

Some Don'ts

Not everyone can use a service guarantee. Your organization might not be ready for one. If a guarantee of "complete satisfaction or all your money refunded" makes you shudder, you first need to change the organization to make it more service-oriented.

Companies tremble when they think of the payouts they might have to make. This probably explains why some companies have vague guarantees. They think they will have to shell out.

And it is shifty to put out a service guarantee as an advertising or market-boosting device, without any interest in actually changing the organization or your delivery process to guarantee the service you promise. This also betrays the fear that forking out refunds is money down the tubes.

The truth is, not guaranteeing service is money down the tubes.

Many companies that have adopted guarantees have discovered that their refunds over a year are much lower than expected. And they discover that in living by the guarantee, they more than make up for payouts by gains in repeat business.

The Five Essentials of a Guarantee

Hart lists five qualities of a good service guarantee.

1) *The guarantee is unconditional.* Unconditional means without exceptions or hidden clauses. No if's or but's. The customer is satisfied or the customer is not.

2) *The guarantee is easy to understand.* Plain language expresses your promise clearly. It conveys honesty and a willingness to

stand by your promise. The customer knows what to expect and so does the employee. Guaranteeing "quick service" is vague. "Service within five minutes" is precise. Companies shy away from precision because it commits them to words they don't want to stand behind. Being precise means you are willing to put yourself at risk, because a precise offer of service can be measured. Customers appreciate that approach.

3) *The guarantee is meaningful.* Your guarantee should offer what your customers want most out of a company like yours. Federal Express, for example, offers on-time delivery, because that is what people expect from a courier company.

The refund should also suit the product and service. Obviously you don't offer a free trip to Hawaii if the pizza you delivered is late. On the other hand, giving the customer a 10 per cent discount coupon on their next purchase is chintzy, and fails to address the matter at hand: the pizza the customer is holding has been delivered late.

4) *The guarantee is easy to invoke.* In other words, don't make the customer go through any more trouble than he or she already has. If customers want a refund, they shouldn't have to go to great lengths to get them. The customer shouldn't have to fill out a form, have the form approved by the manager, then come back tomorrow between noon and two to collect the refund.

Apart from the inconvenience, a drawn-out refund procedure makes the customer feel like he or she is trying to pull a fast one on the company to get a free meal. Often, the customer will wind up wishing he or she hadn't complained.

For another example, consider stereo stores. They would often promise to beat any price in town. Trouble is, you had to get written proof of an offer from another store and bring it around to the stereo company before they'd knock down the price. The customer doesn't appreciate the inconvenience.

The solution is to empower employees to give refunds on the spot. Or even anticipate them. If a waiter knows a dinner group has been getting slow service all night, he or she could beat them to the punch by offering them a complimentary dessert before they complain.

5) *The guarantee is easy for the customer to collect on.* Many credit card companies immediately credit your account when you phone in a complaint, no questions asked. So don't wait three weeks before giving a refund, or promise the customer a refund then tell them they have to come down to the store and fill out a form before they can pick it up.

Internal Service Guarantees

To make a service guarantee effective for external customers, it is good practice to have a service guarantee for internal customers. An internal guarantee holds as much force as an external one.

For instance, a newspaper production unit may offer the distribution unit a guarantee that the evening run will be ready at a fixed time. If production fails to have the papers sitting on the dock ready to go at the prescribed time, it refunds the distribution unit out of its own budget. This arrangement will naturally encourage departments to work together to speed the internal delivery process and make it really work. It will also eliminate silos between departments and prevent unrealistic demands.

A MISCELLANY OF LESSONS

Below is a collection of lessons learned, good and bad service experiences, things companies have done to raise their level of service, and words to the wise that, I hope, will serve as a review or summary of Total Quality Service.

You will notice at the end of each entry a number in parentheses. This number refers to the chapter where you can find more information about the subject discussed in the anecdote.

Something for the Wall

The Miami Herald (December 25, 1989) collected a list of customer service do's and don'ts from various sources. Here are a few. They're good little reminders about all I've talked about in the previous chapters.

➤ Don't underestimate the effort required to attain good service.

➤ The customer's definition of service — not yours — is what matters. Know what your customers expect.

➤ Promising more than you can deliver will alienate customers.

➤ Follow up by asking customers if they are satisfied. It shows you care and gives you immediate feedback on how the problem was handled.

➤ Portray the customer service staff as internal consultants to the company. Don't position them as a buffer between irate customers and the company.

➤ Cost pressures prompt short-sighted managers to sabotage service by cutting staff or demanding higher productivity.

➤ Customer service is a moving target. Consumer expectations change.

➤ It's more effective to say "I'm sorry" than it is to say "we're sorry."

We Take the Hamburger More Seriously Than They Do

"If we want to compete in the '90s, we'll have to give service more than lip service," says John Young, Senior Vice-President of Human Resources at Four Seasons Hotels & Resorts. "We'll have to feel the same obsession about service that Ray Kroc felt about hamburgers.

"Explaining why McDonald's leads all its competitors, Kroc said, 'We take the hamburger more seriously than they do.' " (1)

The Modern Customer

The training manual of Service Guaranteed Eateries of Seattle offers the following service example, which to me exemplifies the service environment needed for the '90s.

You have recently bought a pair of shoes from a downtown store. A week later, the sole starts to come off. So you drive downtown. You spend 15 minutes finding a parking spot. The salesperson happily gives you a new pair of shoes. But are you happy?

Well, you got your shoes, but getting them was a hassle. The salesperson did nothing to make it up to you.

What should the salesperson have done instead?

He should have given you a new pair of shoes *and* thrown in something extra, like a pair of socks. The store would have not only replaced an inferior product, but made up for the inconvenience that replacing the product caused the customer.(1)

The Edge in Service

Facing increased competition from U.S. trucking firms because of free trade, Canadian truck-transportation firm Reimer Express feels quality and service are the best way to differentiate itself from the new competition. "Everybody on the highway has basically the same kind of truck," says John Perry, Vice-President of Training and Quality, "and no one has invented a new way to drive it." (1)

The Edge in Tough Times

Tough economic times force retail stores in malls into making a difficult choice.

To survive, stores must seek either low-end business or high-end business. If you have a retail store on the high end, you have the added responsibility of giving high-end service. Customers today have the luxury of being fussy.

Those who run the malls are now giving service extras to bring people into their mall rather than have them go elsewhere. Some employ runners to help customers take their bags out to their cars. Others offer battery-boosting services.

Mall users are getting older, too. So malls have put in more automatic doors. More wheelchair services. More rotundas with palm trees under which elderly people may sit down and rest their feet. And there are pickup and drop-off services for neighborhood senior citizens. (1)

Do Companies Care About Quality of Service?

In 1989, the Business Travel Division of American Express took the big step. It put in a quality service training program for employees.

Today, it is well ahead of the competition.

At Business Travel Centres across Canada, the company's internal "quality index" increased to 93 per cent from 75 per cent in two years. Because of its drive to deliver high quality service to its corporate clients, the Business Travel Division retained 96 per cent of its account base. And that meant more digits on the bottom line. A million dollar account returned to Amex after a year away trying out the competition. The reason it gave, says the manager of the Montreal Business Travel Centre, was Amex's quality of service. (1)

The Secret of a Deming Winner

Robert Tallon, President of Florida Power & Light (the first American firm to win the Deming Prize), says "The best way I know to hold on to a customer is with quality — a quality product, quality service, and quality management." (1)

Customers will always pay for quality and service.

We Never Hear From the Customer

According to *Service America*, 96 per cent of problems customers have with a firm are never reported. And those old customer survey standbys, comment cards, reveal only 4 per cent of the problems. (1)

Lines for a Plaque

What is quality?

What the customer sees in you.

What is quality service?

Exceeding what the customer expects from you. (1)

Public Sector

I am often asked whether Total Quality Service has to be applied differently to organizations in the public sector. Just like those in the private sector, public service organizations (for example, a health department or a public utility) must revamp and rethink the way they do business.

Today, the role of government in business affairs is more important than ever. Global competition requires that governments give more assistance to the business community, especially in research and development. Another demand on the public sector is fiscal restraint — there is a need to balance quality and efficiency, especially in the area of customer service. As well, customers are demanding better access to and better performance from government services. Government services must be more accountable and their operations must be more transparent. They have the difficult job of balancing the conflicting requests of interest groups while not losing sight of them as customers. (1)

Quality Service Is Not Fancy Extras

Many executives think offering good service means luxury extras like in-seat telephones on airplanes or plush seating in restaurants.

Alaska Airlines, heavily in the black while everyone else in the industry is waving for help in a sea of red, stresses an almost family attitude to service on their flights. Their senior chef pops aboard every month to check with passengers on how they like the food. In 1991, he told *Business Week*, "I don't want to be identified with airline food." (1)

Get Modern

William Sheehan, the CEO of Omni Hotels, has a warning for executives too obsessed with taking the cost-cutting route to business success. "Any industry in today's environment that has backlogs of latent raw materials (empty hotel rooms or 10,000 widgets, for example), undirected and passive employees (trained to fill a slot on an assembly line or to perform a single function) and undefined customers will fail.

"What the principles of TQM (Total Quality Management) define, quite simply, are as basic as your business: what do you sell and what are your production costs, who is doing the selling and what your customers expect and are worth to you. If you don't care about defining any of these, why bother? (Or, why are you worrying about insignificant details like market share?)" (1)

Doing That Extra Bit

At Halloran House in New York, the concierge gives guests a walking tour of the neighborhood surrounding the hotel to familiarize them with stores and services. (1)

What Does the Customer Want?

The Edison Electricity Institute annually researches the needs of electricity consumers. In the late '80s, it found one interesting tendency among customers: residential customers contrast their perception of the product with their perceptions of the utility's service. That is, the customer will not quibble over high prices if he or she knows that high-quality service comes with it.

The people at Standard Register Company stress the same idea in one of their print advertisements: "We asked our clients what they wanted from a business forms company. (The last thing they said was business forms.)" (1, 2)

Another Line for a Plaque

Give bad service and your competition prospers. (1, 2, 3)

Yet Another Line for a Plaque

The only reason a person buys from your company and not from someone else is that they expect a lot more from you. (1, 7)

T.Q.S. Means Emphasizing Process, Not Productivity

Here's a story. A company had shown staff a customer service video to help improve customer service. But service didn't improve. In fact, customers reported that staff seemed to have become ruder: "They seem to want to get us off the phone fast."

The staff were asked by a consultant what the problem was. "We all read his messages," one employee said of the CEO. "We saw the video. But we're not walking the talk. You see, every time we complete a customer call, we put a checkmark down here on this form." He pointed at an elaborate complexity of lines on a single sheet of paper. "The more checkmarks we make, the more we get paid." "So you see," said another employee, "we could theoretically get paid more for being rude to 25 customers than we could for satisfying 10 customers over the same time."

The President Is a Customer, Too

When Levi Strauss first made 501 jeans, it put rivets on the fly and the pockets to make them survive wear and tear. Most of the rivets disappeared over the years into the mists of fashion, but the fly rivet remained, even though outdoorsmen said they didn't like it. In the '30s, President Walter A. Haas Sr., wearing a pair of 501's on a fishing trip, was kneeling down beside the campfire when he noticed that the rivet had suddenly become very hot; at once, he understood why so many customers had complained about it. The rivet was removed from the line of jeans shortly thereafter.

Hard Lessons in the Public Service

David Couper, the Chief of Police of Madison, Wisconsin, discussed the many hard lessons he learned about quality while on the job.

Writing in *Quality Progress* (October 1990), he made a few observations that you don't hear often enough:

➤ Quality improvement and politics don't mix. In fact, they butt heads with one another. Too often, politicians, accustomed to short-term goals, haven't the patience or inclination to run a two- or three-year quality program because they can't expect to see a payoff during their term. Couper says politicians must shake themselves free of their political aims and think of what long-term benefit quality improvement would have for the country instead. (3)

➤ While the private sector has readily embraced new ways of doing business, Couper says, government bodies are still stuck in a nineteenth-century love of authoritarian work systems. This is at a time when there is plainly a lack of leadership in bureaucracies and constant pressure to maintain the status quo. This must end. Change begins at the top; leaders must empower workers. (1, 3)

➤ Couper believes that our society, especially our work society, is more authoritarian than we like to admit. And we are more comfortable with it that way. "Employees do what they think their bosses want — more than their bosses think they do," Couper writes. We do our leader's wishes, which is a fine thing, but only up to a point. Employees watch their superiors very closely, and are sensitive to everything they do. At a time when we need to encourage creativity and independence of action and thought, bosses who give even a hint of falling back on the status quo, or who use fear to direct the company, will have the employees scuttling back to the silence from which they came. No innovations will surface again for a long time. (6, 7)

► Couper sees the greatest hindrance to quality improvement in North America in our predilection for "cowboy management." Couper's theory is that cowboys work alone. They want to be heroes, to solve a problem in the grandest, most heroic way possible. A problem can be fixed "by force: force of will or force of fear." Cowboys are "lords of their environment." The trouble with cowboy management is that it discourages importance of the group, of input of ideas, of people working together to solve problems. "Cowboy management should be as out of date in the workplace today as a cowboy is in Manhattan." (3)

Similar to the cowboy mentality is the "ego" problem: putting the "I" ahead of the "We." To put it another way, the individual is more important than the team. Anyone who has played sports knows that teams win, individuals don't. The power of the whole, as it were, is greater than the sum of the parts. Leaders who don't recognize teamwork, who don't encourage it, who take credit for work done by others, rob the other members of the organization — and they will never contribute again. (3)

How Much Time Is Spent on Service?

"Far too much time is spent in meetings talking about internal issues that have no relevance to customer needs," says Jeff Rushton, speaking on the many service changes made to his organization, Mediacom. "To solve this, we have changed the focus of our internal meetings so at least 50 per cent of all management meetings are customer-oriented." (4)

Don't Write, Phone

Research by AT&T discovered that 86 per cent of consumers would rather call a 1-800 number to register a complaint or make an inquiry than write a letter. If that's not enough reason to put in a toll-free line, AT&T also learned this: 62 per cent of consumers are more likely to do business with a company if it provides 1-800 services. (4)

Where's the Gap?

Procter & Gamble surveyed its internal processes and discovered that 40 per cent of its invoices were incorrect. But the problem didn't lie with the invoice handlers, as the company expected. It surveyed how orders were placed (that potential service gap between front-line staff and the customer) and found that 80 per cent of the errors stemmed from inaccurate or incomplete information on the order placement. (4, 5)

Team Handling

Federal Express organized one of its U.S. offices into self-managed teams of five to 10 people. The result? Handling problems like inaccurate bills and misdirected packages went down 13 per cent within a year. (4, 5, 6)

Tracking Customer Preferences

Holt Renfrew, almost an institution in the Canadian fashion industry, has been building a database of customer purchases for the last few years. The computer system records the color, size and style of outfit purchased. It also keeps track of customer birthdays and anniversaries. Using this information, friends of the customer can ease the difficulty of making a gift decision by checking the computer to see what their friend likes. And, having recorded customer preferences, Holt Renfrew can contact customers when a particular item they may like appears on sale. (4, 7)

Cut Sales, Increase Profit

Levi Strauss, the dean of jeans makers, has reorganized itself in a way that has a Japanese feel to it.

First, the company abandoned its diverse collection of clothing lines and went back into jeans. Then it changed its attitude toward its employees. There are 80 task forces at Levi Strauss whose goal is to improve the relationship between managers and staff. There are now profit-sharing plans for assembly-line workers. And employees have been free to organize their workplaces as they see fit.

The result? The company's sales have gone down — while its profits have risen. (4, 7)

Redesign the Environment

From the day he first opened his doors, Barry Steinberg, the President of Direct Tire, hoped his tire outlets wouldn't become like those speed shops with grimy floors and calendars with scantily clad women on the walls. He feels that customers don't like to sit around in this kind of environment anymore than he does.

He told *INC.* magazine that he's discovered that a key service differentiator is *not* being a typical tire shop. Not being typical means that the waiting area is clean and tidy. There are interesting and up-to-date magazines on the racks. Fresh coffee is available. And no girlie calendars either — 40 per cent of his customers are women, and he wants them to feel comfortable visiting his company. (5)

At the Touch of a Button

Service is the speed of light at the big Canadian chain Delta Hotels & Resorts. Messages for guests are immediately transferred on-line to the customer's room, where they appear on a television screen. There is also a light on the telephone that flashes when the guest has a waiting message. If guests want to check out, they can do so from their room: the television issues user-friendly instructions to enable the guests to check out, and they can pick up a printout of the bill at the front desk on their way out. The same equipment is used to tell the front desk staff whether a room is ready for a new guest; housekeeping staff clean the room, then contact the front desk on-line to say that the room is ready.

24-Hour Service

Mediacom has a 1-800 number that is open 24 hours a day, seven days a week. Says Jeff Rushton, "The key component of the 1-800 number is not so much that customers can report problems, because these problems should not happen in the first place, but that customers receive 24-hour turnaround on their problems. And even if we cannot resolve the individual problem within 24 hours, we get back to the customer and let them know what we are doing to resolve the issue.

"The interesting thing is that Brian McLean, Mediacom's President, personally phones every customer who phones in on the 800 number to ensure the issue was resolved to their satisfaction, thus showing to both customers and employees that top management is committed to our service issues." (5, 7)

Design Service Around People

A fast-food company was baffled about why, after all sorts of motivational seminars and rewards systems, employees still seemed to be listless.

Management had observed that front-line staff spent a lot of time standing around, waiting for things to happen. They were worried the customer would see this as negative value being added to their product. At first, they thought that increasing automated processes would speed up customer service. Then they discovered, after a service gap analysis, that automation was the problem, not the solution.

The automated equipment was forcing staff to stand about while they waited for some process to be completed. Paradoxically, automated equipment was standing in the way of good service. So the company cut back on it, letting staff do more; staff became motivated, more "into" their jobs, and they served the customer with a level of enthusiasm that management had never had before. (5)

Now That's Weaving Service into the Fabric of the Organization

I was at the head offices of Amdahl recently. The logo for its quality service program is a "Q" in a triangle. As I walked down the hall to a conference room, I suddenly noticed that this logo was the pattern in the carpet. (5)

T.Q.S. Is a Straight Road

Your goal is to simplify the service process. You want a straight road from management to customer, not a crooked grid of lanes, pathways, and ostensible shortcuts that looks like a roadmap based on the principle of a maze. (5)

Another Line for a Plaque

If employees don't buy into your objectives, there is something wrong with your objectives. (5)

Innovators are Easy To Find

A study by *The Economist* found that half of the innovations introduced by a company will fail, but that those originating at the bottom of the organization are the most likely to succeed. (5, 6)

"I Know What the Customer Wants"

Companies *think* they know what the customer wants. But when you ask how they know, as the Sandy Corporation did in a survey of service industries in the United States, it was revealed that 42 per cent of companies did not use customer surveys, 62 per cent did not provide customer comment cards, a whopping 70 per cent had no customer service departments, and 19 per cent said they used no customer monitoring programs at all! (5, 7)

Service Means Having a Long Memory

The Delta Hotels & Resorts chain keeps a computer history of all its past guests' preferences in rooms, breakfasts, and the like. It also offers secretarial services for corporate clients. And photocopies. And in-house day care. The chain has seen the need to adapt to changing customer wants. And Delta does one more thing: anyone in the hotel is authorized to give out a night's free accommodation if the customer feels he or she has not had a complaint satisfactorily resolved. (6)

Warning Signs

Communications Briefings magazine listed the telltale signs that employees are losing interest in the service initiative:

➤ People start speaking of customers as impositions on their time rather than as service opportunities.

➤ Employees develop an orientation toward the rules of business school rather than a value orientation that considers spirit, excellence and contributions.

➤ People begin to have different understandings of words such as "responsibility" and "service."

➤ Leaders start to rely on structures instead of people.

➤ Pressures of day-to-day operations push aside concern for vision and risk.

The Ultimate Test of Empowerment

At the Banff Springs Hotel, the famous resort in the Canadian Pacific/Doubletree chain, there is a main hotel and a separate building called The Manor, with about 250 rooms.

The management team of the hotel decided to try a pilot project called "Self-Directed Work Teams." They wanted to remove the supervision of housekeeping room attendants in The Manor.

The executive housekeeper told management of the success he felt he'd had, as department head, in hiring the right people through structured interviews. He felt he'd been able to identify, then hire, people who naturally love to clean. Therefore, he asked, why do these people need supervisors to always check the rooms? Instead, why not hire people who can clean the rooms properly and give them an incentive to do so?

So, The Manor eliminated floor supervisors and developed an incentive program. Once a month, a management committee (made up of the human resources director, a housekeeper, a person from Rooms and a person from Catering) conducts spot checks of rooms in The Manor.

The team has a checklist of what to look for in terms of cleanliness, and they pass out cash incentives every month to the room attendant who has the highest scores on the checklist. They also give cash incentives to the most improved performer over the previous month.

Then they take the winners out for a special VIP dinner in the hotel. Says Carolyn Clark, Vice-President of Human Resources, "The people are cleaning the rooms just as well, if not better, than when we had paid supervisors. So, what we've been able to do is flatten the organization structure and give more responsibility." (6)

Vision

Dave Clark, President of Campbell Soup, believes that the quality vision at his company will make people line up at the door to work there. "Not that we're going to pay the most," he cautions, "although I hope the pay is competitive. Not that we're going to have the most luxurious offices or anything like that — far from it. But rather that Campbell Soup is going to be such a satisfying place to work because you really can make a difference. You can be empowered." (6)

The Corporation Is a Family Business

Amy Lyman, a lecturer in behavioral sciences at the University of California at Davis interviewed 78 business owners in that city to find out if family-oriented businesses offered better service. She wanted to know how service was perceived by family and non-family businesses.

She found that non-family owners of a business would refer to customer service in strictly financial terms; there was little connection between their own values and the value of service to the customer. Family owners regularly stated that their notion of service grew out of personal values. Good service, they felt, reflected something about them personally or was part-and-parcel of family values learned in childhood.

Interestingly, non-family-owned businesses had written service agendas, while family-owned businesses generally did not. Written service plans seemed to carry an atmosphere of "follow-the-rules"; employees chafed under the noose of having to follow policy when they knew the customer was in the right. Informal practices, by the absence of written rules, allowed personal feelings to enter the service transaction.

Lyman also made an interesting insight into human nature. When a front-line employee is faced with the problem of a customer trying to return merchandise he or she has obviously damaged but claims to have bought in that condition, close to two-thirds of family businesses said they would back down from obvious dishonesty and give the person their money back. Just under a fifth of non-family businesses said they would. (6)

What If You Were President for a Day?

Thousands of people worked for Buck Rodgers. When he took over as President of IBM's Data Processing Division, he asked each employee to finish this statement: "If I were president of the Data Processing Division...." Employees knew that their suggestions would be taken seriously (the best ideas were eligible for corporate awards), and they responded with several thousand suggestions. (6, 7)

The Pygmalion Effect

"Raising our expectations of employees' capabilities, in our experience, raises performance," says John Young of Four Seasons. "In a famous motivational study, Rosenthal and Jacobson concluded that student achievement often mirrors teacher expectations even more than student ability. They called it the "Pygmalion Effect." As Eliza Doolittle says in Shaw's play *Pygmalion*, "The difference between a lady and a flower girl is not how she behaves, but how she is treated." (6, 7)

Player of the Week

A housekeeper at the Halifax Sheraton Hotel won a Player-of-the-Week award for the following bit of service generosity:

A young man approached her late one evening wanting to know where he could buy a bouquet of flowers. He had just become engaged. The housekeeper gave him a fresh bouquet: the one she had received that day for her birthday. (6, 7)

Instant Reactions

At London's Heathrow and Gatwick airports, British Airways has installed "Video Points," electronic booths for travellers to record their impressions of BA's service on arrival. (7)

Open Door

Federal Express has a formal "open door" policy to handle employee complaints or questions. An employee or group of employees submits a query to the Employee Relations Office, where it is routed to the person who can most suitably attend to it. The person who receives an Open Door inquiry, no matter who they are in the organization, has 14 days to respond.

Federal Express's "Blueprint for Quality" cites one example in which part-time employees working at desirable locations in the delivery network were bumped from their jobs by full-time employees wishing to move from less-desirable locations. The company's solution was to allow part-time employees to accumulate seniority points to allow them to apply on an equal footing for full-time positions. (7)

Sorry

A Nashville hotel owner describing her customer service policy: "Sorry is not an answer here."

TOTAL QUALITY SERVICE

Below is a fair summary of T.Q.S. It's not from me. It's from Mediacom. What I like about it is the way in which the company has embraced each one of the essentials that goes into making a service culture. And it has made a good one! Here's Jeff Rushton:

Teams: "First, we are setting up what we call a 'cat' process, which is cross-functional customer action teams that allow individuals within each region to set up a team and get the resources needed to solve issues that directly affect customer delivery."

Evaluation: "We have also established a customer service council comprised of long-term members of the firm from different functional areas whose purpose is to

1) establish quality service goals and review progress of customer service programs;

2) review the recommendations of the customer action teams;

3) administer the customer service reward system; and

4) co-ordinate the communication vehicles needed to support our customer service philosophy."

Internal customers: "We are also looking at establishing a program that recognizes the importance of the internal customer concept in delivering true customer service. Modelled after similar programs in place in other companies, the 'count on me' program will reward employees who have gone out of their way to help other employees satisfy customer needs."

Commitment: "All of our senior management is involved directly with our top customers."

Standards: "One of the more important pillars of Mediacom's customer service philosophy is delivery. True customer delivery occurs when the company recognizes that what may be considered acceptable delivery internally (because it meets internal standards) may not be acceptable to your customers."

Measurement: "In essence, service standards must be established based on defined requirements from your customers, and for these standards to be meaningful, they must be measurable so improvement can be shown over time. Service guarantees must be easy to execute and meaningful to your customers.

"Next, in order to ensure you are keeping pace with trends, it is important to measure your company against verifiable quality report cards such as the Baldrige Canadian awards for business excellence criteria."

Continuous improvement: "Finally, no matter how good your internal system areas, mistakes will occur, and it is important that all mistakes are investigated with corrective measures communicated throughout the organization."

External customers: "The customer service program must be externally focused because service is only service if it is what the customer wants. All too often, companies tend to develop their internal system to what they think customers want, rather than the actual customer expectations. To help this external orientation in our system planning, we have begun to change our focus from generating internal reports to generating useful information in a format usable by our customers."

The long term: "One of the key things that has happened over the past years at Mediacom is a refocusing of the long-range plan on how to deliver value and quality to our customers. A customer plan that attempts to solve customer issues is now at the centre of Mediacom's long range plan."

IS THE JOURNEY OVER?

You have finished the book, but the journey is not over. In fact, for some readers the journey is about to begin. As a first step, why not take the PULSE challenge (Appendix I). For those of you further along, have you reviewed your internal and external research (Appendix IV)? Do you know where your service gaps are? Or, if you have identified your gaps, have you mapped them (Appendix V)? Do you need to revise your customer bill of rights (Appendix III)? Do you need more information on suggestion programs (Appendix VI)? Could you use a glossary of Quality Service terms (Appendix X)?

Getting Around To It

Finally, for those of you who need that extra push, a reason to finally get around to it, to embark upon the quality service journey, to develop that service culture, I offer you the following Tuit.

Photocopy it, put it on your desk or your wall, and good luck on your journey.

A Round Tuit

This is a Tuit. Guard it with
your life as Tuits are hard to come by,
especially the round ones. This is an indispen-
sable item. It will help you develop a Service
Culture. For years you have heard people say,
"I'll do it as soon as I get a Round Tuit."
Now that you have one, you
can accomplish
all those things that you've
put aside 'til you got a
Round Tuit.

THE NICEST CUSTOMER IN THE WORLD

Remember my customer at the beginning of the book? Here's the other side of that person, the alter ego of today's typical customer:

I'm a nice customer. You all know me. I'm the one who never complains, no matter what kind of service I get.

I'll go into a restaurant and sit quietly while the waiters and waitresses gossip and never both to ask if anyone has taken my order. Sometimes a party that came in after I did has their order taken first, but I don't complain. I just wait.

And when I go to a store to buy something, I don't throw my weight around. I try to be thoughtful of the other person. If a snooty salesperson gets upset because I want to look at several things before making up my mind, I'm as polite as can be. I don't believe rudeness in return is the answer.

The other day I stopped at a full service gas station and waited almost five minutes before the attendant took care of me. And when he did, he spilled gas and wiped the windshield with an oily rag. But did I complain about the service? Of course not.

I never kick. I never nag. I never criticize. And I wouldn't dream of making a scene, as I've seen some people do in public places. I think that's uncalled for. No, I'm the nice customer. And I'll tell you who else I am.

I'm the customer who never comes back!

APPENDICES

APPENDIX I

PULSE AND THE SERVICE E.D.G.E.

How far along the Quality Service journey have you progressed?

On the pages that follow we provide the PULSE questionnaire. By completing the questionnaire you will be able to conduct a self assessment of your progress along the Evaluate, Design, Guide, and Encourage Excellence Quality Service journey.

A note of caution. Most organizations do well in terms of Design and Guide. Unfortunately, they are not as well grounded as they could be and do not have a firm foundation based on a solid Evaluate stage [check your answers to questions II 5, 6, 8 a); III 1 a), 1 b), 3, 10]; they also fall down in the Encourage Excellence phase [questions include II 7, 8 c), III 4, 5, 6, 7, 8 b)].

Take the challenge and complete the questionnaire. Your responses will provide you with a self assessment of your degree of development in each of the E.D.G.E. phases.

PULSE

A Program to Understand the Level of Service Excellence in the Business Community

A confidential assessment of your preparedness to meet the future needs of your customers or clients.

Sponsored by:

Canadian Pacific Hotels & Resorts

 AMERICAN EXPRESS

 CANTEL®

FEDERAL EXPRESS

 ⊕ MANPOWER® TEMPORARY SERVICES

"Service. Everybody talks about it, but not too many people are happy with it. Yet quality service is becoming more and more important in business today. Service is a critical factor for survival - the competitive edge in many organizations.

> Creating the Service Culture:
> Strategies for Canadian Business

It's very difficult to dispute this statement, yet surprisingly, little sustainable action in improving the quality of service has been taken by many organizations. Our research suggests that the primary reason for this is a lack of information on the successful practices of others, together with insufficient information on customer needs. Management requires strategic information which can identify "service" gaps (gaps between customer needs and actual delivery by the organization). With this information in hand, management can then focus on filling those gaps and building strength for the future.

Our study sponsors, in association with Price Waterhouse, would like to assist you in this process. A survey, similar to the one which follows, will be conducted with executives within the retail, financial services, hospitality, manufacturing and business services segments. Responses to these questions will help to establish a database of trends and practices in the industry.

In return for completing this questionnaire we will provide you with a computerized analysis, comparing your results to industry and national responses. Results for individual respondents will be confidential and mailed directly to the survey respondents.

How to answer this questionnaire

Your responses should be based solely upon your perception of your own company.

Please respond to the questions by marking the appropriate box. Unless otherwise instructed, (✔)only one box per question.

Price Waterhouse

I. Service Issues as a Consumer

Research has shown that, in the eyes of the consumer, Quality Service can be represented by the following five terms:

- Reliability — The ability to provide what was promised, dependably and accurately
- Assurance — The knowledge and courtesy of employees and their ability to convey trust and confidence
- Empathy — The degree of caring and individual attention provided to customers
- Responsiveness — The willingness to help customers and provide prompt service
- Tangibles — The physical facilities and equipment, and the appearance of personnel

Depending on the service being delivered, one term may be regarded as more important than others.

1. As a consumer, which of the above five terms is most important to you when being provided with "service" by organizations in each of the following segments? (only ✔ one entry per column)

	(a) Retail	(b) Financial Services	(c) Foodservice	(d) Lodging and Recreation	(e) Business Services	(f) Manufacturing	(g) Government
	(5)	(6)	(7)	(8)	(9)	(10)	(11)
Reliability	1	1	1	1	1	1	1
Assurance	2	2	2	2	2	2	2
Empathy	3	3	3	3	3	3	3
Responsiveness	4	4	4	4	4	4	4
Tangibles	5	5	5	5	5	5	5

2. Name an organization which excels in providing quality service in each of the following segments.

Retail: _____ (12 - 13)
Financial Services: _____ (14 - 15)
Foodservice: _____ (16 - 17)
Lodging & Recreation: _____ (18 - 19)
Business Services: _____ (20 - 21)
Manufacturing: _____ (22 - 23)
Government: _____ (24 - 25)

3. In general, in the past six months, do you believe that the quality of service you have received overall as a consumer has:

☐1 improved   ☐2 not changed   ☐3 declined   ☐9 don't know   (26)

4. In each of the following industry segments, in your opinion which of the following requires the most improvement?

	(a) Retail	(b) Financial Services	(c) Foodservice	(d) Lodging and Recreation	(e) Business Services	(f) Manufacturing	(g) Government
	(27)	(28)	(29)	(30)	(31)	(32)	(33)
Reliability	1	1	1	1	1	1	1
Assurance	2	2	2	2	2	2	2
Empathy	3	3	3	3	3	3	3
Responsiveness	4	4	4	4	4	4	4
Tangibles	5	5	5	5	5	5	5

5. How often do you purchase products or services from a business that provides excellent service but higher prices rather than lower prices and less service? (✔ one box only)

☐1 all of the time   ☐2 most of the time   ☐3 sometimes   ☐4 rarely   ☐5 never   ☐9 don't know   (34)

II. Service Practices in Your Organization

1. Does your organization have a strategic mandate or mission statement that includes mention of the words quality service or a dedication to achieve that in the future?

☐1 yes   ☐2 no   ☐9 don't know   (35)

2. How strongly does the concept of quality service figure in the strategy of your organization?

☐1 very much   ☐2 a little   ☐3 not at all   ☐9 don't know   (36)

3. Does your organization's strategic mandate include a statement acknowledging the role of the employee in achieving quality service?

☐1 yes   ☐2 no   ☐9 don't know   (37)

4. Does any one department or individual have responsibility for ensuring that quality service is to be delivered to your customer base?

☐1 Yes...One department/individual is responsible   ☐3 No . . . There is nobody responsible
☐2 Many departments/individuals are responsible   ☐9 Don't Know   (38)

5. Approximately what percent of the total number of employees in your organization are involved in the delivery of quality service?

☐1 0% – 10%   ☐4 31% – 40%   ☐7 61% – 70%   ☐10 91% – 100%
☐2 11% – 20%   ☐5 41% – 50%   ☐8 71% – 80%   ☐99 don't know   (39 - 40)
☐3 21% – 30%   ☐6 51% – 60%   ☐9 81% – 90%

6. Do you believe that there is a budget set aside for your organization's quality service initiatives? (41)

　☐₁ yes ☐₂ no ☐₉ don't know

7. On a scale of 1 to 10, how committed is senior management to quality service? (Circle one answer only) (42 -43)

　　　　1　　2　　3　　4　　5　　6　　7　　8　　9　　10

　very committed　　　　　　　　　　　　　　**not very committed**

8. On a scale of 1 to 10, how would you rank your organization, as a whole, on its dedication to: (Circle one answer only for each)

　(a) The **delivery** of quality service? (44 - 45)

　　　　1　　2　　3　　4　　5　　6　　7　　8　　9　　10

　very dedicated　　　　　　　　　　　　　　**not very dedicated**

　(b) Communicating its **commitment** to the delivery of quality service to its employees? (46 - 47)

　　　　1　　2　　3　　4　　5　　6　　7　　8　　9　　10

　very good　　　　　　　　　　　　　　**very poor**

　(c) Communicating its **successes and failures** in the delivery of quality service to its employees? (48 - 49)

　　　　1　　2　　3　　4　　5　　6　　7　　8　　9　　10

　very good　　　　　　　　　　　　　　**very poor**

9. Over the next two years do you expect your organization to pay more attention, less attention, or about the same of attention to quality service as it does now? (50)

　☐₁ more ☐₂ less ☐₃ about the same ☐₉ don't know

10. How often do you believe your customers purchase products or services from businesses that have an excellent service but higher prices rather than a business with lower prices and less service? (51)

　☐₁ all of the time ☐₂ most of the time ☐₃ sometimes ☐₄ rarely ☐₅ never ☐₉ don't know

III. Related Service Practices

1. Does your firm have a formal market intelligence system to track:

　(a) the external environment (economic, political and international trends)? (52)

　☐₁ yes ☐₂ no ☐₉ don't know

　(b) your competition? (53)

　☐₁ yes ☐₂ no ☐₉ don't know

2. In general, do you view your competition as having more, less, or about the same dedication as your organization to the delivery of quality service? (54)

　☐₁ more ☐₂ less ☐₃ same ☐₉ don't know

3. Do your customers/clients view your competition as having more, less, or about the same dedication as your organization to the delivery of quality service? (55)

　☐₁ more ☐₂ less ☐₃ same ☐₉ don't know

4. Is there provision in your organization's employee compensation package to reward superior performance in quality service? (56)

　☐₁ yes ☐₂ no ☐₉ don't know

5. How often do you believe that reward provisions are used? (57)

　☐₁ frequently ☐₂ occasionally ☐₃ seldom ☐₄ never ☐₉ don't know

6. Are there reward provisions for quality service at all levels in your organization? (58)

　☐₁ yes ☐₂ no ☐₉ don't know

7. Can employees profit monetarily from the long-term performance of your organization in the area of quality service? (59)

　☐₁ frequently ☐₂ occasionally ☐₃ seldom ☐₄ never ☐₉ don't know

8. (a) Do you have a formal, regularly scheduled training program dedicated to quality service? (60)

　☐₁ yes ☐₂ no ☐₉ don't know　　Skip to 8(c)

　(b) What percent of employees receive quality service training? (61 - 62)

　☐₁ 0 – 10%　☐₂ 11 – 20%　☐₃ 21 – 30%　☐₄ 31 – 40%　☐₅ 41 – 50%
　☐₆ 51 – 60%　☐₇ 61 – 70%　☐₈ 71 – 80%　☐₉ 81 – 90%　☐₁₀ 91 – 100%

　(c) Does your organization use "quality circles", brainstorming, or other methods to encourage ideas? (63)

　☐₁ frequently ☐₂ occasionally ☐₃ seldom ☐₄ never ☐₉ don't know

9. (a) On a scale of 1 to 10, when your organization recruits new employees at a junior level position, how important is their attitude to customer service? (64 - 65)

　　　　1　　2　　3　　4　　5　　6　　7　　8　　9　　10

　very important　　　　　　　　　　　　　　**not very important**

(b) On a scale of 1 to 10, when your organization recruits senior level employees, how important is their attitude to quality service? (66 - 67)

1	2	3	4	5	6	7	8	9	10
very important									not very important

10. Does your organization periodically seek customer input on their perceptions of your company on its service delivery? (68)

☐₁ yes ☐₂ no ☐₉ don't know

IV. Classification

Please complete the following to describe your organization.

A. **Industry category** (✔ all boxes that apply)

☐ Manufacturing 1 (69)
☐ Retail 1 (70)
☐ Financial Services 1 (71)
☐ Business Services 1 (72)
☐ Lodging/Recreation, Foodservice 1 (73)
  (restaurants, fast foods, etc.)

☐ Health Care 1 (74)
☐ Government 1 (75)
☐ Primary Resource Industries 1 (76)
☐ Transportation, Communication & Utilities 1 (77)
☐ Other (please specify) 1 (78)
_____

B. **Company ownership**

Type (✔ all boxes that apply)

☐ Public 1 (79)
☐ Private 1 (80)

☐ Family-owned or controlled 1 (1)
☐ Franchised (in whole or in part) 1 (2)

Location of Corporated Headquarters

☐₁ Canada   ☐₂ U.S.   ☐₃ Other (please specify) _____ (3)

Note: For Questions "C" through "E", if the required figures are not available, your closest approximation is sufficient.

C. Approximate annual sales revenue (in Canada) in 1990: $ _____ ,000.00 (4 - 12)

D. Approximate number of full-time employees (in Canada) in 1990: _____ (13 - 17)

E. Your position in the Organization:

☐₁ First Tier (Chairman, President, C.E.O.)
☐₂ Second Tier (Vice-President, all staff reporting directly to the First Tier)
☐₃ Third Tier (includes all other members of in the organization) (18)

Thank you for completing this questionnaire. Your individual responses will remain confidential at all times.

Please return this questionnaire to Price Waterhouse for tabulation. No postage stamp is necessary if mailed in Canada. Fold this document in three on the dotted lines with the address on the front, and the words PULSE on the back. PLEASE TAPE THE SIDES; DO NOT STAPLE THE SIDES.

If you would like to receive a report comparing your results to a summary of those in your industry and across the country, please write your return address in the space provided.

If you have any questions, please contact Stanley A. Brown at (416) 863-1133 (call collect).

Name: _____
Title: _____
Company: _____
Address: _____
City and Province: _____
Postal Code: _____

Fold here

Fold here

Business Reply Envelope

No Postage Required
If Mailed in Canada

||| 12004

Price Waterhouse, Management Consultants
Suite 3300,
Box 190
1 First Canadian Place
Toronto, Ontario M5X 9Z9

Attention: Stanley A. Brown

APPENDIX II

SERVICE STRATEGIES — LEARNING FROM BEST PRACTICES

In the pages that follow we provide you with a selected number of service strategies and philosophies of some of the more well-known Quality Service organizations as well as those that we highlight as Service Masters. Service Masters are those organizations that received the highest mentions in our PULSE study in their respective sectors.

The service masters include the following companies:

Retail	Nordstrom; Wal-Mart
Financial Services	Royal Bank; American Express
Foodservice & Hospitality	Marriott; Four Seasons; Canadian Pacifis Hotels & Resorts
Manufacturing	Toyota; Honda
Business Services	IBM; Xerox; Federal Express

Other strategies, visions and mission statements include those of:

➤ Campbell Soup Co. Ltd.

➤ NCR

➤ Reimer Express Lines Ltd.

➤ Credit Union Central of Ontario

➤ Stew Leonard's

The *Campbell* Commitment

Our Vision:
Campbell Canada: A dynamic, market-oriented, growth company excelling in the "well-being" business

Our Core Values:
To transform this vision into reality we will emphasize and rededicate ourselves to the core values that built the reputation our Company has enjoyed for more than half a century. The three values, which form the core of our corporate philosophy are:

An obsessive desire to satisfy our customers and our consumers.
In each of our activities, from the growing of fresh produce to the preparation and delivery of our finished product, we will focus on meeting consumer needs with products and services of the highest possible quality and the best possible value.

A Passion for creative risk-taking.
Innovation is the hallmark of all leading companies. By fostering an environment in which creativity flourishes, we will remain on the leading edge of the Canadian food industry.

A profound respect for people.
What better way to engender positive motivation, abiding loyalty and lasting satisfaction among all who work with us, provide us with goods and services, or consume our products?

CANADIAN PACIFIC HOTELS & RESORTS

Mission

Canadian Pacific Hotels & Resorts is dedicated to being the leading Canadian hotel company providing uniquely satisfying hotel experiences.

We will earn the loyalty of our guests by consistently exceeding their expectations for personal service and warm hospitality, and by welcoming them in distinctive surroundings.

Our actions will create a sense of pride and long-term commitment for everyone associated with the Company, and generate a competitive rate of return for our shareholder.

In all we do, we will be guided by a commitment to the following principles:

- We will act with integrity under all circumstances.

- We will build an environment of individual trust and respect, enabling all employees to realize their full potential and decision-making ability.

- We will reward performance, and encourage all our people to become professional members of our industry.

Credit Union Central of Ontario
Quality Service Mission Statement

Credit Union Central of Ontario (Central) is a co-operative organization committed to delivering excellence-in-service, to ensure a strong, unified credit union network in the Province of Ontario and to support and further the collective interests of its customers/members.

Our Quality Service Commitment

Central employees recognize that each of us has a customer/member, internal and external, in everything we do, for every business process. Each customer/member has the right to receive timely and reliable service from all Central employees and departments, all of the time.

Our customers/members have the right to:

- speak to the appropriate department without waiting, and receive timely, accurate feedback and resolution of problems or concerns.

- receive courteous, empathetic and equitable treatment at all times, regardless of the reasonableness of the request.

- be kept informed and be treated with extra care in the event of any delays.

- receive superior quality, innovative and competitive services.

- receive regular, current communication about the financial services industry in general, and Central's services in particular.

- question our services and offer suggestions for improvement.

FEDERAL EXPRESS

Federal Express's service policy is to create a satisfied customer at the end of each transaction. We will achieve 100 per cent customer satisfaction by performing 100 per cent to our standards, as perceived by the customer. To realize this goal, we will strive relentlessly to enhance quality in order to improve productivity. This proclamation is signified by the following symbol used to represent our commitment to achieve 100 per cent customer satisfaction (quality) and 100 per cent service levels (productivity), while remaining dedicated to the principles of our People-Service-Profit philosophy.

Source: *Blueprints for Service Quality*

FOUR SEASONS HOTEL

The Four Seasons Service Strategy is best conveyed through a three-word expression and a series of statements made by its President.

The three-word credo — **"facta non verba: deeds not words."**

The company's statement of purpose — "Our goal is not selling our product. Our purpose is not gaining market share. Our first concern is gaining customers. Our goal is a satisfied guest. If we make this our first concern, we'll always beat the competition, sell the product, and gain market share.[1]

"Our success is totally dependent upon our ability to anticipate what our guests want. We want to make sure that they have everything they need so that they aren't distracted from their real reason for travelling."[2]

[1] Tourism Outlook Conference, November 20, 1989
[2] *Maclean's*, June 5, 1989, Special reprint for Four Seasons Hotel

THE NCR QUALITY POLICY

NCR is dedicated to providing products and services that continuously satisfy the needs and expectations of our customers. To accomplish this, we will constantly improve the quality of our products and services and the processes that create, market and support them by striving for excellence in the execution of all operations.

We believe:

- The ultimate measure of quality is customer satisfaction.
- A commitment to superior quality is the hallmark of leadership.
- Mutually rewarding, long-term relationships with customers and suppliers are key to achieving excellence.
- Superior quality derives from attention to specific requirements for quality in all operations.
- Dedication to quality leadership requires continuous assessment, adaptation, and advancement.

The NCR Quality Policy is deployed through the NCR Quality Strategy, which expresses a fundamental prevention orientation.

OUR COMMITMENT TO QUALITY

Provide Error-Free Services to Our Customers by Meeting Requirements and Performing Our Tasks Right the First Time.

D.S. Reimer
Chairman and Chief Executive Officer

A.G. Kraemer
President and General Manager

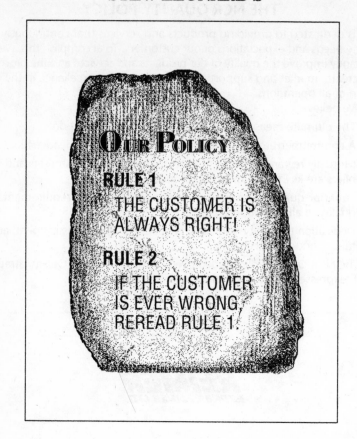

APPENDIX III

CUSTOMER BILLS OF RIGHTS

Quality Service does not happen because senior management created a quality service strategy and we all followed it. There must be a recognition of the customer, both internal and external, and their rights and expectations from the organization.

The following will provide you with some guidance in constructing your own bill of rights; however, it is only the first step.

The true test of management's belief in the bill of rights is its willingness to post and communicate these rights to the customers themselves. The following should act as an important guide; but don't forget — you must be prepared to measure performance against these standards and reward appropriate behavior.

AIR CANADA
THE CUSTOMER BILL OF RIGHTS

Accurate information, courtesy, comfort and punctuality. These are some of the basic rights to which every Air Canada customer is entitled. And no one is more qualified than you to see to it that these rights are protected.

- The Customer has the right to get through to reservations without waiting and to receive prompt, friendly, courteous service and accurate information.
- The Customer has the right to cheerful and efficient service at the sales offices, cargo terminals, airport check-ins, and departure gates.
- The Customer has the right to a hassle-free flight, a comfortable seat, a good meal, friendly service, and an entertainment system that works.
- The Customer has the right to be serviced in the official language of his or her choice.
- The Customer has the right to depart and arrive on time.
- The Customer has the right to receive his or her baggage and/or cargo promptly and in good condition.
- The Customer has the right to be kept informed when there are delays or when things go wrong, and to be treated with extra care in these circumstances.
- The Customer has the right to receive prompt decisions concerning compensation.
- The Customer has the right to be treated with care and compassion.

AMDAHL'S CORPORATE VALUES

Customer Problems Are Our Problems

Because we strive to establish long-term relationships with our customers, we take their needs and requirements seriously. We have an obligation to maintain the highest standards of product performance, value, and service. To do this we must:

- Listen closely to our customers to understand their needs.
- Make the satisfaction of our customers' needs our primary mission.

We Do It Better

We seek innovative ways to apply advanced technologies to products that are recognized for their quality, performance, and value. Our success derives from products and services that earn us the respect and loyalty of our customers. To earn this we must:

- Accept the risks of long-term research and development.
- Be a leader in providing innovative technological advances.
- Deliver products and services that are competitively priced, conform to requirements, and provide more value.

People Are The Company

The ability, commitment, and enthusiasm of our people are central to the success of our company. We continuously strive to develop and encourage these qualities. Therefore, we must:

- Attract exceptional people who will work together to produce superior products and services.
- Treat our people with honesty, fairness, and consideration.
- Provide a challenging environment that encourages growth and personal satisfaction.
- Encourage our people to be productive, take initiative, and be innovative.
- Expect every individual to take responsibility for quality products and services.

TOYOTA - Customer Bill of Rights

1. The right to a clear explanation of the reasons for all recommended repairs and adjustments.
2. The right to know in advance of the cost of repairs to your car.
3. The right to approve any work done on your car beforehand.
4. The right to a clearcut, understandable schedule of charges.
5. The right to quality repairs.
6. The right to the lowest cost repairs with good quality, safety of operation, and compliance with emission control and safety legislation.
7. The right to delivery of your car when promised.
8. The right to deal with courteous and concerned people.

XEROX

In the race for quality, there is no finish line.

Of all the goals we set for ourselves at Xerox, none is more important, more worthy of our efforts than the satisfaction of our customers.

It is with this in mind that we have committed ourselves totally and absolutely to quality in the products and services we offer.

At Xerox we understand that the commitment to improve, to set still higher standards and then achieve them is one means by which we can assure customer satisfaction.

It is for this reason we will continue to run hard and fast in a race without end.

To have won the Canada Award for Business Excellence in the Quality Category was a meaningful milestone in this race.

It means that as a result of our efforts our customers are winning. And that is the way it should be.

We answer to you.

APPENDIX IV

RESEARCH — EXAMPLES OF INTERNAL AND EXTERNAL SURVEY TOOLS

But where do you start, whom do you research, what types of questions must you ask, and how do you ensure that they are posed properly?

In the pages that follow we provide excerpts from questionnaires used by:

➤ NCR   ➤ Federal Express

➤ American Express   ➤ Toyota

➤ Amdahl

The questionnaires show the need to research internal as well as external customers, to provide an opportunity to monitor trends, and where possible, to solicit qualitative as well as quantitative information.

As well, one will find examples of how organizations can chart progress through the use of:

NCR CANADA LTD

QUALITY OF SERVICE ENHANCEMENT SURVEY   Page 1 of 3

GENERAL AREA OF NCR SERVICES

SPECIFIC SERVICE FUNCTION OR PRODUCT

Level of Importance		Level of Satisfaction
		1 - Poor
1 - Completely Unimportant		2 - Fair
2 - Not Very Important		3 - Average
3 - Important		4 - Good
4 - Very Important		5 - Excellent

1/ DELIVERY & INSTALLATION

4 3 2 1 N/A	**1A/ HOW WOULD YOU RATE NCR'S DELIVERY SERVICES OVERALL?**	( ) 5 4 3 2 1 N/A
4 3 2 1 N/A	- EQUIPMENT NORMALLY ARRIVES WHEN NEEDED?	( ) 5 4 3 2 1 N/A
4 3 2 1 N/A	- USUALLY ON-TIME TO PROMISED DELIVERY?	( ) 5 4 3 2 1 N/A
4 3 2 1 N/A	- COMPLETENESS OF SHIPMENTS?	( ) 5 4 3 2 1 N/A
4 3 2 1 N/A	- CARRIER HANDLING (DAMAGE, ETC.)?	( ) 5 4 3 2 1 N/A

4 3 2 1 N/A	**1B/ HOW WOULD YOU RATE NCR'S INSTALLATION SERVICES OVERALL?**	( ) 5 4 3 2 1 N/A
4 3 2 1 N/A	- NCR'S SITE PREPARATION CONSULTATION/ADVICE?	( ) 5 4 3 2 1 N/A
4 3 2 1 N/A	- SYSTEMS INTEGRATION, IF REQUIRED?	( ) 5 4 3 2 1 N/A
4 3 2 1 N/A	- SYSTEM PRE-STAGING, IF REQUIRED?	( ) 5 4 3 2 1 N/A

FOR PRODUCTS INSTALLED BY NCR:

4 3 2 1 N/A	- NCR'S PRE-INSTALLATION INTERACTION?	( ) 5 4 3 2 1 N/A
4 3 2 1 N/A	- AVAILABILITY OF F.E.'S FOR INSTALLATION(S)?	( ) 5 4 3 2 1 N/A
4 3 2 1 N/A	. TIMELY ARRIVAL OF F.E.'S FOR INSTALLATION(S)?	( ) 5 4 3 2 1 N/A
4 3 2 1 N/A	. INSTALLING F.E.'S APPARENT KNOWLEDGE LEVEL?	( ) 5 4 3 2 1 N/A
4 3 2 1 N/A	. COMPLETENESS OF NCR'S INSTALLATION SERVICE?	( ) 5 4 3 2 1 N/A
4 3 2 1 N/A	- SYSTEM PERFORMANCE ON INITIAL INSTALLATION?	( ) 5 4 3 2 1 N/A

AMERICAN EXPRESS
CUSTOMER SATISFACTION STUDY

The purpose of this study is to determine how well we provide service to you, our valued customer. Thank you for taking the time to tell us.

1. What was your primary reason for calling American Express? (Check all that apply.)

  (a) To inquire about my bill .... ☐ 1-1

        To find out my account balance .... ☐ -2
        To find where to send my payment .... ☐ -3
        To find out if my payment was received .... ☐ -4
        To find out when my payment was due .... ☐ -5
        To request a copy of my statement or charge ...... ☐ -6
        To report an error on my bill .... ☐ -7
        To dispute a charge .... ☐ -8
        Other_____ ☐ -9
           (SPECIFY)

  (b) To inquire about a Cardmember service or benefit .... ☐ 2-1

        To ask a question about Express Cash .... ☐ -2
        To ask a question about Sign & Travel .... ☐ -3
        To ask about another Cardmember service .... ☐ -4
        To ask about a promotional offer .... ☐ -5
        Other_____ ☐ -6
           (SPECIFY)

  (c) To report a lost or stolen Card or request a replacement .... ☐ 3-1
  (d) To ask a question about American Express merchandise .... ☐ -2
  (e) To ask a question about an American Express magazine .... ☐ -3
  (f) To return a call from American Express .... ☐ -4
  (g) Other_____ ☐ -5
           (SPECIFY)

2. Do you recall if you were able to get through to American Express on your first attempt?

  Yes, got through on first attempt .... ☐ 4-1   **SKIP TO QUESTION 4**
  No, did not get through on first attempt .... ☐ -2   **CONTINUE WITH QUESTION 3A**
  Don't remember .... ☐ -3   **SKIP TO QUESTION 4**

3a. If you weren't able to get through on the first attempt, was it because:

  The phone was never answered .... ☐ 5-1
  You got a busy signal .... ☐ -2
  You got the wrong number .... ☐ -3

3b. And, how many calls did you have to make before you finally got through to American Express?

  1 call .... ☐ 6-1
  2 calls .... ☐ -2
  3 calls .... ☐ -3
  4 or more calls .... ☐ -4
  Don't remember .... ☐ -5

4. When you did get through, do you recall how long it took for the telephone to be answered by a representative?

  Immediately .... ☐ 7-1
  1 - 3 rings .... ☐ -2
  4 or more rings .... ☐ -3
  You received a recorded message .... ☐ -4
  Don't remember .... ☐ -5

AMDAHL CORPORATION CUSTOMER
SATISFACTION SURVEY

	Very Satisfied		Neutral		Very Dissatisfied	Not Applicable	12 Months Change		
							Better	Unchanged	Worse
Software support for Amdahl licensed program products:*									
5 • Timeliness	1	2	3	4	5	x	x	x	x
6 • Effectiveness	1	2	3	4	5	x	x	x	x
7 • Professionalism	1	2	3	4	5	x	x	x	x

Comments: _____

c _____

*Amdahl licensed program products include UTS®, UTS/F, AMDEREP, MAP, MVS/CCSP, MVS/RMS, SURF.

	Very Satisfied		Neutral		Very Dissatisfied	Not Applicable			
Software support for non-Amdahl licensed program products:									
8 • Timeliness	1	2	3	4	5	x	x	x	x
9 • Effectiveness	1	2	3	4	5	x	x	x	x
10 • Professionalism	1	2	3	4	5	x	x	x	x

Comments: _____

d _____

Product installation:									
11 • Timeliness	1	2	3	4	5	x	x	x	x
12 • Effectiveness	1	2	3	4	5	x	x	x	x
13 • Professionalism	1	2	3	4	5	x	x	x	x

Comments: _____

e _____

Customer services management:									
14 • Responsiveness	1	2	3	4	5	x	x	x	x
15 • Effectiveness	1	2	3	4	5	x	x	x	x
16 • Professionalism	1	2	3	4	5	x	x	x	x

Comments: _____

f _____

Amdahl education services:									
17 • Instruction	1	2	3	4	5	x	x	x	x
18 • Course content	1	2	3	4	5	x	x	x	x
19 • Facilities	1	2	3	4	5	x	x	x	x

Comments: _____

g _____

FEDERAL EXPRESS

Survey-Feedback-Action (SFA)

HOW TO ANSWER: Read each statement carefully. Then to the right of each statement mark the bubble which best expresses your agreement or disagreement with the item. Mark only one answer for each item, and remember to respond to all items. Remember that "workgroup" means all persons who report to the same manager as you do regardless of job title.

	STRONGLY AGREE	AGREE	SOMETIMES AGREE/DISAGREE	DISAGREE	STRONGLY DISAGREE	UNDECIDED/DON'T KNOW

1. I feel free to tell my manager what I think. — SA A AD D SD U
2. My manager lets me know what's expected of me. — SA A AD D SD U
3. Favoritism is not a problem in my workgroup. — SA A AD D SD U
4. My manager helps us find ways to do our jobs better. — SA A AD D SD U
5. My manager is willing to listen to my concerns. — SA A AD D SD U
6. My manager asks for my ideas about things affecting our work. — SA A AD D SD U
7. My manager lets me know when I've done a good job. — SA A AD D SD U
8. My manager treats me with respect and dignity. — SA A AD D SD U
9. My manager keeps me informed about things I need to know. — SA A AD D SD U
10. My manager lets me do my job without interfering. — SA A AD D SD U
11. My manager's boss gives us the support we need. — SA A AD D SD U
12. Upper management (directors and above) lets us know what the company is trying to accomplish. — SA A AD D SD U
13. Upper management (directors and above) pays attention to ideas and suggestions from people at my level. — SA A AD D SD U
14. I have confidence in the fairness of management. — SA A AD D SD U
15. I can be sure of a job as long as I do good work. — SA A AD D SD U
16. I am proud to work for Federal Express. — SA A AD D SD U
17. Working for Federal Express will probably lead to the kind of future I want. — SA A AD D SD U
18. I think Federal Express does a good job for our customers. — SA A AD D SD U
19. All things considered, working for Federal Express is a good deal for me. — SA A AD D SD U

TOYOTA   NEW VEHICLE SALES AND DELIVERY SURVEY

OUR RECORDS SHOW THAT YOU PURCHASED

FROM

PLEASE PROVIDE:

HOME TEL: _____

BUSINESS TEL: _____

If you did not purchase this vehicle, please check here and return this survey unanswered ☐

HAVE YOU **PREVIOUSLY** PURCHASED A TOYOTA VEHICLE? ☐ YES ☐ NO

IF YES, PROVIDE **MODEL** _____ **YEAR** 19 ____

FOR EACH OF THE FOLLOWING QUESTIONS, PLEASE CHECK THE BOX THAT BEST REFLECTS YOUR FEELINGS.

1. **When you purchased your new Toyota, how satisfied were you with the performance of the dealer's sales staff on EACH of the following items?**

	Very Satisfied	Somewhat Satisfied	Neither Satisfied Nor Dissatisfied	Somewhat Dissatisfied	Very Dissatisfied
Courtesy and friendliness	5	4	3	2	1
Knowledge of Toyota products	5	4	3	2	1
Professionalism	5	4	3	2	1
Fulfillment of commitments made during sale	5	4	3	2	1
Overall handling of sale by salesperson	5	4	3	2	1

2. **At the time you took delivery of your new Toyota, did someone at the dealership . . .**

	Yes	No	Don't Know
Explain the vehicle service maintenance schedule	2	1	9
Explain the new vehicle warranty	2	1	9
Provide information about the dealership's service and parts departments (such as hours open, appointments, etc.)	2	1	9
Offer to demonstrate vehicle features and controls	2	1	9
Give you a copy of the Vehicle Delivery Certificate	2	1	9

3. **How satisfied were you with the condition of your new Toyota at the time of delivery on EACH of the following items?**

	Very Satisfied	Somewhat Satisfied	Neither Satisfied Nor Dissatisfied	Somewhat Dissatisfied	Very Dissatisfied
Cleanliness of the exterior	5	4	3	2	1
Cleanliness of the interior	5	4	3	2	1

4. **Did your salesperson or a dealership representative follow-up by contacting you after delivery about your satisfaction with your overall sales experience?**

In Person ☐	By Phone ☐	In Writing ☐	No Contact ☐

YOUR OVERALL EXPERIENCE

5. **Would you recommend this dealer as a place to buy a new vehicle?**

Definitely Recommend	Probably Recommend	Might or Might Not Recommend	Probably Not Recommend	Definitely Not Recommend
5	4	3	2	1

3, 2, 1, PLEASE EXPLAIN WHY: _____

IMPORTANT - PLEASE SEE REVERSE SIDE OF THIS SURVEY

APPENDIX V

SERVICE MAPPING — EXAMPLES OF PROCESS MAPS

In Chapter 5 we described the service mapping procedure in broad terms. In the pages that follow, we provide samples of maps created by other organizations. Remember — the maps can be broken down into finer detail to describe actual paper flow or interaction within a functional department or a division. Your objectives in creating your first maps are to provide a preliminary top-line overview so that you can determine where to establish your priorities.

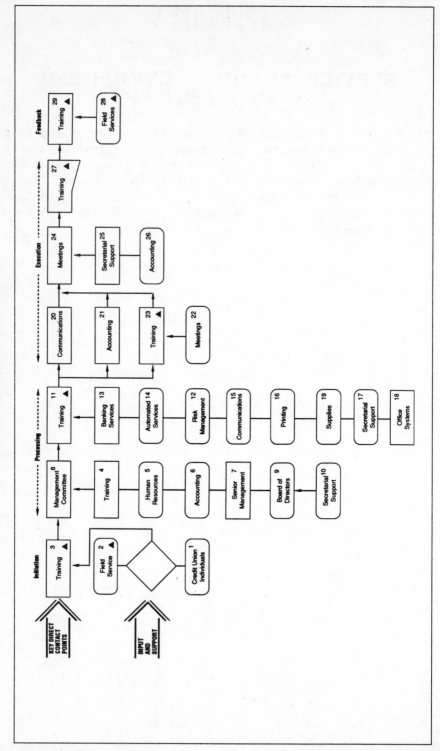

Credit Union Central
TELLER TRAINING COURSE

PROVIDING SERVICE AT A RESTAURANT

APPENDIX VI

SUGGESTION PROGRAMS —
INTERNAL AND EXTERNAL

Internal Customer Programs

Innovation is not creativity; rather it is observing the practices of others, modifying and then adapting them to suit your organization. These ideas and suggestions may come from your internal as well as external customers. The following provide examples of the forms used by Quality Service organizations to encourage these ideas and thoughts.

External Customer Programs

Most customer comment cards focus primarily on rating the service delivered or the quality of the product or service rather than on soliciting ideas from their customers for improvement opportunities.

The forms and comment cards that follow will provide you with some guidelines on the practices of others, and a base upon which you might create your own programs.

Tell Us How We Did Today!

We're Listening - We want to serve you better!

● My opinion about the service received at Eaton's Yorkdale: YES NO

- The Salesperson greeted me courteously
- The Salesperson assisted with my purchase
- I would like this salesperson to help me again
- The department was easy to find
- I found the merchandise I wanted

If No, what did you require
_____

- I found the store clean

● If No, please comment

Additional Comments or suggestions:

_____
_____
_____
_____
_____

Salesperson's Name _____
Dept. _____
Your Name _____
Optional; Phone: Bus: _____
Home: _____

EATON'S
YORKDALE

Please deposit in our customer comments box located at escalators and elevators.
Thank You! Your interest will help improve our service to you tomorrow.

TOYOTA CANADA INC.

EMPLOYEE SUGGESTION PROGRAM

DATE:_____   NO.:_____

USE A SEPARATE FORM FOR EACH SUGGESTION. PLACE THE WHITE AND CANARY COPIES IN THE ENVELOPE PROVIDED AND DEPOSIT IN THE SUGGESTION BOX. RETAIN THE PINK COPY FOR YOUR RECORDS.

SUGGESTION:_____

_____

_____

_____

_____

_____

_____

_____

_____

_____

BENEFITS TO T.C.I.: _____

_____

_____

_____

_____

_____

_____

_____

_____

NAME: _____ TITLE: _____
          (PLEASE PRINT)

DEPARTMENT / ZONE / DISTRIBUTION CENTRE: _____

SECTION: _____ SIGNATURE: _____

SUGGESTION COMMITTEE RESPONSE. DATE SUGGESTION RECEIVED: _____

THANK YOU FOR YOUR SUGGESTION WHICH HAS BEEN REVIEWED BY THE COMMITTEE. AS A RESULT YOUR SUGGESTION:

☐ *IS UNDER STUDY. YOU WILL RECEIVE A DECISION OR UPDATE WITHIN 60 DAYS.*
☐ *HAS BEEN SUBMITTED PREVIOUSLY WITHIN THE LAST TWELVE MONTHS AND IS INELIGIBLE.*
☐ *HAS BEEN REJECTED. AN EXPLANATION WILL FOLLOW IN 15 DAYS.*
☐ *HAS BEEN ACCEPTED.*   **AWARD: $**_____

COMMENTS: _____

_____

SIGNATURE: _____ DATE: _____

WHITE AND CANARY COPIES TO SUGGESTION COMMITTEE: PINK COPY · EMPLOYEE RECORD.

POSITIVE
ACTION
REQUEST

PAR NO.
03005

Your job area? - Please Check

FROM: _____
(Print your name)

LOCATION: _____
Where do you work (based)

DATE: _____

☐ OPERATIONS ☐ SALES
☐ HIGHWAY ☐ OFFICE
☐ MAINTENANCE ☐ OTHER

"I AM AWARE OF A PROBLEM THAT IS CAUSING A ROADBLOCK TO MEETING REQUIREMENTS AND KEEPING ME AND/OR OTHERS FROM PERFORMING ERROR -FREE WORK."

PLEASE CHECK: ☐ IN MY OWN JOB OR ☐ IMPACTS ON THE COMPANY

THE PROBLEM OR SUGGESTION IS:

Press Firmly

RECOMMENDED SOLUTION:

PAR RECEIVED BY: _____   POSITION: _____
(Print your name)

**A
C
T
I
O
N**

☐ IMMEDIATE SOLUTION IMPLEMENTED.

☐ PASSED ON TO MY QMT.

QMT ACTION

☐ CAT FORMED

☐ RESOLVED

☐ TO QUALITY OFFICE FOR STEERING COMMITTEE.

PLEASE HAND ALL COPIES OF PAR TO YOUR SUPERVISOR.

DISTRIBUTE: White - Supervisor/Manager. Canary - Quality Office. Pink - Kept By Employee.

APPENDIX VII

COMMUNICATION/NEWSLETTERS — A RANGE OF IDEAS

Quality Service does not just happen and then you forget about it. You may start the engine but the car will stop without sufficient fuel.

Communication, both internal and external, is an essential tool. Some organizations have more elaborate programs than others. Tools used include magazines, videos, simple newsletters, and even one-page flyers. Here we show excerpts of a sample of these communication vehicles.

December 20, 1990 Issue 69

A Publication for the People of American Express Canada, Inc.

CIBC

"Becoming Canada's No. 1 Financial Retailer"

DELTA VIEW

INDIVIDUAL BANK

Vol 2 No 2 Fall 1990

DELTAVIEW — VIEWING THE CHANGE TO RETAIL BANKING

FYI
EDITORIAL

"W orking smart-
er" or "doing it right
the first time,
everytime, on
time and with value" — are phrases that
you are going to be hearing frequently from everyone in the Individual Bank.

Higher Personal productivity and the
have become increasingly important at CIBC, and
impact not only on our short term performance but
position in an increasingly-competitive financial marketplace.

But, what do we mean by better "cost management," and
increased productivity"? Does it mean shifting our customer
Service Quality focus back to one of
cutting costs and moving paper?

Absolutely not! And I cannot emphasize this enough. Effective cost

Cabinet Members Join Service
Quality Team Leader Workshop

"W e're all in
this together."
The notion
that Service
Quality involves everyone at
CIBC was again proven as
Individual Bank cabinet mem-
bers recently joined team leaders
and managers from the Greater
Metropolitan Toronto region for
a two-day workshop.
The workshop sent a clear

Candid discussions added value
to the workshop as senior
management and branch em-
ployees addressed critical issues
involving customer service and
front line support.
Everyone donned their Team
Leader hats and glasses to
exchange ideas and observations
gathered from employees in one
of CIBC's largest and diverse
markets.

executive vice-president, Cliff
Shirley, executive vice-president
Rodney Chand, executive vice-
president, Ron Britten, executive
vice-president, Steve Lenard,
senior vice-president, William
Hamilton, vice-president
and Keith Sjoerch, senior vice-
president.
The session focused on the
management support required to
build teamwork both within

APPENDIX VIII

MODELS
FOR CONTINUOUS IMPROVEMENT

There is no single methodology to bring about a cultural transformation and a focus on continuous improvement.

The Service E.D.G.E. is one such methodology, as are the methodologies that follow. Please remember, they are much more than fancy flowcharts. Behind each of these strategies exists a detailed action plan, together with quality teams, communication, training, and reward programs. By considering all of these methodologies or process improvement models, a process within your organization may also be developed and nurtured.

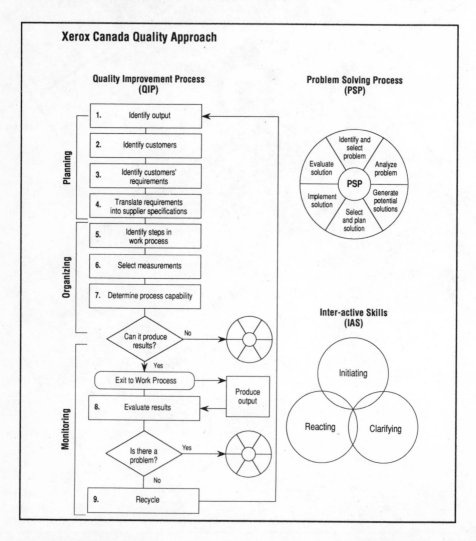

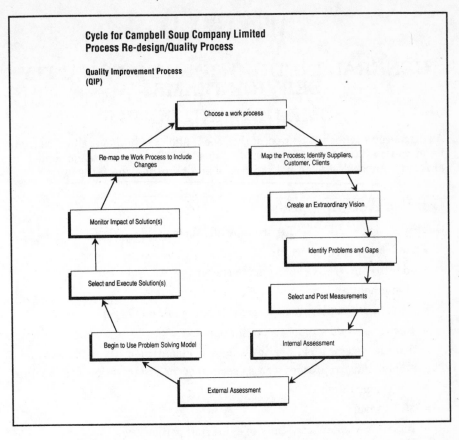

**Cycle for Campbell Soup Company Limited
Process Re-design/Quality Process**

Quality Improvement Process
(QIP)

Choose a work process

Re-map the Work Process to Include Changes

Map the Process; Identify Suppliers, Customer, Clients

Create an Extraordinary Vision

Monitor Impact of Solution(s)

Identify Problems and Gaps

Select and Execute Solution(s)

Select and Post Measurements

Begin to Use Problem Solving Model

Internal Assessment

External Assessment

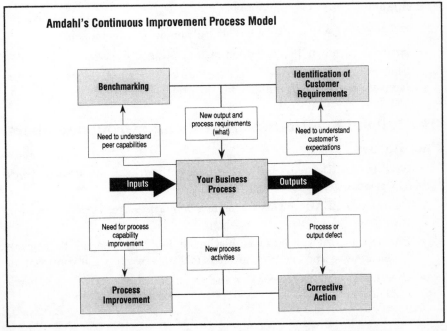

Amdahl's Continuous Improvement Process Model

Benchmarking

Identification of Customer Requirements

New output and process requirements (what)

Need to understand peer capabilities

Need to understand customer's expectations

Inputs

Your Business Process

Outputs

Need for process capability improvement

Process or output defect

New process activities

Process Improvement

Corrective Action

APPENDIX IX

GENERAL INSTRUCTIONS FOR QUALITY SERVICE TEAMS —
SOME DO'S AND DON'TS

As discussed earlier in the text of this book, effective teams are necessary to build and maintain a lasting service culture. The following provide some general guidelines which will help to create and maintain these teams.

Quality Action Teams

Quality Action Teams (QATs) are typically formed to:

➤ Address quality concerns

➤ Identify innovative solutions to concerns

➤ Implement and monitor viable changes

➤ Involve all employees in improving the quality of service

➤ Encourage and support a team approach

➤ Encourage cross-fertilization and inter-departmental communication

These teams must represent a cross-section of the organization and must be:

➤ Interdepartmental

➤ Multi-level

➤ Based only on effective mix of skills and perspectives

At a minimum, each team must have a:

➤ Facilitator (CANNOT be a member of senior management)

➤ Scribe (which can be rotated for each meeting)

➤ Shared responsibility — EVERY group member individually and collectively shares responsibility for the group's work

The Role of Facilitators, Scribes and Group Members
Facilitators

➤ NOT TO LEAD the discussion but ensure that the group stays on track so work can get done

➤ Guide (NOT LEAD) the discussion in a non-aggressive, assertive, win-win manner

➤ Ensure that EACH group member has an EQUAL opportunity to speak up, be creative and feel that he/she is making a worthwhile contribution

➤ Create a climate necessary for each member to be heard and to learn from others

Scribes

- Eliminate the need for note taking of other members
- Record ALL ideas and suggestions
- Distribute a summary of meeting to all members before next meeting
- Prepare an agenda for next meeting

Group Members

- Contribute opinions, knowledge and experience to discussions
- Encourage each other to participate (invite suggestions — THERE ARE NO RIGHT OR WRONG IDEAS)
- Prepare for each meeting (for example, may involve some information gathering)
- ATTEND ALL GROUP MEETINGS

Guidelines for All Group Members

READ THESE GUIDELINES BEFORE EACH GROUP MEETING.

REMEMBER, EVERY group member individually and collectively shares responsibility for the group's work.

1. Stay on track, on task, and focussed.
2. Suggest — do not state — alternative methods or concepts.
3. Encourage participation from each and every member of the group.
4. Ensure all efforts at participation are met with respect, acceptance and courtesy.
5. In the event of a conflict, try to find win-win solutions.
6. Avoid siding with any opinions.
7. Avoid evaluating a group member's idea or suggestion.
8. Work for consensus on decisions.
9. Ensure that all group members will support the outcome as if it was their own — even if it wasn't.
10. Maintain a high energy, positive atmosphere. Have a WE CAN DO IT attitude and help each group member find his/her own CAN DO position.
11. Speak up, listen, learn, appease each other, and demonstrate your team spirit.
12. As needed, refer back to these guidelines, and encourage others to do so as well.

Guidelines for Facilitators

READ THESE GUIDELINES BEFORE EACH GROUP MEETING.

We all give each other visual, auditory and verbal messages. Be aware of how you are communicating in all of these ways.

Visual Messages

1. Sit or stand in a relaxed but erect posture.
2. Make eye contact easy between yourself and the group members.
3. Show when you are attentively listening — a genuine smile or serious expression are signals of your involvement.
4. Move comfortably among group members and address them easily both collectively or individually.
5. Avoid barriers (such as desks, easels or folded arms) and antagonistic signals (such as pointed fingers and a raised voice).
6. Be relaxed and demonstrate confidence.
7. Show the group that you are having FUN.

Auditory Messages (refers to the tone or attitude you project)

8. Be enthusiastic and energetic.
9. Try not to speak in a monotone or in a low volume (modulate your rhythm, volume and pitch).
10. Do not use skepticism, sarcasm or a tone of superiority.

Verbal Messages (refers to the spoken words)

11. Carefully choose your words. (Use "we" instead of "I," "When" instead of "if," and "and" instead of "but.")
12. Address group members by their names.
13. Gently boomerang questions directed to you back to the group to come up with ideas and solutions.
14. When necessary, paraphrase or restate what you have heard to give the speaker a chance to confirm or clarify meaning.
15. Enlist the group's assistance in helping you remain neutral.

Additional Process Suggestions

16. Set time limits for each meeting, and adhere to these limits.
17. Fifteen or twenty minutes before allotted time is up, guide the group to reach conclusions and formulate a summary for the scribe. Ask group members for input into the summary. Before closing, review the summary with the group to ensure it truly reflects the group's conclusions, and set an agenda for the next meeting.
18. Avoid giving singular credit or blame.
19. Help the group stay focussed and on task.

20. Make suggestions when the group is stuck.

21. Encourage and reward participation.

22. Keep discussions win-win.

23. Work for consensus on decisions. Stay NEUTRAL at all times.

24. Remind members of their role, agreements and ground rules, gently and appropriately.

Guidelines for Scribes

READ THESE GUIDELINES BEFORE EACH GROUP MEETING.

1 Listen for key words. Capture basic ideas rather than writing down every word.

2. Write legibly.

3. Don't be afraid to misspell.

4. Number all pages consecutively.

5. Record all comments (don't be selective or edit meaning).

6. Don't assign a name to a comment.

7. Don't add your own commentary to the summary.

8. Distribute summary to all members promptly.

9. Ensure that the group provides an agenda for the next meeting.

10. Distribute the agenda for the next meeting.

Self Assessment

For Group Members

Did I contribute to the meeting?

Did I stay on track?

Did I talk too much?

Did I use active listening/feedback?

Did I prevent anybody from voicing their opinions or ideas?

Did I encourage group members to voice their ideas?

Did I dominate the meeting at any point?

Did I remain calm and objective?

Did I get defensive when questioned or criticized?

Was I enthusiastic and energetic?

Do other group members feel comfortable working with me?

For Facilitators

Did I help the group develop a process for the meeting?

Was I effective in keeping the group on track?

Was I able to keep the meeting moving along smoothly?

Did I talk too much?

Did I use active listening/feedback?

Did everyone have a chance to voice their opinions or ideas?

Did I protect group members and their ideas

Did I keep any one person from dominating the meeting?

How well did I handle disruptions?

Did I remain neutral and not take sides?

Did I get defensive when questioned or criticized?

Did I project an image of enthusiasm and energy?

Do other group members feel comfortable working with me.

For Scribes

Did I record all ideas appropriately?

Can I provide a useful summary of the meeting from my notes?

Did I slow the group down?

Did I edit or leave out any comments or suggestions?

Did I prepare and distribute the meeting summary promptly?

Do I have an agenda ready for the next meeting?

APPENDIX X

A GLOSSARY OF QUALITY TERMS

It is absolutely critical that all members of the organization speak the same language as well as walk in the same direction.

Amdahl publishes a booklet which is given to all of its employees. Not only does it describe the company's Quality vision and each stage of its Continuous Improvement Process, it also provides a Glossary of Quality Terms. The terms and definitions that follow are primarily those prepared by Amdahl (reprinted here with their permission), with additions prepared by the author. The latter are indicated by an asterisk.

Assure*
The act of establishing a confidence level that a predicted result will occur. This type of action is the primary action mode of a "quality assurance" staff function.

Benchmarking
The process of comparing our products, services and processes to similar products, services and processes of our best competitors or recognized leaders in other industries.

Brainstorming
A technique used to encourage creative thinking, to generate ideas in a short period of time, and to achieve group participation in problem identification and/or solutions.

Breakthrough*
The ability to design and activate products or services that revolutionize an entire industry's rules of the game. In doing so, new standards for consistently meeting or exceeding customers' service needs and expectations are set.

Breakthrough Service*
A service which is substantially differentiated from that offered by an organization's competition on those issues important to the customer and the manner in which it achieves its results.

Business Strategy
The set of decisions and activities which describes the approach the organization will take to accomplish long-term business goals.

Cause and Effect Diagram
A visual representation of a problem or defect and all the possible causes related to it. Often represented as "fishbone" diagrams, cause and effect diagrams clearly illustrate the various factors impacting a process by grouping and sorting all the related causes.

Check Sheet
A data collection tool in which one tallies, or checks off, the number of occurrences of a particular event. It is the logical point to start a problem-solving cycle.

Competitive Requirements
The requirements, including extra features beyond the customer's stated requirements, that we establish to make our products and services better than the products and services our competitors offer. Usually determined through benchmarking.

Conformance to Requirements
Our processes and outputs meet our agreed-to requirements.

Continuous Improvement Process
The concept that improvement is a constant and necessary set of activities to ensure ongoing customer satisfaction and improved efficiency, effectiveness, adaptability and control.

Continuous Improvement
A standardized process used by employees to plan, control and improve work processes and output.

Control
The process of regulating and guiding operations to detect, avoid or prevent defects and taking corrective action when a defect occurs. The goal of process control is to eliminate final inspection.

Control Chart
A control chart is a run chart with statistically determined control limits. Control charts are used when there is a need to discover how much variability there is in a process, in order to determine statistically whether the process is in control.

Control Tools
A group of measurement methods that allow you to statistically assess, monitor and track processes to determine if they are producing output that meets requirements.

Corporate Values
A set of ethics, standards and principles that govern the actions of the Corporation.

Corrective Action Process (CATs)
The process for identifying and correcting the root cause of recurring defects. The focus of this activity is on preventing the defect from occurring again. Corrective Action tends to produce incremental or evolutionary changes to the process.

Corrective Action Teams
A group of employees who work on identifying and correcting errors within a single process.

Customer
The receiver or purchaser of a product or service.

Customer Bill of Rights*
A series of statements outlining the elements of quality service that the customer (internal and external) should expect in its day-to-day contact with the organization.

Customer Delight* (Super-faction)
Going beyond merely meeting the stated requirements in order to build and maintain customer loyalty.

Customer, External
The ultimate purchaser of a product or service.

Customer, Internal
The next user (individual, group or organization) that uses your work product or service.

Customer Requirements
The set of measurable attributes required of our product and services that the customer agrees will satisfy particular customer needs.

Customer Satisfaction*
The state in which customer needs, wants and expectations throughout the product or service's life are met or exceeded resulting in repeat purchase, loyalty and favorable word-of-mouth.

Cycle Time
The time from the beginning to the end of a specific work process, or the amount of time it takes to complete one transaction through a work process; for example, the time it takes to process one vendor invoice, start to finish.

Defect
Any occurrence of an output not meeting an output requirement, or any occurrence of a process not meeting a process requirement.

Ensure*
That act of making certain, or attempting to do so, that prescribed actions are taking place and prescribed results are being accomplished. This type of action is the primary means of implementing "quality control" and is the responsibility of the line personnel directly responsible for the product or service.

Flow Charting
A pictorial representation of the steps in a process. Flow charts provide excellent documentation of a process and are useful tools for examining how various steps in a process relate to each other.

Functional Business Planning
Planning at the organizational level directed at achieving the short and long term goals of the function and the Corporation. This planning has goals and objectives that cascade, top-down and bottom-up, throughout the organization. It focuses on "How we will accomplish it."

Global Economy
We do business in an environment where our customer base spans the entire globe and our competition can come from any country, worldwide.

Hierarchy
Persons organized according to rank or authority, e.g., President, Vice-President, Director, Manager, etc.

Histogram
A graphic display of the frequency distribution of like data, for example, temperature or dimensions. A histogram reveals the amount of variation a process has within it, categorized by type.

Improvement Goals
Goals which specifically address improving a process or output.

Improvement Objectives
Specific tasks to achieve the improvement goals. Objectives are assigned to organizations, work groups or individuals. They have specific time frames, and individual and group performance is measured by the achievement of those objectives.

Improvement Tools
A set of methods and tools used primarily in activities related to quality improvement.

Infrastructure
The organization's structure and set of roles and responsibilities which support and facilitate the quality improvement process.

Innovation*
Looking beyond the organization to identify standards and processes which can be adapted and modified and brought into the organization.

Long Range Plan
Long term, corporate level planning, based on the Company's strategy and mission; it includes products, business processes, finances and quality — "How we would like it to be."

Measurement
Any form of statistical or objective data used for the evaluation of process or output performance.

Mission Statement
A statement that guides an organization's directions by identifying what the organization does and whom it serves.

Moment of Truth*
Any moment in time when your customer interacts with a product or service that you provide which influences his or her level of satisfaction with the total experience.

Output
The material or information provided to customers, internal and external. The result of your business process.

Output Defect
An output that does not meet the requirement set for it. An error in output is a defect.

Output Measurements
Measurement to ensure or determine that an output is defect free. A measurement should be in place for each requirement.

Output Requirements
Specifications for your output based on customer and competitive requirements. Requirements are specific and measurable.

Pareto Analysis
A method to display graphically the relative importance or the frequency of various causes of defects.

Partnership
A term used to describe how a supplier and a customer work together to establish agreement on input and output.

Performance Measures*
Indicators of the work performed and the results achieved in an activity, process, or organizational unit. Performance measures may be financial or non-financial, qualitative or quantitative. A traditional example of a performance measure of an activity is the number of defective parts per million or errors per thousand invoices processed. An example of a performance measure in an organizational unit is return-on-sales averages, sales per order, or number of calls per minute.

Planning Tools
A set of methods or tools used primarily in the planning activities related to quality improvement.

Problem
A situation or condition that is considered undesirable and will continue to exist in the future unless corrective action is taken.

Problem Solving Methodology
The process of first defining the problem, then establishing the criteria for the best solution given your resources and objectives, and finally evaluating all the sets of possible solutions against the established criteria to determine the one solution that best meets the criteria.

Problem Statement
A statement that clearly identifies the basic underlying problem.

Process
A system of work tasks and work flows that produce specific outputs or work products from input. A work process describes how work is done, how outputs are achieved and how value is added to the inputs and the work product.

Process Capability
The ability of a process to produce a product or service within the limits set for it, and the ability to meet specific process requirements.

Process Control
Activities and measurements directed at proactively ensuring, with reasonable confidence, that a process meets the requirements set for it and will produce defect free output.

Process Defect
The process itself is not meeting the requirements set for it. Cycle time or capacity deficiencies are examples of process defects.

Process Design
The planning of activities within a process, based on input and output requirements, to maximize the efficiency, effectiveness, resource utilization and capability of a process. Process design includes documenting, standardizing, and testing of the process and control methods to ensure that the process produces defect free output.

Process Documentation
The recording of a process in such a way that it can be clearly communicated to everyone who participates in the process.

Process Improvement
Activities aimed at improving the reliability, effectiveness, efficiency or capability of a process. The focus is on the redesign or restructuring of work processes, and results tend to be revolutionary.

Process Improvement Groups (PIGs) or Teams (PITs)
Groups who are chartered by management, because of their expertise, to design or redesign a process when the process is not able to meet the requirements set for it. PIGs and PITs are usually cross-functional teams. The focus is on defining how to minimize cost, reduce cycle time, eliminate activities that add little value to the finished product, and achieve defect free output.

Process Management
The process of ensuring that processes are documented, controlled, compliant with standards and continually improved.

Process Measurements
Measurements directed at ensuring that the process meets the requirements set for it. A process measurement should be in place for every process requirement.

Process Owners
The designated person responsible for process documentation, clarity of roles within the process, updating, administration, and process integrity. Process owners provide leadership, support, direction, and measurement to the process. They are accountable for customer satisfaction, and they have the authority to change the process when it no longer meets requirements.

Process Requirements
Specific and measurable standards associated with a work process and derived from customer and competitive requirements.

Process Specifications
Customer and competitive requirements are translated into specifications for process capability.

Process Standardization
Developing a written procedure to assure that a process is done in the same way by each person who does it. Standardization prevents defects because everyone involved in the process consistently performs tasks in one "best way."

Product Performance
The characteristics of a product that distinguish its fitness for use.

Product Requirements
Specifications set by the producer of a product through the process of translating customer and competitive requirements into terms and language usable by the producer.

Quality
Conformance to requirements. The outputs of work processes meet the requirements agreed to by our customers (internal and external), and our work processes conform to the requirements set for them. The totality of features and characteristics of a product or service that bear on its ability to satisfy stated or implied needs.

Quality Assurance*
All those planned or systematic actions necessary to provide adequate confidence that a product or service will satisfy given requirements for quality.

Quality Audit*
A systematic and independent examination and evaluation to determine whether quality activities and results comply with planned arrangements and whether these arrangements are implemented effectively and are suitable to achieve objectives.

Quality Circle Teams*
See Corrective Action Teams.

Quality Commitment
Our pledge to our customers to produce products and services that meet their requirements and add substantial value in comparison to our competition.

Quality Control
Methods or techniques that ensure that a process will produce an output that is defect free this time.

Quality Councils
The management systems and organizational structure that provide leadership and focus for planning, controlling, and improving quality. Quality councils are made up of senior and line managers.

Quality Fundamentals
A set of principles that guide individual employees and organizations in meeting our quality commitments to our customers.

Quality Improvement Process
Activities aimed at continuously improving the reliability, efficiency, effectiveness, and capability of our processes, products, and services through corrective action or process design and improvement activities.

Quality Improvement Strategy
The set of decisions and activities that describe the approach an organization will take to accomplish quality goals.

Quality Management*
That aspect of the overall management function that determines and implements the quality policy.

Quality Measurements
Measurements that enable us to compare actual performance to output or process requirements.

Quality Methodology
A system of interrelated activities, procedures, processes, and practices that focus on the continuous improvement of processes, products, and services and accomplish the three aspects of quality: quality planning, quality control, and quality improvement.

Quality Planning
The process by which customer and competitive requirements are gathered and translated into goals and objectives, specifications, and/or products or services.

Quality Policy*
The overall intentions and direction of an organization that determine and implement the quality policy.

Quality Service*
The end result/deliverable goal to which an organization must strive. How an organization is seen in the eyes of the consumer/client/guest — and in the eyes of those involved in the service delivery chain. It is a perceptual and quantifiable result.

Quality Service Continuum (Service Delivery Chain)*
The chain of connected critical moments that begins with an initial contact with the organization and ends when contact with the organization has been completed.

Quality System*
The organizational structure, responsibilities, procedures, processes and resources for implementing quality management.

Quality System Audit*
A documented activity performed to verify, by examination and evaluation of objective evidence, that applicable elements of the quality system are suitable and have been developed, documented and effectively implemented in accordance with specified requirements.

Requirements
Specific and measurable standards and characteristics associated with output or processes.

Root Cause
The original or primary cause for non-conformance of process or output. The factors in a process that, when changed, will eliminate the defect.

Service Guarantee*
An investment in customer satisfaction and loyalty. But to be effective, the guarantee must be unconditional, meaningful and easy to invoke, collect on, understand and communicate.

Service Delivery System/Process
A chain of activities which describes the interaction between functional groups within an organization in delivering a service to a customer. The sequence must include the initiation, processing, execution and follow-up to the external customer and would describe the internal and external standards of performance required to meet or exceed customer expectations.

Service Mapping*
A procedure to flowchart the service delivery chain. The procedure traces backwards through the organization those functions which are involved in a particular service delivery.

Service Quality*
Internal, departmental service and quality goals towards which the organization must strive. Once these goals are met and exceeded, the organization will be regarded as a quality service provider.

Service Strategy*
A statement describing the vision of the organization in delivering quality service to both internal and external customers.

Statistical Process Control
The use of statistical techniques to monitor a process or its output in order to achieve and maintain a state of control and to improve the capability of the process.

Suppliers
The sources of information and materials used in a process. They may be internal or external to the company, organization or group.

Trends
A view of data points, over time, that indicate a direction or pattern. Attention should be paid when the direction or pattern of data does not compare favorably with predetermined goals, objectives or specifications.

Total Quality Management*
Organized activities involving everyone in a company — managers and workers — in a totally integrated standards-based effort toward improving performance at every level. (This term has many meanings and is still constantly evolving.)

Total Quality Service*
A process by which an ethos of service commitment is instilled within the organization which encourages autonomous effort on the part of the employees to improve and maintain the quality of service on their own.

Value-added Activity*
An activity that is judged to contribute to customer value or satisfy an organizational need. The attribute "value-added" reflects a belief that the activity cannot

be eliminated without reducing the quantity, responsiveness or quality of output required by a customer or organization.

Waste*
Resources consumed by unessential or inefficient activities.

Work Improvement Teams (WITs)
A group of employees who perform like jobs working together to improve or standardize the work processes or outputs within their own work group.

World Class
The best in the world in a particular category.

Zero Defects
Error free outputs and processes which consistently meet requirements.